# THE
# SHARING
# SOCIETY

# THE SHARING SOCIETY

by

## EDWARD LAMB

~~~~~~~~~~~~~~~~~~~~~~~~~~~~~~~~~~~~~~~~~~~~~

Lyle Stuart Inc.   *Secaucus, N.J.*

First edition

Copyright © 1979 by Edward Lamb
All rights reserved. No part of this book may
be reproduced in any form except by a newspaper
or magazine reviewer who wants to quote brief
passages in connection with a review.

Queries regarding rights and permissions
should be addressed to Lyle Stuart Inc.
120 Enterprise Ave., Secaucus, N.J. 07094

Published by Lyle Stuart Inc. Published simultaneously
in Canada by George J. McLeod Limited
Don Mills, Ontario

Manufactured in the United States of America

Library of Congress Cataloging in Publication Data

Lamb, Edward.
    The sharing society.
    I. Lamb, Edward.   2. Businessmen—United States—
Biography.   3. Lawyers—United States—Biography.
I. Title.
HC102.5.L28A37     332′.092′4   [B]     79-18669
ISBN 0-8184-0284-9

*It took millions of years for human intelligence to develop and then to explore the possibilities of the wheel and interplanetary travel. During the twentieth century humankind has achieved something even greater —the building of a framework for a world community. We have laid the foundations of humanity's home.*

*We possess a truly universal and international United Nations. To this noblest of human institutions I dedicate this book.*

# Contents

# THE SHARING SOCIETY

# CHAPTER

# I

~~~~~~~~~~~~~~~~~~~~~~~~~~~~~~~~~~~~~~~~~~~~

# Introduction

I am often called a rich radical. I would not quarrel with that description. I have spent many decades operating more than fifty corporations and making a great deal of money. I have acquired banks, leasing and manufacturing companies, and several television stations. I am an example of the extremely successful businessman in the capitalist United States.

I suppose I should be called a radical because I do not believe in the system that I have had the knack of operating. I became a multimillionaire in a system that is not in the best interests of the majority of people in the United States or elsewhere.

Many books have been written on how to get rich by the evangelists of free enterprise. My story may give my readers some useful notions about how to play the financial game. Yet as a successful participant who so seriously questions the basic tenets of capitalism, I shall also, I hope, offer some frank and perhaps more lasting ideas.

Let me go back a bit. I have come a long way from my humble beginnings as the ninth child of Mary and Clarence

Marcellus Lamb. I was born when my mother was forty-seven years old, but this remarkable exercise in middle-aged productivity was not my mother's final achievement for she gave birth to my younger brother eighteen months later.

My father was a commercial fisherman on the shores of Lake Erie, and it was on these fishing grounds that I began my career building shipping boxes and cleaning fish. We hauled our catches off to market: herring, white fish, perch, pickerel, catfish and mullet. At twelve I had had enough of a fishing career and its uncertainties. I wanted to be a lawyer. After all, lawyers make a good living and go to Congress and sometimes even to the White House.

I was born a white, male American with the puritan ideal of earning and saving money. I also grew up believing the words of our Declaration of Independence: "We hold these truths to be self-evident: That all men are created equal; that they are endowed by their Creator with certain unalienable rights; that among these are life, liberty and the pursuit of happiness." It was quite all right with me that, being born in the Midwestern United States, I had more equality than, say, a youngster born in Asia, Africa, Harlem, or rural Georgia. With our advantages and an education handed us, we could go places and become professionals or entrepreneurs. Other men could take care of themselves. Our heritage let us know that it would be normal to aspire to the prestige of a pope or to the power of a president. One isn't born a doubter or an iconoclast. One gradually thinks one's way into such heresies. And I have, let me admit right away, been thinking myself into a good number of heresies ever since I was a child.

Uncle Frank Lamb was one of my early idols because he had so much common sense. He was suspected of sleeping around a bit, but neither he nor his wife, Helen, minded his extracurricular activities. She took care of the household and distributed his paycheck. He sweepingly identified himself with the whole human race and stood ready to solve the big problems of the world. Lesser men envied him. No one could call him a simpleton, although his solutions may now seem oversimplistic. He insisted, for instance, that every human being in formulating his life's purpose has a freedom to choose between two philosophies, one based on the way people live, the other upon the state of the universe. To affect one's fellows, to be a part of society, to lead a meaningful existence, to help organize humankind seemed to him to be so much the more useful and exciting choice.

Charles Darwin and others had already persuaded my generation that man evolved over centuries into an increasingly effective creature. His *Origin of Species* supplanted the Bible as a fountain of faith for us. Darwin suggested that man emerged out of the war of nature, "of strife unending," and that all things progress toward perfection. In the long journey man had survived the savagery of the organic realm and innumerable biological imperfections. By trial and error and a developing perception, the human animal had embarked on the roadway to excellence. Could this mean ultimately a society without ideological chains or national boundaries? Many of us grew increasingly optimistic about man's ability to control and direct his own destiny and achieve a better life.

As Dr. Carl Sagan of Cornell University has illustrated, if all the changes on this planet since it began were compressed into a period of one year, the whole of human history would represent only ten seconds. The rate of change is accelerating, and the human being must, like any other creature, adapt or perish. We are bound to ask ourselves whether human intelligence will enable man to make the necessary adaptations fast enough—or will man become just one more on the list of extinct creatures? This must depend, among other things, upon our being able to develop the techniques of organizing our world and its societies along more just and rational lines than at present.

I do not live alone on this planet. Enlightened self-interest dictates that somehow every person should participate in a government that is just and fair to the largest possible number. Governments should belong to, and serve, all. The United States Constitution was doubtless written with this in mind; and since we know from experience that all power seeks to increase itself, we Americans set up a kind of obstacle course by balancing powers among a national executive, a judiciary, and a congress.

Yet in the United States during the period of its greatest affluence, the era when private ownership became recognized as the ultimate power, the control of government moved away from the people and into the hands of fewer and fewer owners. In the United States today the individual feels that he can do little, and is of little consequence. The security and well-being of our people are being eroded. We ask whether the mass of our citizens will ever regain control. Is there a practical way for us to take hold and achieve a more just economy?

The United States government, through its various regulatory agencies, such as the Federal Communications Commission, the Securities and Exchange Commission, and the Immigration and Naturalization Service, requires its citizens, especially its businessmen, to sign affidavits attesting to their non–Communist party affiliation. Many of us have no difficulty signing such affidavits since we are not expected to attest to the purity or sanctity of the competitive, free-enterprise, or capitalist system.

I am a progressive human being with increasing doubts about the viability and permanence of our private, uncontrolled capitalist system. These doubts exist in spite of my own entrepreneurial successes which give me control, through personal trusts and various leverage arrangements, of companies with assets in excess of six hundred million dollars. Such assets are growing rapidly, presently at the rate of ten million dollars a month. Such an accumulation of wealth is one of the dangers to the capitalist system. It's also obvious that such individual affluence in the midst of world poverty can't continue for long.

We can be certain that there will not be any voluntary, or even forced, redistribution of the individual's wealth. American citizens and corporations under the Fourteenth

Amendment are protected from governmental seizure of private property without "due process" or compensation.

I outline in this book a different approach—a technique to achieve a more equitable path to the future, the roadway to the Sharing Society.

# CHAPTER

# II

≈≈≈≈≈≈≈≈≈≈≈≈≈≈≈≈≈≈≈≈≈≈≈

# The Enigma

As we go through life, we all suffer some battle scars. There has been hardly a time since my early labor-lawyer days when I have not been black bagged, my movements shadowed, my records rifled and phones tapped, my friends and associates interviewed and harassed. Even so, I was amazed at the data when my files were finally secured from the FBI and the CIA under the Freedom of Information Act. Information ranged from the ridiculous to the innocuous. Forgotten nightmares were revived. It is fascinating to know that so many thousands of man-hours and dollars were invested to prove data that had been published in *Who's Who* for thirty-five years. Irrelevant tidbits like my collection of old masters, such as paintings of Rubens, Van Dyke, and Gainsborough, were included. My correspondence and telegrams to friends in the Soviet Union were opened and copied by the CIA. My many trips to Fidel Castro's Cuba—stories exhaustively covered in the American press—were given "top-secret" labels.

One of the episodes in my life—a strenuous Washington witch hunt with its great publicity in the early 1950s—provided more than twenty-five hundred pages of "scoops" for the Federal Bureau of Investigation. The experience at the time caused me anguish and inconvenience—and litigation expenses in excess of nine hundred thousand dollars. (Not everyone can afford to clear his name through the courts as I was able to do.) Yet the FBI had built up an enormous bureacracy and what could keep them better occupied than ferreting out the dissidents among us?

When a person gets involved in a serious cause, he rather expects to be smothered in controversy. Indeed, it can be fun. I still believe that the full life of an activist is better than the fence-sitter who watches the world go by. I was a dissenter; I argued that socialism—call it communism—should be studied to see if it offered worthwhile alternatives to our own system. I might give the FBI and the CIA an A for effort but an F for failure to secure results. I could have furnished them more information—good, juicy, meaty stuff—had they asked me for it. But their abortive searches and their inept detective work clearly breached my most elementary rights of privacy. And I didn't see any need to reward their clumsiness gratuitously.

No matter how much the FBI and the CIA pursued me, and pursue me they did for more than forty years, my net worth increased enormously. My financial status became a source of mystery and anger to federal regulatory agencies. To them it was an anomaly that a multimillionaire industrialist should espouse a way of life that directly threatened American's affluent profit making.

In 1933, about the time Franklin D. Roosevelt's positive social proposals provided some of us with a degree of hope, I made my first extended trip to Soviet Russia. I saw that socialism was a living reality. After that trip to the U.S.S.R. I felt that the Soviet experiment was a genuine and potentially successful effort at human betterment. Much of the Soviet struggle was hard for me to understand—yet I decided to try. This was the fact: a planned economy was emerging before our eyes and seemed to offer promise of a better world. Millions of people who were born into capitalism began to wonder during those depression days why in a so-called free-enterprise system we had so much hunger, unemployment, depression, and disarray. Irrespective of any subsequent criticism or controversy, I saw that this was the basic fact of our existence.

It was all there in the FBI and CIA files, revelations about my attempts to help improve the human condition. As a labor lawyer, I instituted the significant Portal-to-Portal case in the federal courts and won a far-reaching decision in the U.S. Supreme Court on June 6, 1946 that put hundreds of millions of dollars into the paychecks of American workers. Corporate executives and business organizations were furious. I tried dozens of cases for the steelworkers and various national unions against the giant companies. Over the years I earned the reputation, which has never left me, as a troublemaker, a maverick, a hair shirt on the capitalist system.

I was helping my less fortunate fellowmen, but no one ever claimed that I was a fuzzy idealist. I seemed to know something about the art of money making. I learned how to organize assets, and I admit I enjoyed the game of creating profits. The study of law teaches the nature of the social structure—and reveals its operating guidelines. It showed me how money begets money. The opportunities to use credit or derive income from the use of money are almost limitless. The formula was simple—ingenuity allied to a bit of cash, small down payment, long payout, and capital gains. I learned one rule at the outset: invest and continue to invest in a basic industry led by good management—better if it were a mix of technological, marketing, and organization strategies but always headed toward one goal—profitability.

Real estate, corporate reorganizations, individual ventures—all were attractive. But an alternative—the growth of the service industries—became more apparent over the years. In our uneven society there are many easy ways to wealth. It's always a safe bet to get control of material resources such as land or the oil that gave fortunes to John D. Rockefeller, J. Paul Getty, H. L. Hunt, Andrew Mellon, and so many others. I don't happen to feel that big money is made by gambling at Las Vegas or by dealing in securities on the stock exchanges. The big buck comes when one accumulates capital or credit. When an individual fixes his eye on a sound company and concentrates on buying stock until he gains a substantial block or even control, he's on his way. In these days of bigness, by mergers or takeover, the holder of stocks in target companies has done quite well.

I soon learned that in any corporation there is only one ultimate voice of authority, and that is ownership. But ownership is not enough; someone must be in charge who can run the store. Professional, skilled, scientific managers are trained to analyze problems and make decisions. The responsibility of management is always to ownership. In our society there is only one goal—profits. The annual report appears and dividends are declared, but no matter how one reads it, only the bottom line counts. In the past, American corporate wheelerdealers might have tolerated sloppiness and waste in the executive suite, but in today's competitive market it is safe to say that the efficiency of most American institutions is significantly improved.

An important question, from the social point of view, is how to achieve managerial competence in a system that alters the basic premise of ownership. Corporations in private control grow larger and larger in the United States—the trend toward monopoly capitalism is being constantly intensified. It takes us away from the true economic, political, and social democracy. Can state ownership of the means of production achieve this democracy while retaining managerial excellence?

And another question. Can one individual, you or I, do anything to improve the condition of an irrational world? Every human being in the capitalist world has to answer this question for himself. There is no dogma or guideline for all. I admit that a capitalist competitive society, despite its flaws and its suspect social objectives, does stimulate research and product improvement and personal incentive. But if we disregard the waste and inequity of experiment and transition for the moment, I maintain that scientific management, operating in a planned economy, actually offers more hope for a majority of mankind.

In America we're frustrated and uncertain. We exaggerate external demons. We build Soviet bogeymen and reach the peak of absurdity as we seek to be militarily number one in a world loaded down with nuclear weaponry. Communism is not the challenge to the American culture —the challenges are worldwide hunger, ill health, and poverty. Internally the challenges involve the future of the capitalist welfare state: the growth and stability of our political structure to formulate and execute wise policy decisions, both domestic and foreign, and a rational and farsighted energy plan. No wonder the drive for political remedies has tapered off—indeed, few young people look upon a career in politics as self-fulfilling or effective.

Dollars rather than service has become the objective and badge of many in government service. The big dollar often goes to the biggest scoundrel who leaves office and writes a bestseller. Most Americans realize that the real action and the power are on the economic front where the signals are forwarded to those who hold political office; however, they see that they are effectually blocked by a stalemate. We mouth words about individual "rights," suggesting that the constitutional right to vote or assemble is more important than the universal human right to eat, work, and live securely. The well-organized, well-financed right wing in America keeps both major parties anchored to a tedious, conservative consensus. People are saturated with propaganda about the merits of free enterprise. We are told that our freedoms lie in protection from government—our government.

Marxists are splintered. The American labor movement decades ago abandoned social idealism and progressivism; its aged leadership is often busy feathering its own nest. Throughout the world the mild left is confused; liberalism, as we know it, utters safe, century-old Populist theories. It's impossible to tell the difference between the moribund, antiquated, look-alike programs of Democrats or Republicans where the outs campaign against the ins. It seems a large part of the world is disillusioned with the milk-toast social-democrat programs.

The protestor, the nonconformist, even the political independent of today, becomes an againster—against Vietnam and Watergate, against communism, against big government, the CIA, and taxes. Millions of dollars are spent in the battle for a single congressional or gubernatorial seat. We have a maze of indecision—where do we look for the affirmative, positive program for building a sensible, secure future? I believe our answers will be found in a rational, planned, secure, and international society.

I question the viability of the political systems now used by the industrialized countries of Europe, North America, and Asia. Many of the ideas bandied about in commercial circles sound like a plan for a special American brand of fascism. Further, I can't overlook what is happening in the developing countries. Although I am a veteran of a highly developed nation, I want to add my personal observations on two nations we have victimized, two Third-World nations with a future—Vietnam and Cuba.

Americans watch their candidates make ridiculous promises to increase social-welfare programs and reduce arms expenditures. We've seen these same men, as presidents, add tens of billions to military spending, impartially shipping arms to potential friends and foes alike. We are only five percent of the world's population but we are responsible for a third of the world's annual arms expenditures. We are truly the world's greatest seller of violence. We justify our overkill by saying that we're saving ourselves from the Russians, protecting our allies of the moment, and creating jobs on the home front. Can this charade go on forever in a nation suffering fifty billion dollars annual deficits and a trillion-dollar national debt that will never be repaid?

We in America are not living on a magnificent island, apart from a troubled world. Nor will we settle the problems of the world by unilateral decree. We are beginning to recognize our total interdependence with the rest of the world. The dream of each of us, a utopian objective, is practical and achievable. Once we face up to the serious realities of today, we shall be taking the first step toward tomorrow's rational society.

Recently at lunch with Bill Moyers, the famed television reporter, at New York's Four Seasons restaurant, I was asked to explain my "incongruities." "Here you are, Ted, possessed of wealth and great assets in television broadcasting, skilled in the fields of law and scientific management. You even seem to enjoy your role as an independent businessman or controversial social activist. You know the role of the Establishment in the operation of our society, and you know how the industrial-political complex can hit you as a dissenter. Yet you openly applaud government political attacks on the private sector. Why? Do you seek a satisfaction of the ego, the fun of accomplishment, the delivery of a message —or what?"

I told him, "Bill, I hate clichés and pat answers as much as you. I am a human creature enjoying a short stay on this planet. I seek to further a man-made structure that will permit us all to live together sharing more equitably our global assets and opportunities. I am what I am, a very privileged person, born a white male in mid-America at the peak of its eminence. Preceding my time there were many changes and revolutions fought with fists, swords, or machine guns. Today the revolutions are more sophisticated and involve exercises of the mind. Technological advances, like the computer, occupy our attention. But other changes are occurring, including a clarification of the economic or ownership base of our social order. Karl Marx and Nikolai Lenin were among those who clarified the nature of the new world.

"In today's world of change, orderly or otherwise, the worth of any one of us will be measured by a single yardstick, and it is not money or monuments. We will say, 'What did this one life do to bring about a society where all of earth's children taste the joys of social and economic fair play?' It is imperative that we obtain an international structure with ultimate power to maintain world order. I propose to do everything in my power to bring about this new society."

~~~~~~~~~~~~~~~~~~~~~~~~~~~~~~~~~~~~~~~~~~~~~~~~~~~~

# Philosophers, Politicians, and Profits

Who would deny that the residents of Paris, Bogotá, Tokyo, and Chicago live better because men of peace, like Michelangelo and Herbert Spencer, lived on this planet? Yet we heap honors upon the Napoleon Bonapartes and the Julius Caesars for conquering their worlds. It's about time that we recognize that Spencer, the English philosopher and evolutionist, spoke truly when he said, "Whatever fosters militarism makes for barbarism; whatever fosters peace makes for civilization."

We have lived in a turbulent, unruly world. Our presidents and kings, armed with convenient ideological shields, piously railed against war, yet seized neighboring lands. We justified terrorism—when practiced by our military allies, the good guys. We're realists—war is oh so profitable to the winners. Only the people are the losers. The holocaust in Hitler's Germany, the bombing of refugee camps in Palestine, the indiscriminate slaughter of civilians in Vietnam were patently terrorist acts repulsive to the nonaggressive.

Through it all, we became reconciled to one reality—

those in power in any society, fascist or socialist, have as their top priority remaining in power. We know too well what happened to the democratically elected Marxist leadership in Chile. President Salvador Allende, democratically elected and truly a friend of the working people, didn't protect the tenure of his regime. Can we expect that non-violent efforts to change things will succeed any better in the future? Change is more often brought about by violence. A professor friend of mine, who doesn't get bogged down by the semantics of nonviolence during a transition of power, says, "Whenever anyone mentions devolution to me, I reach for my revolver." Cynical—and realistic.

Under such conditions, how should you and I proceed to build a more rational world of law and order with a strong central authority? At least we can examine an available alternative to jungle warfare and secure a structured society. We'll dream and act to make firm a meeting place where mankind can effectively control the violence of nation against nation; we'll find a planet where we can work, play, and live. We see an individual human being, a tightly controlled, behavioral machine with mechanisms of learning and memory operating as a highly evolved organism. Other animals, ranging from the little bee to the larger dolphin, act in much the same way as man. Now our species has added certain new dimensions—we've developed an ability to make decisions; a fantastic development. Where risk and uncertainty exist, such as in economic planning, in adjusting resources, or in carrying on political campaigns, we will call in the modern computer and use it to solve problems usually thought to require human judgment. Even before the age of cloning we prepare for the computerized person!

We should simmer down and consider two simple objectives in life: *one,* help build the bridges of mankind and achieve a feasible structure for a World Community; *two,* help set up the operational procedure, including the use of advanced scientific management skills that would best permit mankind's global organization to function. Man has battled over the form of the international structure and created troublesome, complex relationships that arose from his na-

tional self-serving illusions. Recently we saw African and
Asian social systems begin to shake and flounder. Private
ownership was merely operating behind national boundaries.
Capitalistic affluence decried restraints upon its privileges.
It became clear that control over any enterprise in which
the big get bigger would not be easily surrendered. Private
enterprisers could build images of their welfare impulses,
but they could not eliminate the incongruities of the competitive jungle.

Many questions have bothered me, and I don't know
that I'll ever find the answers. Still, it's more difficult to
answer questions like Why do the birds sing? than Why do
people struggle so hard to obtain and retain property? I
never could find a moral imperative to justify capitalism.
Surely, it's not just the raw greed built into us; neither
could it be mere craving for security, status, and power.
Whatever the reason, our present political system, our government, is built on this economic base, this foundation
of private property. Our ideologies, including the so-called
Protestant ethic, actually extol the accumulation of property.
Many of our contemporaries of the Western industrialized
world arbitrarily oppose any social order that requires a
more equitable sharing of property. They whip up fear of
communism, to justify the accumulation of wasteful arsenals.
This kind of approach, coupled with self-righteous smugness, will doom society as we know it.

I am the first to admit that it's easier to espouse the cause
of social justice if one's financial rating tops several million
dollars. Lecturing to college audiences in defense of my
beliefs is a favorite pastime. I have even enjoyed appearing
before some of the new "free enterprise" seminars under-
written by our giant American companies. Private enterprises in the oil, banking, auto, and other industries are
supported by enormous advertising campaigns. Today many
American colleges beset by lack of funds are willing to
teach anything, especially that modern "ideologies" yield
bigger personal salaries and stockholder dividends.

Businessmen on leave from their companies become pro-
fessors and find the experience a quick, rewarding method

of recruiting their future executives. When I question the tenets or lasting qualities of capitalism, a voice from the back of the hall may ask me, "It's easy for you to be a rich liberal and hold extremely progressive views. But what about us? We still have to get jobs, possibly get married, pay for the car, make lease and mortgage payments—maybe even to your bank." I reply that I held progressive and controversial views both before and after the time I practiced a profession or accumulated big money.

I see now, more clearly than ever, that there is need for radical adjustment in our political and economic order. I've experienced the pressures applied against the person who makes waves or files complaints. While I was a labor lawyer trying cases against powerful corporations, the courts, with the active cooperation of the established legal profession, tried to disbar me. As a television broadcaster, my competitors and my government put me through a long, difficult, and expensive communist witch hunt. The experience had benefits—it made me question whether we could have an objective judicial system able to defend individual rights against the awesome power of the wealth that controls government.

Scars or no scars, as I matured, I became more, not less, questioning. Experience does have the virtue of permitting one better to understand what makes any society tick. Our young people begin to understand that capitalism breeds monopoly as the big get bigger, and doesn't necessarily allow either freedom of enterprise or the protection of human rights. Such developments will occur only when we modify, change, and grow with a governmental structure dedicated to the welfare of all of us. Whether government is stacked against the little guy or not—our task will be the wedding of the two revolutions—social ownership and managerial know-how—into the beautiful international world of tomorrow.

The campus crowd today in the United States is different. American students are interested primarily in their own economic and social status. In the roaring 1960s campus activists seeking change had their eyes opened. Students

opposed the Vietnam war and the "domestic establishment."
The Vietnam debacle and the Watergate, Koreagate, and
Chilegate episodes discouraged trust in our government
processes and leaders. Through the ensuing years the whole
world shuddered at the perfidy of the Richard Nixons, Spiro
Agnews, and John Mitchells and their extralegal actions.
In our so-called political democracy the very scum of our
nation seemed to have risen to the surface. Nor would its
problems be settled by born-again idealists. Sooner or later,
we told ourselves, our leaders would be compelled to look
at the economic base of a nation that tolerates the dominance of giant monopolies.

Why generalize or get bogged down in semantics—leftists
are not always Marxists and rightists aren't always fascists.
We all hoped that the new reformers who identified with
consumer and environmental causes would bring a bit of
order and stability into our society. As we watched developments, we saw taxes unfairly reduced for the rich,
national deficits mount, unemployment and inflation escalate. Occasionally we shudder at the massive inertia on today's campuses. Students aren't showing noisy, slam-bang
demands for change. Rather, graduates rush to the best-
paying service industries. The architectural, medical, and
law schools are buried in admissions applications. Professions are the road to the good life. Many believe that their
future personal security lies in their ability to advance
within a national economy that they suspect is uncertain
at best. "Let me get mine while the getting is good. We
cannot know the lifespan of our capitalist, nuclear-laden
society." They are more interested in getting good-paying
jobs themselves than in adequate national health and welfare plans for all.

Students in the schools of business administration know
where the goldmines are. They are taught how best to
operate the system to extract the most ore. They accept as
priority one their own goal of personal and material enrichment. Operating in a free-enterprise system, they become proficient in devising stock options and pension and
bonus incentives, and they know the meaning of shelters

and capital gains. Their "managerial talents" are useful in all human institutions, profit and nonprofit; indeed, they seem to know how to make the human institutions tick. However, it won't be long before American youth begin to look at their system and ask themselves whether they can continue to defend the indefensible.

Although I found myself wanting to change the system radically so that it can meet its social obligations to all our fellow humans, I came to believe that I knew what programs I was against better than what I was for. Maybe that is why revolutions are led by the young. Maturity makes one less able to wear identification tags and labels, like Republican, Democrat, socialist, or independent. American political parties are not noticeably different—and provide no alternatives.

To the chagrin of my contemporaries, especially in the business world, I came to be critical of many American institutions. I emphasized belief in many of the economic analyses of Karl Marx, Friedrich Engels, and Nikolai Lenin as I looked at the alternatives they offered. The guidelines for the socialized society were designed to provide more equitable sharing of assets among all individuals and nations. History shows us that social changes can occur rapidly, but no prophet at any time can claim to know society's ultimate shape. Nor do I wear blinders. I recognize weaknesses in Marxism. One such weakness is its slowness in accepting a trained elite professional group of scientific managers able to plan, operate, and run human organizations.

It simply makes sense to recognize planning as an integral part of living. It is such an essential part of what is called the management function. Planning is not a mysterious, unfathomable science. It is simply "the continuous, dynamic process of clarifying scope, purpose, and mission— identifying and evaluating capabilities, environment, and future developments—establishing and revising goals, objectives, priorities, and strategy; developing and implementing programs and projects; allocating essential resources; and seeing that acceptable results are accomplished on schedule." Fancy words for operating a railroad or a nation —or a planet.

Today we watch the building of hundreds of schools, hospitals, and, of course, corporations. Each project presents the same challenge and identifies various phases of the planning procedure: (1) gathering facts and information; (2) analyzing the information and making decisions; and (3) devising strategy to carry out the decisions. In other words, where are we, where do we want to go, and how do we get there?

The role of the manager as he studies the human condition cannot be overemphasized. The decision he makes today affects the future happiness and welfare of mankind and possibly the continuance of life on earth. Those who would manage this earthly habitat must recognize the interdependence of all peoples and the need for a new world order. We have watched fantastic technological innovations in transportation, communications, and energy. It's not a question of loyalties or which nation is stronger. Human goals remain the same—adequate housing, food, jobs, and essential services for people. It is amazing that although civilization has reached this point, poverty and hunger are still everywhere. If our social managers would plan us into a better world, they must look at horizons beyond national, color, and racial boundaries. Barbara Ward, in her work *The Home of Man* (Norton, 1976, page 293), noted that the old philosophers and the new scientists may possibly bring about a "fusion of new knowledge and ancient wisdom and release a more potent explosion of moral energy than any earlier attempt to convert humanity from the false gods of greed and power. It is much easier to overlook words of wisdom, however eloquent, than to override the solid, incontrovertible evidence of material reality."

Without underestimating the importance of the political state, we sooner or later grasp the significance of economic determinism in molding the course of history. A change in the ownership of the means of production from the private-enterprise system may be a necessary prelude to effective operation, but it alone is not enough. There is still a missing ingredient—the art or science of management. Someone must be around who knows how to operate the organization. It has been said that management is the single discipline that has transformed the findings of all the physical and social sciences into the towering achievements of our age. Such a program attempts to harmonize relationships between classical management techniques and all the behavioral sciences.

I have visited the campuses of many schools of business administration—Harvard, Boston, California, Chicago, Michigan, Stanford, Columbia, the Tuck School at Dartmouth, Western Ontario, and many others. We have hundreds of thousands of students in these business schools training to be future managers of our economy. They receive basic management experience, specializing in multiple subjects like accounting, computer sciences, quantitative methods, finance, and economics. These students are not just dilettantes with a smattering of knowledge in contemporary management techniques. They reach into the areas of policy making and problem solving. These schools are developing the successful managers of the future, possessed of a proficiency and familiarity in many job areas, such as marketing, manufacturing, finance, and systems. The manager remains a generalist with a peripheral knowledge of the wide areas of human activity. The professional manager, trained to operate an enterprise, makes a much greater contribution to social progress than do my contemporaries who are loudly engaged in preserving property "rights."

The really striking thing about today's manager is that he looks beyond the four walls of his own specialty. He spans the world, opens vast new horizons, and finds numerous options. As a leader of an emerging society, he understands personnel relationships and motivation, statistics, long-range planning, production and distribution, cost analysis, and finance, all to the end that he may generate programs and satisfy man's needs for goods and services. He asks questions, learns the facts, and resolves issues. He is the trained professional problem solver. We should feel safer with such people around us.

A student of management soon discovers that the principles of good management are universal and apply to all industries wherever situated. He discovers that managerial skill utilizes the latest cultural and scientific knowledge of worldly man. The developments of our technological age permit these skilled problem solvers to reach the heights of leadership in any social system of which they become a part. If our own nation can't absorb its graduate students, the socialist countries offer a beckoning invitation. Cuba, Rumania, the U.S.S.R., the Peoples Republic of China all provide pleasant and challenging invitations to our scientific-management graduates.

I have recruited into my employment dozens of managers. I like lawyers in management least of all—they look backward for precedents, try to drive by looking through the rearview mirror. I like best the business-school graduates, masters of business administration—MBAs. The new breed of manager is aware of the big problems and opportunities presented in modern social systems, but he is also the professional problem solver and the decision maker. It's probably true that a majority of today's MBAs are blindly devoted to the preservation of the capitalist system of which they are such a privileged and vital part. But these specialists have a refreshing and objective approach to problem solving, and their political-party preferences are not paramount and may not be determinative of society's future.

## WE'VE DEVISED THE CORPORATION— WHAT NEXT?

We grow alarmed as we look at the institutions man has created. We have adopted so many ideologies and religions. We even tried to confine ideas within geographical boundaries. We look at the Catholics warring against Protestants in Northern Ireland, Jews against Arabs in the Middle East, or Muslims against Christians in Lebanon. Each faction claims to fight to preserve lofty, ideological abstractions; each claims contact with man-made divinity. We might better take the time to appraise the effectiveness and reality of some of our current human institutions.

Of all the instruments of capitalism for carrying out man's ideals and purposes, none equals the corporation, a central vehicle that is now moving into most economies. Take a look at this powerful, impersonal entity, the modern supercorporation, a monster that actually replaces nation-states. Conglomerates may have indeed become the principal governing force in many parts of the Western world. No one would claim that under such an impersonal instrument we'll ever achieve a more equitable distribution of income and wealth. Our giant corporations, as mere creations of the state, will probably be the first to amend or disappear in a new social order.

After all, corporations are motivated not to enhance the community welfare, but to stimulate profitable sales, obtain larger credits, limit personal liability for corporate mistakes, stimulate production, and make a profit. They have helped create monopolies in most industries. They have set the patterns for the international cartels in commodities. Large-scale investments in the multinational corporations have been seen to cause instability in the lives of the peoples of the Third World.

Corporate officials decide our fate. When the president of an American knitting mill decides to move his plant from Rhode Island to Georgia, whole communities are uprooted. When corporate headquarters move to Westchester County, the tax basis of New York City is eroded at the very time that the city's ghettos house an ever-increasing number of unemployment welfare "cases."

The corporation's single function is growth and profit, but it does have a remarkable ability to build its own image as a citizen of the community. It easily handles questions of corporate bribery at home or abroad; after all, it "makes jobs." The corporation is detached and devoid of social consciousness or responsibility. Practically every new technical advance has as its objective the displacement of human labor. Any talk of a "corporate soul" concerned with the common welfare is so much baloney.

In support of apartheid or anti-union legislation the multinational corporation can manipulate and export large numbers of jobs. The corporation exercises enormous political clout. In the United States it has adopted techniques long used by its labor antagonists—they call it grass-roots lobbying. Ten thousand lobbyists operate in Washington, D.C., and generate calls and floods of letters and postcards to senators. Small businesses are enlisted; a blitz can scuttle congressional or executive action. Corporate political-action committees spend millions to prevent legislation they don't like. Mass-media advertising has barred political reform to the point of nullifying effective tax reforms. To put it bluntly, the American political apparatus is now under the total control of business.

As a practicing attorney , I watched the influence of the legal profession decline. One reason is that lawyers are becoming the handmaidens of the corporation. Their job is to worship the past and protect the *status quo*. I labored in the rich vineyards of a profitable law practice for two decades to the material benefit of my clients. Yet I always wondered if there was any great social significance if Client A owned building X rather than his adversary, B. Indeed, I questioned our whole adversary system of jurisprudence. In criminal cases it was the state against the individual. Why shouldn't the lawyer, like every other member of the community, be charged with getting the truth out into the open and justice accomplished promptly? In protecting individual freedoms, why shouldn't lawyers also have the obligation of developing and safeguarding the common welfare?

While lawyers look at historical precedents and tell other people what to do, the professional managers, in dissecting current issues, direct and operate vast economic and social institutions. Their objectives ought to include the satisfaction of social needs. The manager, irrespective of his cap or his title, must take responsibility for achieving goals. Responsibility is fixed, performance required. The manager is human and mobile; he can shape a private corporation or any institution within which he functions; the institution is what he makes it.

A nation worthy of survival must allocate its capital and

resources into line with a people's urgent priorities. Our American corporate dominance is responsible for many social failures. Forty percent unemployment among our black youth can hardly be consistent with any government's obligation. Ownership in the United States lives behind a heavy corporate cloak, but crisis will follow crisis—and poverty and disillusionment under politicians will introduce us to a new revolution under skilled managers.

Bringing corporations, with their wealth and power, under immediate public control in a capitalist "free market" economy may be unrealistic and won't be accomplished without a major struggle. The accumulation of power under the corporate shield must assume its share of blame. Federal charter of all corporations is but a single small step, but it's a step in the right direction. At least all business will operate under larger guidelines. But you may be sure that special interest lobbies will not allow Congress to take action. Nevertheless, as a creation of the state, bearing responsibility to the community, the child cannot forever control its societal parent.

Another change in the governance of our corporations involves an increase in employee participation in work-place decisions. Worker participation in management and ownership is becoming better established in many countries, such as West Germany and Sweden. American laws have not required social responsibility and have tended to emphasize the impersonal and protective aspects of the modern corporation. Thus, people buy or sell the securities of a corporation the way they play craps in Las Vegas or the horses at Churchill Downs.

There are encouraging signs. Rapidly growing consumer cooperatives and credit unions are positive steps toward worker involvement and enrichment. There is abroad in our land, not as much in America as in the other industrial nations, some support for public ownership of utilities and land, even of banks and small loan agencies. The forthcoming economic crises will bring these issues to the forefront.

Although the nature of the American political administration changes slightly every four years, the control of government by self-interest groups will grow apace. Our federal government's involvement in the economy and its attempts to accomplish social objectives is imperiled by the adoption of private interest restraints. No matter how the federal political establishment is debated, the issue of corporate dominance of our nation remains. The struggles of the future will largely revolve around this matter of who runs America. Under the "free enterprise" system corporations will predominate; under a planned society a democratic people will govern.

# CHAPTER
# IV

~~~~~~~~~~~~~~~~~~~~~~~~~~~~~~~~~~~~

# The Power
# and the
# Glory

At the age of seventeen, with the hopeful arrogance of the very young, I wrote a document, still in my files, outlining my campaign plans for the presidency of the United States. My strategy was drafted while I worked as an office boy in the Toledo law firm of Brown and Geddes. I secretly felt that one day posterity would find the document, a truly historic gem, tucked away in the effects of my estate. It would teach future generations that any bright-minded, ambitious youngster could realize that ultimate goal. The sketch also revealed juvenile horizons and emphasized a childish conviction: happiness requires prestige, comfort, power, and money. There was but one path to glory, and it would be achieved through political office. Election merely meant that a person must get a majority of the votes—it was that simple.

The American Dream, we were told, was big enough to harbor all religions and even the less-favored minorities. My privileged status as a white male American was the good work of a good God. God? Could this be another word for man's conscience? Such questions began to bother me. Were all those monumental cathedrals and historical buildings laboriously constructed by men throughout the ages to glorify an illusion? The idea of "success" began to get troublesome. Would my life reach out to glory and would fame equal success?

Maybe it was impossible for a youngster in that affluent environment to see that there could be another, even a better, world—a world in which ultimate success lies in the fulfillment of dreams of social change and a more equitable sharing of the world's goodies. Alas, most of my century saw America at war. We had become a superpower. I was faced with a quandry—become president of the most powerful nation on earth or work, inconspicuously, perhaps, for social and economic justice and ecological sanity.

For the benefit of worried historians I listed my accomplishments in high school, including my skills in pole vaulting and football. My carefully prepared autobiography didn't include such items as the presidency of the literary and debating societies, the senior class, the dramatic club, and the senior play. At the time such matters were trivia, not to be classed with athletic prowess. My football coach, Bill Wright, who sold insurance and headed the Young Men's Christian Association, added a point—"Don't get bogged down in doubts, avoid controversy, have faith in God, religion and your fellowman. Otherwise, you'll never get anywhere." Frankly, all of us looked upon higher education as a means of commanding a better-paying job in the economic system.

My plan called for graduation from Williams College in 1924, Harvard Law School in 1927, a short stretch of practicing law, and then election as state senator in 1930, governor of Ohio in 1941, U.S. senator in 1946, and president in 1948. I would run as a Republican to carry on the tradition of my father. No matter that he was only a precinct chairman, the lowliest office in the whole political spectrum.

My father's personal alienation from politics came within a few years. He was a plain, hardworking, honest commercial fishermen. Our large, urbanized, mechanized society was under the domination of local politicians like John

O'Dwyer in East Toledo, who built up corrupt political machines and got away with rake-offs on contracts. Big graft money helped keep his people in office. Often the bosses stood openly at the election booths and passed out beer and dollar bills. It was not uncommon in our wards to have more votes tallied than voters registered.

The boom was cut short by the stock-market crash in October 1929. Like everyone else, I lost almost all my material possessions. But I still had my license to practice law. In that profession one has only to be curious and innovative. People are always in trouble; someone always needs a lawyer! And the devastating years of the 1930s opened up big opportunities to acquire business bargains. Yet bargain hunting in depression times wasn't pleasant. It often meant taking possession from farmer or homeowner. People couldn't get jobs; banks and industrial concerns went bankrupt. Just about everything went haywire in our confused, unplanned society. My home city of Toledo issued scrip instead of wages—and the scrip itself became practically worthless. Hunger existed in the midst of food surpluses. Warehouses held huge hoards of commodities until an owner could get his price. The system wasted more than enough food to feed tens of millions of hungry people.

As I reflect on those ugly days, I realize that we were part of a crazy, irrational world drama. As a nation, we refused to look at fundamentals. We naïvely thought that somehow a falling stock market or lack of money in circulation caused unemployment. Our "economists" wouldn't admit that we might be seeing the collapse of the world's political and economic systems. Sociologists and politicians saw unsolvable problems—each of us thought only of survival. We weren't prepared to think of creating a sane society in which the world's abundance could be shared. We had heard from some of our American soldiers who intervened in Russia's New Society during 1918–20 that the Bolsheviks were wild men who raped women and that peasants were starving.

I met Franklin D. Roosevelt on several occasions, and I made friends with many New Dealers. They dared not say so openly, but they were slowly discovering some of the weaknesses of our profit-motivated economy. Favorable mention of Marx or Lenin could have separated them from their jobs in Washington. As the country lay helpless, we heard some preachments on the primacy of the government's responsibility for satisfying social needs.

My law practice grew handsomely. However, I began to wonder about the morality of my allegiance to the American economic system.

My corporate law practice withered away as I moved into the camp of unorganized labor and civil libertarians. I became active in the formation of the Steel Workers Organizing Committee and the CIO. Before long I was representing John L. Lewis, Phil Murray, and John Brophy in several controversial and stormy labor cases. I represented the striking shoe workers in Portsmouth, Ohio, and in the process I defeated the clumsy attempts of the corporations' attorneys to disbar me. It was natural enough that when I took the labor side I should lose my wealthy clients—I just didn't expect it to happen so quickly.

I experienced many real satisfactions in taking the law claims of the workers. It's thrilling to correct any injustice, but the massive inequity of a social system seems to go beyond the efforts of any single person. Alliance with other reformers is a truly great and warming satisfaction. Fighting for a cause can even become more exciting than election to office—and much more fun than making a financial killing. Beyond all else, it fulfills one's life and enriches one's sense of usefulness.

In those early days our major objective became the organization of giant trade industrial unions in the mass-production industries. We wanted to get more democracy into the unions. A clean, trim labor organization would then have the muscle to deal effectively with the emerging industrial giants. We began to talk about the philosophy of state ownership of the means of production. But any nation's first priority is to get a plan for a firmer grip on the economy. There was widespread opposition to permitting the study of communism in schools or factories. It was obvious that the New Dealers didn't dream of basic changes; they settled for stimulating and organizing mass consumer purchasing power. They allowed the owners to set up monopolies as they wanted, hoping only that the people could somehow be protected.

Back in 1924 Senator Robert M. LaFollette of Wisconsin founded the Progressive party. It was my first exposure to populism. As a college student, I campaigned for his political and social programs. I attended LaFolette's provocative lectures on street corners and on campuses. Soon I was speaking to groups of unemployed. I probably gained a few votes and fewer converts for the Progressive party. But the experience taught me firm lessons, especially when I later waged my youthful campaign for the U.S. Senate on the Republican ticket. I learned some political facts: either get behind the established political Republican organization or get out. Shortly after the 1929 crash, I got out. I was impressed by LaFollette's emphasis on the need for farmers and trade unions to organize and cooperate. Like countless others, I decided that a progressive American could hardly travel the path of the conservative Republican party.

We recognized that reformist programs couldn't stop at our national borders. We also wondered if a dedicated group of enthusiasts could help improve international relations through economic-trade, cultural, and political exchanges. What about including all countries in a sweeping treaty of friendship—even Soviet Russia and other newly organized socialist countries in strange, faraway, dangerous places? Would it be possible to move peacefully into internationalism, or would we wait until forced to share our vast resources? Couldn't we understand that a voluntary sharing of a nation's assets with others must remain just a childish dream?

I ran again for the United States Senate—this time as a progressive Democrat. I came out attacking the giant corporate monopolies. Again, I got licked. I ran for the office of attorney general of Ohio on the Democratic ticket with disastrous results. All this chasing of political office and failing should have told me something. At least I was impartial in taking my political beatings at the hands of party political bosses who had one thing in common—they all opposed my leftist views. And for myself, I began to wonder if all politicians weren't playing charades.

As a trade-union attorney with clients like my close friend August Scholle of Detroit, head of the Committee for Industrial Organization in Michigan, I began to carry some political clout. In spite of reservations, I became a member of various state Democratic political committees. It was impossible at the local level to see much difference between Republican and Democratic parties except that one group was in and the other out. The incumbents had the spoils and found it easier to raise money. With my trade-union contacts I soon learned how to get funds channeled into the campaign coffers of various candidates. Money determined elections—and funding progressive candidates became one of my specialties. Some of them, like Congressman Vito Marcantonio of New York City and Maury Maverick of Texas, were notoriously radical, and I helped their kitties substantially.

By the mid-1940s the organization of industrial trade unions was nearly completed. Labor leadership, especially those under Catholic and other church influence, grew more and more regressive. I doubted my ability to retain unswerving loyalty to the leadership of such worker organizations, whether headed by a John L. Lewis or the likes of reactionary George Meany.

Unions in autos, steel and haulage developed bureaucracies as their members achieved security and status. Affluence caused them to float toward the right. We did have some vigorous public debates about the possibility of truly sharing property. We asked ourselves if religious tolerance and an effective internationalism could make more progress in the socialist countries. Practically all union officials upheld the capitalist nations where man's top priority is gauged by the accumulation of wealth. I pointed out that the pursuit of individual welfare or a change of economic status would never permit drastic alteration of industrialized societies. Ideologies, especially among the religious, always seemed to support the state's efforts to preserve the *status quo*. Sects throughout the ages have claimed a special connection with a god.

With his theory of economic determinism, Karl Marx emphasized that ultimate power is in ownership. The course of events in the United States proved the accuracy of the thesis. During those wretched depression days with owner-ship "bargains" galore, I began to acquire newspapers and radio, television, and manufacturing companies. It wasn't too difficult. I simply made small down payments. The sell-ers themselves financed the long-term payouts. It was equally obvious that in a capitalist society ownership of the com-munications media could influence policies. With hindsight I regret that I took so long to acquire ownership of the in-stitutions controlling vast sums of money, like banking and insurance companies.

Businessmen avoid getting too far out front; many prefer to give the appearance of holding themselves aloof from political activities. They prefer to let their lieutenants speak for them—spokesmen who include lawyers, trade associations, and lobbyists. Corporate executives take off for the Florida beaches and leave management and public-relations outfits to create images. Corporate presidents maintain the com-pany's more significant contacts and attend White House functions. Enormous funding of politicians is simple. Financ-ing, big financing, can be accomplished by underwriting testimonial dinners for politicians and political parties. Un-der our system, the fund raiser is always in. Millions of dollars are poured into a campaign.

But a campaign to humanize business deserves our atten-tion. We certainly favor programs advancing the human-potential movement. The disillusioned young may well find business a respectable way to make a living. After all, we are alert to the ideological changes taking place in con-temporary society. Certain radical change of the current scene is not being directed by the Communist party. Wouldn't it be surprising if socially sensitive graduates of our business schools could be the leaders of the movement for the basic structural changes necessary to make our so-ciety more responsive?

I helped finance the campaigns of people and programs I liked, but I do not believe I ever asked a favor of any politician. I enjoyed making substantial gifts to many of the more progressive congressmen, hoping to affect their policies. I provided several politicians, including presidential candidates, with transportation on my private plane. The walks I took in Oregon with the great progressive Senator Wayne Morse were delightful and effective in cementing my friendship with a worthy man. Political contributions give donors a certain ego satisfaction—and tickets of admission to the offices of the mighty.

Politicians in America have difficulty being statesmen or spokesmen for great and noble principles. They are elected by courting their own local constituencies. Frequently congressmen are little more than errand boys. I doubt whether any politician in Congress would care to disclose the background of all his financing. Without mentioning names, I have slipped dozens of money envelopes to my progressive political friends. Money given to congressmen has no party allegiance, only client allegiance. Corporations work their wondrous ways by greasing both sides of the road.

According to *Congressional Quarterly,* August 7, 1978, one Republican congressman in California, Robert F. Dornan, said with some emotion, "Corporate managers are whores. They don't care who's in office, what party or what they stand for. They are just out to buy you." Republican Senator Paul Laxalt of Nevada said simply, "We find that our 'friends,' the Fortune 500, are playing both sides." As a large donor to individual Democratic candidates and to the party itself, I served several times as delegate to Democratic national conventions. Always I told myself that I aided the progressive cause in the country. At least my causes, like campaigns for the United Nations or for recognition of the socialist states, were always in the open.

He who disturbs the entrenched money and power centers can expect to be assaulted with bricks in return, as those of us who went through the witch-hunt days of Senator Joseph McCarthy can testify. There were many inconsistencies. No matter how I was criticized as a progressive, I found that I could make money—big money—in a world where money speaks. It's comfortable to sit in a room with bankers and know that I can speak their language. Many have known that I allocated sizable funds for unpopular causes.

Many liberals, especially in business and the professions, run away in a crisis. They're glad to forget the witch hunts of Richard Nixon's and J. Parnell Thomas's Un-American Activities Committee. A nation watched their headline attempts to massacre Alger Hiss. They also charged that I was a member of the Communist party. I was ultimately cleared because big money proved that such smears and frameups can be defeated.

Expensive public-relations experts change images. For several years my name appeared in print as "the radical Toledo lawyer." After I acquired substantial property, I became the milder "controversial Toledo industrialist." Now it's "American banker." I like being called "radical" better.

The process of gaining respectability is simple enough. I never blamed the American financial community for being disturbed by my push for radical causes. At least there was so little my critics could do about stirring up another smear against me—unless they wanted to go through one big rousing battle in the law courts. I had proved that I could win battles—and stay out of jail! When my intellectual, liberal or union labor friends moved to the right and deserted the cause, as many of them did, I continued to urge nationalizing our steel, transportation, and defense industries. When the labor unions became protectionists and demanded tariffs, I campaigned for more free trade—and increased trade with the socialist nations.

During the post-Watergate days when rampant corporate-government bribery was exposed, many industrial leaders had their hands full explaining their questionable actions. A lull set in. Inasmuch as I wanted nothing more than my independence, I didn't have to equivocate in my opposition to the Vietnam war and tax increases or my support of effective wage and price controls and full trade and diplomatic relations with all the nations of the world. I took stronger positions on such issues as abortion, integration, full employment, détente, health planning, and a strong central governmental authority.

There are in our midst brave souls, fellows who put their jobs on the line in resisting an unjust war or joining up with liberation movements, like those in Spain or Vietnam. I also had great personal admiration for businessmen like Cyrus Eaton of Cleveland and Marriner Eccles of Salt Lake City. Throughout the turbulent 1960s they not only expressed vigorous approval of trade with socialist nations, but also showed their outright opposition to war. They challenged anyone to accuse them of a Communist "taint."

Although I admired the dignity of such beautiful people in quieting critics, my own put-down of my detractors was a simple "Screw 'em!" and get on with the cause! On a personal note, I was glad to broadcast words of encouragement from Cuba to the Vietcong in the late 1960s. Our CIA was disturbed. But I told them that it took greater courage for the brave youths who resisted the draft and were imprisoned or forced to live abroad for so many years.

One night in Mexico City I talked at length with Justice William O. Douglas. I admired him as a man, a jurist, and a social activist. He was an alert and profound author— America's leading authority on First Amendment freedoms. We served together for many years as fellow trustees for the Center for the Study of Democratic Institutions, Santa Barbara, California. At that time he was between wives three and four. He talked that night of the limited personal freedoms enjoyed by a justice of the highest court.

After a few tequila drinks we took turns telling our favorite stories. We laughed over the antics of his critics, like Barry Goldwater, Spiro Agnew, and Richard Nixon. After dinner, he expressed envy as I took off for a large party with a pretty delegate to the conference. Douglas, always conscious of his position and image, feared doing anything more to feed the gossips. At that very moment his impeachment was being sought by a Republican congressman named Gerald R. Ford. My own lively activities that evening were of total disinterest to anyone else. Anonymity has its rewards!

I don't know every trick in the book about making money, but I know a few. I didn't become successful in the commercial community as an idealist wedded to orthodoxy. Nor do I claim to be representative of my fellow American industrialists. I often predict the eventual doomsday for capitalism unless we adjust our economies to the reality of today's world—in other words, accept rigorous worldwide planning techniques.

America faces the stark fact that the overall economy of the United States is not functioning. It will not work in the future unless we change to a more cooperative, planned, sharing society. Rather than accept our role as a partner in an interdependent world, American political leadership has sought, even in a post-colonial era, to defend unilaterally our *status quo* and national boundaries. What are the alternatives? Our politicians were shocked when Californians adopted a Proposition 13, limiting real estate taxes. What this nation needs is a Proposition 14, compelling our governmental agents to stand up to their responsibilities—raise taxes sufficient to pay our social and economic way.

Planning the private and public sectors has finally become one of the central issues in the United States and other nations. I believe that we can plan to live with the other humans on this planet. André Malraux, French author, in a letter addressed to John F. Kennedy, said: "In the nineteenth century the ostensible issue within the European states was the monarchy versus the republic. In the twentieth century the ostensible issue is capitalism versus the proletariat. But the world has moved on. What is the real issue now? The answer—international cooperation between nations."

We long ago learned that mere discontent does not bring about successful revolutions. Liberation movements and revolutions, with or without violence, use the instrument of government, any government, to achieve their basic purpose: the advancement of the welfare of people who control it. In the midst of crisis, we've listened to the politicians' irrelevant diatribes against communism, for "defense" spending, for big corporations and big unions. It's ridiculous, but we often hear these critics, while seeing their private institutions growing bigger and richer, decry bigness in our federal government. Meantime, big business is unanimous in telling government to keep government's nose out of business's affairs.

Our problems transcend borders. Affluent Americans apathetic toward internationalism became smug and diverted our attention from pertinent and worthwhile programs, such as consumer co-ops, community developments, municipally owned enterprises, and worker-controlled factories. By contrast, our media and giant corporations often use language reminiscent of other decaying societies. But we'll learn. Stresses will intensify until by contact, negotiation, or force we build a multinational medium able to achieve universal world cooperation. Our dreams can be summed up in two priority goals: international cooperation among all states within an effective world organization; and rational societal planning.

I believe that we'll one day recognize the superiority of social ownership of the basic means of production. History decrees differing time schedules for various societies. Such programs have already become a necessity in many Third World countries where only the government has the means to inaugurate and maintain social enterprises. There isn't much time left for Americans to chatter idly about retaining unchanged a private profit system while a vast majority of the world's people cry out for a share, for justice and survival. We face reality. What follows socialism remains to be seen. We've watched nations leave capitalism for communism, but none has returned to a system of private ownership.

∞∞∞∞∞∞∞∞∞∞∞∞∞∞∞∞∞∞∞

# V

# The Managerial Revolt

After I decided to gain control of companies, it didn't take long to find out that operating failures were usually due to inadequate management practices. We should be forgiven for knowing so little about scientific managment—it has such a short history.

In 1911, an engineer named Frederick W. Taylor called together a small group of men to the village of Hanover in the White Mountains of New Hampshire to discuss the possibilities of a new concept in business management. There were many scoffers when he announced that he'd "demonstrate the efficient application of human resources to natural resources." Three decades earlier Taylor's experiments with management methods in the Midvale Steel Company, Philadelphia, had been published in *Shop Management*. His essay "The Principles of Scientific Management" appeared just before the 1911 meetings. Efficiency and productivity summed up the goals of scientific management. He wrote, "The basic responsibility for eliminating waste and improving the output lies with the business manager."

Taylor introduced the concept of time-and-motion practices and efficiency, and he showed techniques for measuring
the "input" required for a given output of the end product.
The treatise immediately caused a furor. Working people
attacked the idea of time-motion studies as "inhuman,"
"demeaning," and "heartless." Strangely enough, opposition
to such a new concept also came from businessmen, the
principal beneficiaries of these studies. Labor, unorganized
and underpaid, demonstrated against the "exploitive managers" who dared introduce machines to take away jobs. The
revolution was on.

Reformers of the day resented Taylor's "standards of
output" as a tool for further exploitation. Several economists
claimed that removing the responsibility for planning methods from the individual worker and turning the task over
to a specialist or manager to organize and plan production
caused the worker to lose his incentive and creativity. He
would become a mere automaton; the industrial worker
would become "efficient" but a nonperson. Taylor replied
that the worker would be freed from the long hours of
labor, that his standard of living would rise and he would
have the income and leisure to become a more complete and
vital member of society.

Taylor, Carl Barth, Harlow S. Person, and others devised
and refined systems for controlling the vast new expanded
economic institutions. They were the first to set down the
ground rules for managing resources in any industrialized
nation. They knew, as others have known, that men do not
live by bread alone, that they want frosting on their cake,
and that they don't enjoy doing anything the hard way.
From the advent of the wheel, men have assumed that the
dominant, if not exclusive, motivation in industry was to
save physical effort.

Planned productivity was introduced, and men learned
to free themselves from menial tasks. With clear hindsight
we see errors in the early theses. No one could be ingenious
enough to foresee the many ways that men could be exploited by the owners of new production facilities. Even

though they envisioned a fuller life for workers, automation meant greater production with fewer hands.

Schools of business administration were established. America's first graduate school of business administration was set up at Dartmouth College, and was directed by Dr. Harlow Stafford Person, the prime organizational force in the scientific-management movement. For seventeen years he served as instructor, dean, and director of the Amos Tuck School of Business Administration at Hanover. He retired from the post in 1919 to continue his labors as editor of the magazine *Scientific Management in America*. In 1936 he wrote the basic outline on scientific management for the *Encyclopedia of the Social Sciences*.

Person, whose name is not as well known as Taylor's,* was also called Mr. Management by succeeding generations. He prepared curricula for schools of business administration, but he insisted that managers should have a solid education in the liberal arts and the humanities. He began to speak of business leadership with a social conscience!

Basically, men like Taylor, Barth, and Person were not interested in redesigning the social order. They recognized inequities in society, but they didn't concern themselves with populist movements that demand social and economic change. True, they were aware of the inequalities, the wealth and the poverty, the inconsistencies of the "free," uncontrolled society in which they lived, but they were not concerned, as were their contemporary revolutionists, Karl Marx and Eugene Debs, with who owned the means of production. As academic engineers, they simply studied how to manage an organization. They wanted to find a way to make the economy work predictably, then move on to the larger problems of satisfying the needs of mankind.

These pioneers in scientific management learned that management is simply the attainment of objectives through

* The Society to Promote the Science of Management later became known as the Taylor Society. As the objectives of Scientific Management expanded, the movement continued for some years under the label of Taylorism.

people. We now seek to prevent management from becoming overspecialized in techniques. We've come a long
way in learning to train decision makers. We realize that
an institution is as good as its management. We're matured
beyond systems, analyses, and goals to the meaningful participation of every person in the operation.

I enjoy watching a good manager function as he translates
the company's goals and acquires the active support of his
full staff, a committed and involved group. Effective management needs neither the carrot-and-stick approach nor
leadership by command. The basic challenge of management
under any social system is *people development*. All people
everywhere want job security, adequate housing, food, education, the satisfaction of human needs. It isn't sufficient to
have people in the modern-day capitalist society, with its
high-anxiety levels, motivated only by job security and
profits.

American corporations offer material incentives, often
enormous financial incentives, to management at all levels,
yet recent surveys show that a majority of managers in American corporations consider themselves "poorly motivated."

The average manager, like other workers, is beginning to
lack enthusiasm for his job and his superiors. He may be
bored, his contribution to society limited and his efforts
and performance unappreciated. The gold gift watch handed
the retiring or long-service employee, even with a smile and
a pat on the back, has its shortcomings. With inflation,
mergers, and takeovers, his future and economic security
are uncertain.

I did not accept the philosophy of scientific management
until I suffered a great many painful upsets. In the various
Lamb Enterprises—television, manufacturing, banking, leasing—we were shaken into adopting modern management
techniques. Heads rolled after we learned the hard way and
mustered the conviction and courage to choose alternatives.
Only then did we achieve some startling successes. A friend
put it grandly: "The corporate gardens of the Lamb Enterprises bloomed only after they brought in people who knew
how to make blossoms bloom."

Our generation has been privy to one of the truly important revolutions in the history of mankind. Here in America we developed the art of scientific management. We went through the age of invention and innovation, we had remarkable political and economic programs, and we learned the technique of massive production.

It is apparent that society's successful entry into the twenty-first century largely depends upon whether the professional manager, recognized the world over for his achievement and skills in industrial management and administration, is given a definitive role in other areas. To our credit, we moved away from the days of the hapless worker epitomized in Charlie Chaplin's *Modern Times*. We have at our disposal men and women trained in planning and administering human affairs who can accept, even on a worldwide basis, responsibility for operating in the public and private sectors.

A quick glance at some of the problems facing the world today leaves us with a crushing sense of impotence: the population explosion, pollution of our shrinking earth, a widening gap between the rich and the poor individuals and nations, the decay of cities, tensions among creeds and races, the exponential rate of change, and the accelerating development of technology, which at times threatens to outrace the imagination of man. We recognize generation gaps and imbalances everywhere—yet we know that young people are dissatisfied with the present state of affairs.

We're in a crisis of giant dimensions. Simple goodwill or the individual's desire to advance human welfare is not enough. After our Watergate and Vietnam experiences, few thinking citizens do not harbor some doubt about the efficacy and adequacy of the American political process. Political democracy is bankrupt. Indeed, our two-party system offers no real alternatives. Men want jobs, housing, and other essentials for a fulfilled existence; the system isn't providing them.

In my own way I have supported popular causes designed to bring peace to the world and prosperity at home. I don't see a solution in any ideology. I am, however, convinced that society must get a new approach and turn to the specialist trained to bring order out of chaos. We need persons trained to use scientific methods, to analyze, correlate, integrate, implement, and accommodate the unknown and the unexpected. Among all the disciplines, only the management specialist has the training and capacity to organize a multitude of concerns directed toward the achievement of what we think is a desirable goal: a better-planned society.

Behavioral sciences tell us a great deal about the human animal as he moves within an operational structure containing all the conflicts and interrelationships common to humanity. As each human is one among many, he's of necessity an "organization man." As a member of a structure, he is aware of certain rights and certain obligations. But he must also recognize some authority.

We have begun to see technology shape man's habitat on a limited planet. As we approach this complex world of reality, we acknowledge the need for a skill to organize systematize, and administer vast and challenging projects. Our pioneers tended to seek only independence and the freedom to wrest wealth from this new land. We like to think that our historical heroes, like Abraham Lincoln, fought a great civil war to free the slaves, but we know all too well as we read the newspapers of that day what the people were thinking about as the crisis unfolded. On February 26, 1861, a few days before Lincoln's inaugural, the Boston Herald's front-page story said, "The chief demand of the age is money, all classes are automated by it, even those who profess to be uninfluenced by it. To such an engrossing extent is the desire for money-making carried that most people think of nothing else. It employs their active exertions during the day and their dreams at night." There was no indication of remorse or even doubts—we have been a nation hell-bent for profit.

Technology created lively new industries in this time of explosive industrial growth in America. Genius in programming for mass production in the huge multiplant operations helped to usher in the new industrial era. The casualties of the market jungle were enormous. Fifteen hundred automobile firms, including Hudson and Maxwell, were established in the early 1900s, but only a dozen would survive: Studebaker, Willys Overland, Ford, and parts of General Motors. Finally, the trend toward bigness and the attrition of free enterprise left only four. There may be even fewer.

The contributions of our American industrialists toward the development of significant management and organization techniques were magnificently intentional, not just intuitive. Before the computer's arrival, such matters as cost studies, inventory control, and internal reporting were performed manually by hit-and-miss means, somewhat the way the earliest pilots flew, not by instruments, but by the seat of their britches. With the fantastic computer our economy grew. It became vital, undisciplined, explosive—somewhat like the frontiers of the land itself.

My father revered his friend Mark Hanna, the early Cleveland industrialist, who, in spite of his stand-patism, taught America some significant lessons. He showed in his exaggerated way that the road to financial power was made easier and faster by acquiring political power. In his dual roles as chairman of the Republican party and United States senator, he helped build the high tariff walls that protected the infant iron, coal, and steel businesses. His protective tariff walls have persisted ever since, even though the infants are now full-grown corporate giants. Our economies may have become interdependent, but our political structures remain as rigid as ever.

About the time ebullient Theodore Roosevelt railed against the giant trusts, big, fat, jolly William Howard Taft joked his way through the presidency. But no president under capitalism, before or since Theodore Roosevelt, ever showed how government could more effectively favor and foster the "prerequisites of business." "Big money talks." He made a pass at antitrust enforcement, but the biggest trusts in autos, food, banking, and chemicals grow ever bigger. Super corporations, like U.S. Steel and Kennecott Copper, were grandfathered into their dominant status by beneficient politicians. Franklin D. Roosevelt and John F. Kennedy may seem to have threatened big business, but their "reforms" and tax adjustments "stimulating capital formation" actually strengthened the corporate elite.

In the early 1900s railroads could be bought, sold, or wrecked by what were, naturally enough, called the Robber Barons. There was savage and destructive competition in the food, drug, chemical, and auto industries. But it became obvious that survival in the jungle of the marketplace would go not only to the big and efficient, but to the well-managed. Our emerging nation had produced creative researchers and innovators, like Thomas A. Edison, who were producing new and exciting products, everything from the telephone to movies, airplanes, and television. We moved into a world of gimmickry and rushed into a loose, unplanned free-for-all. The times were ripe for a bit of sensible self-appraisal and organizational planning.

Most of us are members of large institutions, which are getting bigger and developing ever more impersonal relationships. At the same time we are beginning to recognize our dependence on one another. The modern manager tries to bring about a social cohesion, a big family atmosphere. When I've acquired a corporation, such as a bank, leasing, or manufacturing operation, I've asked my managers to get all employees together so that we can personally discuss our mutual goals and learn to communicate with each other, form a team, and cooperatively share in the fruits of our efforts. I cannot say that the incentives of stock option or employee-ownership plans or profit-sharing plans are total successes, but they are constructive steps.

A good manager develops a certain sense of teamsmanship among all workers from presidents down. Our experience in the day-to-day world—running a church, corporation, club, or any other man-made organization—is always the same. The person at the head largely determines its success.

The graduates of schools of business administration, whether in America or elsewhere, will furnish an increasing number of the future leaders of the world. One of the realities is that the nature of the state itself is changing. National boundaries can no longer confine ideologies or scientific discoveries. Yet we've seen significant human institutions run by leaders who are skilled only in winning popularity and beauty contests, experts only in the art of diverting attention from crucial issues. The world's biggest human institution, the United States government ("of the people, by the people") never has had an effective, competent management team.

The annual pay of chief executive officers in the 1978 *Fortune* list of the five hundred leading corporations runs into the hundreds of thousands. Only the owners can draw bigger funds from the corporate till. These people who own and operate our corporations always take care of themselves; their bottom line glows in good times and bad.

I remain hopeful that we'll get a decent society for America without being forced into it by great social upheaval. When society accepts its responsibility for housing, education, and economic and social security, harnessing the skills and services of people who know how to get results, we'll be on our way.

The imperial president has the ultimate power over much of our domestic welfare programming. Former President Richard Nixon could with a stroke of the pen knock out hundreds of Job Corps training centers. We saw President Gerald Ford take food stamps away from five million people and eliminate hospitals and day-care centers by the hundreds.

An alert professional manager charged with organizing a socially responsive society would act quite differently. It's true that our nation lives under a written constitution and the president must act within his mandated authority, keeping in mind his division of powers with Congress and the judiciary. Our political leaders' judgment is hamstrung by establishment lobbies, political cliques, and preferred constituencies. But the president's task is to respond to the challenges of the modern, complex society he directs. The science of management in government must entertain any technique or any process that permits the social structure to respond to the needs of its citizens.

# CHAPTER
# VI

~~~~~~~~~~~~~~~~~~~~~~~~~~~~~~~~~~~~~~~~~~~~~~

# Two Revolutions

The eighteenth century had its industrial and political revolutions.

At the turn of the twentieth century, mankind witnessed the birth of two additional movements: scientific management (Taylorism) and social ownership (Leninism). Acceptance of scientific management in the socialist countries was delayed, but Nikolai Lenin was first to develop the truly significant revolution. He led the movement to change the ownership of the means of production from the private to the public sector. The Russian Revolution in 1917 succeeded in installing on a sixth of the earth's surface the social ownership of farms, factories, and mines. Other nations followed, so that today more than half of the world's population lives in socialized nations.

Lenin, like Karl Marx, was not concerned with the management or operation of facilities. He and his followers felt that the workers could somehow operate industrial factories or remote farms through a central planning bureau in Moscow. At first these revolutionaries didn't realize that following the seizure of political power, it would become necessary to have managerial cadres. Only in his final days did Lenin recognize the importance of Frederick W. Taylor's *The Principles of Scientific Management*. All subsequent history of the socialist countries is plagued with this failure of earlier Marxists to understand the significance of coordinating human skills—of managing. Quite recently the People's Republic of China began "decentralizing," delegating some responsibilities to lower levels and into their communes. After their "cultural revolution" in the 1960s they sought to join the industrialized society of the twentieth century.

Lenin preached the slogan *Communism means electrification*. The Soviets have learned, as we all must, that it takes longer to install a program than it does to mouth a slogan. Succeeding Soviet leaders eventually followed his advice to electrify and modernize by bringing in management specialists able to make the complex electrified systems function. Today's city of Leningrad on the Neva River at night is a truly memorable sight, a tribute to man's management of electricity.

A remarkable historical item is that Lenin created a form of political structure, while Taylor made it work. There is a certain similarity between the economic development of the United States and the Soviet Union, although Soviet Russia went directly from feudalism into industrialization. Each nation possessed vast natural resources, and each has about the same number of human resources. America's industrial revolution began to click three decades earlier than the Russian because we more promptly developed a professional class of management specialists skilled in controlling and operating economic units.

Can the principles of scientific management be universally applied? Carl Heydel in his *Encyclopedia of Management* suggests that management's province includes "all mankind." He writes, "Management of art and science must be brought to bear wherever effort can be organized on a significant scale—in government, the cultural arts, sports, the military, medicine, education, scientific research, and religion—as well as in the profit pursuits of manufacture and commerce."

From its earliest days I insisted that the economy of the Soviet Union was retarded by the rigid authority given to the central planning cadres and to the steering groups or committees. They were primarily interested in the survival of their system. Early Soviet leaders and the Moscow bureaucracy were unwilling to concede the need for scientific management. They refused to delegate responsibility to a management "elitist class." Faithful party followers found all the answers in the words of Karl Marx. I remember the vehement arguments some of us had in one of the early Moscow sessions held for visiting businessmen. The Russians couldn't find an ideological justification for having anyone except engineering persons as plant managers. On the other hand, American management advisors pushed for a single manager for a single plant charged with coordinating all the human skills under the rubric of scientific management. They covered all the basic principles of management—planning, organizing, controlling, motivating, and communicating. The conference reached no conclusions, but we all felt better for having had the dialogue.

Soviet record keeping was primitive and carried out by bureaucratic pen pushers and bookkeepers. Then came the computer. Though the United States barred its export to the Soviet Union, all the world knew that a new revolution was on its way. The phenomenon could instantly correlate, analyze, and preserve a myriad of facts. Millions of computations rolled out in a single second. Vast operations previously performed without central planning could now be brought together. Our own early tycoons, like Henry Clay Frick, Henry Ford, and Harvey Firestone, may have had a genius for production and organization, but with the advent of the new technology, the rules of scientific management became more understandable, feasible, and institutional. We began to see the possibilities of push-button management of all businesses, large and small, in the operation of the world's assets.

My book *Planned Economy of Soviet Russia* (1934) gave me a chance to study the broad implications of the new socialist economy. Later I learned even more about that historic experiment in the development of a human society. Suddenly I saw a planned society where *all* the levels of power were under government control. In Moscow I often visited with members of Gosplan, the vast national planning agency directing and managing just about all phases of the economy. Setting up such a bureaucracy was a herculean task, and I saw my share of snafus and production failures. Over the years I visited many factories and research centers in the Soviet Union. I was given almost unlimited access to their productive facilities. I saw the struggles to control the economy. But I was also conscious of the economic gyrations happening in the capitalist countries.

The American economy was in the throes of a wild crisis. As industry and society tended toward bigness, the largest institution in the world remained the United States government. America was plagued by unemployment, inflation, and depression. Naturally enough, our involvement in foreign military adventures began to eat up a greater share of our national budget, even as we were required to spend more for our domestic social needs. We were beginning to recognize that if we were to escape serious social upheaval, no matter who was president, no matter which of the two political parties was in control, we would be required to furnish more and not less social services. The need for slum clearance, education, food, shelter, supplies, inter-city transportation had become obvious in the free-enterprise system.

Could traumatic experience stimulate responsible government reform? It was our generation's opportunity—we felt we could obtain the best economic and social security in the history of humankind. One day technology, under the guidance of skilled managers with enlightened attitudes, could give us all the things the politicians had promised!

There were difficulties—the entrenched government bureaucracy, weighted with civil service and seniority systems, makes difficult the recruitment of good administrators. Possibly we have overbuilt hopes for a political democracy. We not only developed an entrenched bureaucracy—but we also too often dredged up the dregs to lead us.

We are left with an anti-elitist group—government by the worst. Distrust, disillusionment, and frustration have taken away the appetite for public service. Recent presidents have included puppets, crooks, fumblers, and rabid religionists. Only a minority of citizens eligible to vote take the trouble to vote. Yet in the private sector we watch major business concerns knock on the doors of our schools of business administration soliciting the cream of available talent. College seniors and graduate students vie for corporate job opportunities, with their better pay scale and chance for advancement, while highly skilled professionals like teachers and technicians remain unemployed by the public sector.

Many young people who try life on the Potomac find, after a year or two in government service, that the nonconformist, the innovator dislikes the "security checks" and the long delays in clearances. The days of suspicion and witch hunts have not passed with McCarthyism or with the Vietnamese or the Middle Eastern wars. In spite of its past scandalous conduct, the Central Intelligence Agency has sharpened its surveillance of government employees.

In the early 1970s I addressed the radical Students for a Democratic Society at the Harvard Club in New York City. Other speakers included various colorful, heavily bearded characters who had precipitated some of the earlier wild campus riots. Many had dropped out of college and joined the "cause." They were full of ideas of how to foment a revolution.

Although I am not an expert on revolutionary techniques, I have talked to many leaders of successful revolutions, like the old Bolsheviks and the younger Fidel Castro. Castro once told me, "Don't send us your young, starry-eyed revolutionists; we've already had our revolution. Send us someone with skills and the ability to show us how-to!" Following the Cuban's suggestion, I advised those would-be radical students, "Irrespective of who owns the means of production, every society has a crying need for someone to be around with the skills necessary to manage the system. Build a new world but be ready to operate it! And get yourself a personal skill; be ready to do your part in building your new society."

It's reassuring that many of our largest American corporations are under the guidance of lively persons under thirty-five. American institutions are learning how to refresh and energize themselves with new blood. The successful company continually evaluates and coaches the managers as it screens out or rearranges the poor performers. It is difficult to think of a successful company today that doesn't emphasize its manpower-training and executive-development programs.

The contrast between the private and public management teams is startling. I shudder when I think of the old men and women setting policies in the Supreme Soviet of the Soviet Union, the Communist party in the People's Republic of China, and our own government.

Peoples of other nations are hungry for our knowledge of the science of management. Russian, Cuban, Chinese, and other students will one day be as cordially admitted to our institutes of business administration as Indian, Belgian, or French citizens are now. We trust that our own specialists will conduct more seminars on the art of scientific management in other nations.

Our dominant role in the science of management is lessening as we realize some of our own shortcomings—both in the operation of our economy and in the training of people to run an effective, efficient government. We do recognize the influence of our managerial performance and its effect on the affairs of all humanity. In appraising our economists, sociologists, and scientists, even our corporate managers—those who make our economy tick—we impose stricter and more meaningful standards. Corporate management's continuance in office is not a matter of winning public acclaim. Getting elected is not their job; they are measured by results.

After one of my conferences in Cuba on the need for scientific management, I was happy to hear Premier (now President) Castro say that he had instructed José Miyar, senior dean of Havana University, to establish a new school of scientific management. This was a significant breakthrough because it was one of the first technical centers for the training of scientific managers ever adopted in a socialist country. Castro is a pragmatist. He reached out to develop a practical ideology compatible with reality and the facts of modern science. He was knowledgeable and astute enough to accept Marxist ideology and couple it with modern scientific methods. By his action Cuba began one of the most significant developments in the history of mankind.

A different slant on the use of scientific management as a historical breakthrough was suggested by Dr. Kenneth Clark, the psychologist and president of the Metropolitan Applied Research Center in New York. He claims it as the humanist approach. He contends that business and industry are the last hope for effecting a change. Solutions based on moral, religious, idealistic, or humanitarian concerns have not worked. Religion in its efforts to cope with problems has produced little more than pious resolutions.

He said, "The ideals of democracy and the practical imperatives of survival in a technological and industrial society reveal that welfare is our greatest weapon for assuring survival and for advancing the well-being of all men; not for building bigger missiles, but in our ability to utilize science to the development of enough of everything to satisfy the material needs of all persons, irrespective of the political or social systems under which they live."

The two revolutions led by Lenin and by Taylor, the revolutions of social ownership and scientific management, may not converge. But they're drawing closer together. Today we can see in socialist and capitalist countries evidence that the principles of scientific management are needed in any political system. The success of future society will be gauged, not only by the identity of the ownership, but by the competence and know-how of its managerial class or profession.

Karl Marx spoke of the class war between owners and workers. Since Taylor, we have heard more of the war between workers and managers. However, the maneuvers between these elements may give way to one more revolution

—the truly managerial revolution. In the future, we'll move toward the sensible society where there is cooperation between peoples of differing disciplines, skills and talents, working under the direction of competent administrators able to plan and bring into existence a new humanity. The emerging nations in their quest for such things as food, shelter, health care, and education take for granted that such matters are an obligation of government. In such a climate each individual will be better able to develop his own interests, and there will be one common denominator—the welfare of all.

We in the United States are in for another rude awakening. The rest of the world is creeping up; some industrial nations have already overtaken us. The Scandinavian nations and other northern-European nations are ahead of us in standard of living, wages, and welfare programs. West Germany and other industrialized states have their economies on sounder ground; their wages and standard of living are the highest in the world. They plan. They tax. They control prices and wages. The state accepts its responsibilities. Negotiations among different segments permit them to achieve a degree of sharing. In a mixed economy their social-welfare programs carry the people into the future post-industrial era. They have long had cradle-to-grave security with a wide variety of social programs. Such a mixed economy may for some time harbor the private and public sectors in peaceful co-existence. There is a teaming up of the interests of workers with those of management as we witness a shift of power from ownership to labor. It may be the wave of the future.

Sweeping changes are taking place, both in the social order and in the relationships of modern man to his fellowmen, to his work, and to his physical environment. Each of us is daily caught in many dilemmas. After all, today's managerial revolution has significance and relevance only to the extent that it affects social change. I have confidence that those who are trained to harness man's skills and disciplines can correct most of man's ills. This is especially true in these times of grave ecological crises. Our energy needs may only await the development of solar cells and solar collectors.

Man's genius can explore the planets. While it lasts, he can exploit and take oil and transport it from distant places, from the north slopes of Alaska or from the deserts of Iran to faraway users. Our governments in the meantime are responsible for protecting our habitat and saving us from the despoilation of the terrain and the ocean floors. The scientific managers of the world, working together, will help solve problems by ingeniously using knowledge to reach global solutions. We look to the managerial revolution itself to improve the lot of mankind.

I live in the web of a capitalist dilemma. I have preached political programs to achieve full employment, and yet I manufacture highly technical labor-saving machines. It is a paradox. I doubt that full employment under uncontrolled capitalism can become an attainable goal. I have spent my adult life pushing progressive, leftist causes. In the meantime my enterprises, especially those engaged in providing services like banking and communication, gained "efficiency," grew, and piled up sizable profits, much of them tax sheltered, amounting to millions of dollars a year. My employees do not have such security.

Always at the core of the dilemma is the concept of property—property, the institution the state, often with the collaboration and toleration of the church and other ostensibly altruistic institutions, maintained in public or private hands. From early times we were taught that thrift, profit, the accumulation of capital, and human physical effort meant success. The machine made its entrance; then came the design of process and product. Then research and more development. There followed the corporation to permit impersonal ownership in the hands of individuals. The mom-and-pop stores gave way to giant chains, distributing goods from enormous manufacturing plants through computerized warehouses and terminals. Farming became a big-scale, corporate activity as ownership went into fewer and fewer hands.

This concentration of ownership of modern society with its billions of interdependent people need not cloud our horizons. A corporate-dominated society still must face up to the social needs of its people—or face revolution. Corporate power is presently vested in self-perpetuating management charged with producing profit for the shareowners. The whole managerial establishment has been beholden to creditors such as banks and insurance companies. We must keep in mind certain lessons of history. The social needs of mankind will prevail over the privileges of entrenched private ownership.

Confusion is heightened when we see how management skillfully maneuvers our economy into the hands of giant legalized monopolies, like American Telephone and Telegraph, or smaller monopolies like my own television stattions. Generally, companies by mere size (General Electric and General Motors) can control markets and prices. Nor were we fooled by the judicial gesture of breaking up a fabulously rich company, such as Standard Oil, into little bits, which didn't lessen their control of vast lands or resources.

Antitrust laws in this country have never been effective; the trend toward bigness is bound to continue. Every industry in America, be it chemicals, autos, steel, or whatever, is now dominated by a few giants. The energy industry, with all its cash flow and tax advantages, will probably never be successfully controlled until the "free enterprise" system itself comes under more severe tests. In the meantime, research and exploration continue to be the province of the big corporation. It is useless to talk about security for jobholders in such a structure.

Great changes are in store for the social system of the United States. I foresee that we'll eventually change our private monopolistic course to a democratic sharing economy. In the meantime, we'll adopt work-planning programs, monetary adjustments, and other temporary reforms at home. Community ownership, not private corporate ownership, will arrive. Managers will remain; only ownership will change. The ascent of managerial talent to power is part of the two revolutions now in progress. America's economic future may well be in the hands of the masters of business administration.

## OMI

In these days we're in a hurry. We use initials for most everything: IBM, GM, U.S.A., U.S.S.R., NATO. I follow the practice in this work—three words will be used to define the keys to mankind's future: Ownership, Management, and Internationalism. Our new call letters will be OMI.

# CHAPTER
# VII

~~~~~~~~~~~~~~~~~~~~~~~~~~~~~~~~~~~~

# The Sun Rising in the East

My initial reaction to the world's first planned economy in the days following the Bolshevik Revolution was one of wonder and shock. It was a strange phenomenon taking place in faraway, mysterious Russia. Who among us was free of curiosity—and doubt? Progressive Americans who showed interest in the Soviet economy were harassed and red baited. We were labeled anti-God and pro-communist. Maybe I came under more suspicion because I spent so much time in Toledo with Karl Pauley, socialist, and Eugene Stoll, communist, and read their pamphlets and books. Of course, it took less courage for Americans to express approval of the event after Franklin D. Roosevelt recognized Soviet Russia in 1933.

As an audacious young attorney and as a self-appointed economist, I traveled to the Soviet Union to explore the workings of the new idea, a country seeking to become the world's first planned society. At the time, no outsider really knew much about what was actually taking place. We merely saw Russia as a nation that had dared adopt Marxism as a working principle of national conduct. I vigorously studied every phase of the socialized society. I researched the role of the church, the status of worker and minorities, the Soviet legal system, factory operations, hospitalization, social insurance, prostitution, and the new prisons. I compared the people's courts with my own legal experiences in the American judicial system. As an ideal, a planned economy offered the Soviets, an economically backward nation of peasants and workers, great hope.

Although few American economists dared to speak out in favor of the Soviet planning process, I developed enthusiasm for the struggle of workers and peasants to build a planned nation. Peoples who had been exploited for centuries were trying to find a new way. In the process of trying to find a more sharing society, enthusiasts claimed that they were developing a "new man."

I was especially impressed by my trips into remote Siberia. A pioneering people were moving into and developing the tundra and the untouched forests of the north and the barren lands of the south. Industrial and housing construction was being conducted by the most primitive manual methods. But they were building a new homeland! The technological revolution of the West would not touch those people for decades.

Every region planned simultaneously its school systems and its villages. Gigantic problems plagued every activity, especially transportation. The rail system was almost in collapse. With horse-drawn vehicles in the wet tundra, the distribution of food was difficult and confused. The people suffered severe famine. The task of building the new society would challenge the most dedicated Russian people. Americans had technology, but except for Henry Ford, few agreed to share their know-how with the Soviets.

It was a time for difficult, ruthless decisions. We tend to be shocked by Stalin's methods but the fact is that he introduced rigid centralized controls and achieved social ownership of land and industry. The Hearst and other newspapers in the United States attacked the efforts of the Soviets to retain power, but retain control they did. It was harsh, but they survived—just as our own revolutionaries had survived almost two centuries before. Power and ownership remained vested in the many, rather than the few.

I saw widespread starvation and suffering in the U.S.S.R. But I also saw economic democracy, entailing self-criticism and discussion, in action. Most outsiders failed to see that this technique of popular participation might lead to the creation of a sharing society. Walter Duranty of the *New York Times*, a longtime correspondent in Moscow, once insisted that I grasp one basic fact: that democracy is "more than a mere right to vote." Economic security, he emphasized, fortified democracy. The people's participation in decision making is evidence of economic and political stability and well-being. For the first time in history a state was accepting and affirming its obligation to provide its citizens with their social and economic needs.

In his low-key approach, Duranty suggested that Lenin might well be correct when he pointed out that the guarantee of decent living standards was the ultimate criterion for a truly democratic society. Duranty didn't need to point out that his ideas were not reflected in the headlines or editorial comments of his New York newspaper. He was beginning to be a bit suspect in headquarters.

In my extensive travels around the Soviet Union I paid particular attention to the treatment of minorities. I was pleased to see that Soviet Russia retained various local cultures, which were allowed to develop in the more than 155 different republics. I studied the extent of the persecution of the Jews in old Russia, the outrageous pogroms when whole villages of Jews were destroyed. I noted that there were, prior to the revolution, six hundred and fifty separate laws solely devoted to limiting the rights and privileges of Jews. I felt that after the successful Soviet revolution the new society tried to eliminate discrimination. At the time there were approximately 124,800 members of the Communist party, four percent of whom were Jewish. Thus, whereas the Jews represented only 1.77 percent of the entire population in Russia, they held more than a proportionate number of memberships in the governing party.

In Moscow I often visited the Central State Planning

Department (Gosplan) in charge of organizing dozens of local, regional, and national scientific institutes. Its departments grew enormously, and I listened to debates on how to make central planning more workable. Collectivization of the farms was going forward. It involved the liquidation of the large landlords or kulaks, often, admittedly, with ruthlessness. I toured the countryside for several weeks. The Russians welcomed visiting outsiders because they were interested in learning "how to." It seemed to me that in spite of the gravity of the situation, there was enthusiasm over economic progress.

To my American eyes, two characteristics of Soviet planning stood out: (1) there were no upper limits imposed on production; (2) production was encouraged and all goods were distributed to consumers. This came as a bit of a shock to me because I had seen markets limited and prices controlled by large American corporations. Foodstuffs were held in our warehouses—and unemployed people starved. I noted that although Soviet production methods were crude, there was no unemployment. There was no inflation because Soviet currency was not convertible into other currencies. The society was unique. We asked ourselves again and again —was it possible a new man might actually emerge out of all this idealism and struggle?

I also wondered how long these two societies with such widely differing economic and social systems could continue their mutual existence on the same planet. I lived in a capitalist world where there were sharp contrasts in people's status. I was born on the wrong side of the tracks, but I could see how easy it would be, with luck, for one private person to become rich. On the other hand the Soviets were building a collective system where the fruits of labor would be more equitably shared among all. I could also see why the Soviets found it necessary to build an enormous defense apparatus to protect their nation from the attacks of outsiders. They, too, wanted to live and survive. They needed to defend themselves against an internal counterrevolution. They knew from experience that the capitalist world would use military and economic tactics to topple a challenging egalitarian society.

Americans couldn't be blamed for watching the Soviet experiment with mixed emotions. A few newspapers published outrageously false stories and overemphasized the famine and pestilence, the miseries of a peasant people emerging from serfdom. The Russians were building a new system. The American people were bent on preserving their own floundering capitalist economy. I began to feel that a saboteur of a socialized society was much more wicked than the looter in the United States, where the crime of theft seemed so commonplace. Once I saw a Soviet looter shot to death as he attempted to steal more than his ration of bread. He was shot because he stole from all his fellows. A hungry American parent may have robbed a food warehouse while the private owner was waiting to get his price.

In the United States, competent engineers and teachers were unable to find adequate work. My own accumulated academic degrees from prestigious institutions meant that I could compete for jobs and increase my earnings. I received a legal degree, passed bar examinations, and became adept at charging fees for telling other people what to do. I could advise citizens of their rights, their obligations, and their defenses. Naturally I charged what the traffic would bear, which, in the case of the affluent, was usually a pretty penny. I dreamed the lawyer's dream—of getting an angry and rich client who was in plenty of trouble and who wanted to fight. On the other hand, in the Soviet Union the student was attempting to learn a skill to better qualify himself to serve his community. Lawyers in the U.S.S.R. became a part of building a planned society.

There are personal problems when an American lawyer gets too far left. He can associate politely with communists or dissidents. He can try their law suits under the principle of defending civil liberties. But if he espouses radical causes, it's different; well-heeled clients and associates simply disappear, and corporate and even family litigation goes elsewhere. Then he often learns who his true friends are.

In my professional and personal life I had some setbacks

and many rewarding experiences. The more my wife's family sought to get her to separate from me—and her society-leader mother was especially insistent that she do so—the more steadfastly she stood by our marriage. Our respect and affection for each other have survived honest ideological differences. We've had our own United Nations.

My family was not difficult, but others asked how I could be such a radical reformer and continue practicing law and even move on to acquire corporations. Was I a communist or a capitalist? I faced still one other question. As a businessman, what would I do if my own properties—banks, manufacturing companies, broadcasting enterprises, transportation companies, or whatever—were to be nationalized or even taxed into public ownership? Would I then start screaming about the glories of free enterprise?

I will not be guilty of being two-faced. I have never opposed government control of any industry or of those commercial activities in which I operated. Through my years as an American industrialist, I have publicly and privately maintained that there is a bigger interest than my own. I insist that public control of industry is a function of government—any government. National policy must encompass all resources and meet society's obligations to its members. Who's kidding who when we seek to shift tax burdens or eliminate welfare programs? How long can we deny that the greatest good to the greatest number is more important than the private wealth of corporations or individuals in America?

It's easy to forget that during the Depression thousands of American factories closed or went bankrupt, farm mortgages were foreclosed, and credit exchanges collapsed. In many parts of the United States we saw a return to primitive barter techniques. We were in a confused, lopsided world: food abundance existed in the midst of hunger, and "surplus" coffee and grains were dumped in the oceans. An enormous accumulation of goods and reserves in agriculture and industry piled up in warehouses. Mortgages were foreclosed. Consumers became jobless. Both imports and exports declined.

We were in no position to help other nations. Each nation scrambled for its own survival. Our national policy, if we had one, was a spectacle of contradictions—in the midst of vast unemployment, we destroyed consumable goods and put our people on the dole. Nations such as Germany and the Arab countries excluded Jews and other "foreign" or minority elements from within their national borders. In our own confusion we sought the obvious way out—we stepped up preparations for war. Our leaders spoke of making jobs. We'd subsidized the farmers and even whole industries. The mad armaments race began among the United States, Japan, Germany, France, and Great Britain.

Lobbies claimed that production of armaments would guarantee our security. We concentrated on military alliances and treaty arrangements—we could deal with the evil ones, the bogeyman and war criminals, later. Nations sought out new territories for their goods and people, hoping to release unemployed or excess populations. We maintained vast military bases overseas to protect American investments on every continent. Japan seized Manchuria; Germany went for the Ukraine, the Polish corridor, and the Saar Basin.

It is easy to look back and see the paradox between the two worlds. It has been more difficult for us to understand the fanatic drive of people, in every period of history, to retain ownership of the means of production. Call it greed or self-interest, it gets all mixed up with patriotism and ideology. We can see why wealthy persons extol the free-enterprise system—it's been good to them. We remember another anomaly of capitalism, where the rich actually get richer in times of adversity than in times of boom. The small and the weak in this competition quickly give way to the giant and the powerful. The banks and the insurance companies pick up the remnants. As in every phase of our economic life, the big get bigger.

The cycle of capitalism in crisis was confusing enough. But there were millions of honest and curious people throughout the world who wanted to learn about the alternatives shaping up in the East. Optimists told us, "Wait a few decades"—and we would find out whether the Soviets would survive. Gradually we learned that the revolution to social change had unbelievably important implications and successes.

Americans lived through wildly traumatic and changing times, periods of war and peace, deflation and inflation, roller-coaster employment levels, depression and prosperity. Now the honest person's task is to advance the building of bridges between two remarkably different societies. Both are superpowers able to destroy all other nations. A major problem of our times has become clear—guaranteeing that the Soviet Union and the United States live together in one world.

# CHAPTER
# VIII

~~~~~~~~~~~~~~~~~~~~~~~~~~~~~~~~~~~

# Broadcasting—the Goldmine Media

Of all my business ventures, I enjoy most my television enterprises. The magic medium has replaced newspapers and magazines in shaping attitudes. It carries enormous influence, for good or ill. It's show business, electronic journalism, imaginative engineering, a legal monopoly, and a license to coin money, all rolled into one.

The video set of the average American family is turned on for more than eight hours every day. National programs are watched by more than one hundred million viewers and it is not unusual to have worldwide audiences of more than one billion. Images are built, elections are won by those with access to the medium.

I suggest that television tends to socialize the family and all other human institutions. It's difficult to develop innovators and unusual thinkers when all our citizens live on the same diet. It's no secret that the programs on commercial television are designed solely to gain mass audiences and appeal to humanity's lowest possible denominators: crime, sex, violence—all highly salable commercial properties. But in the beginning of the TV era, the late 1940s and early 1950s, we optimistically believed that television would advance the cultural level of everyone.

We were realistic enough to know that in our profit-oriented economy our television licenses were exclusive grants to broadcast in a particular area, without any regulation of the charges we made for commercial messages. About the only limit to the extent of commercials was the number of seconds in a twenty-four hour day. That's a lot of commercials. Broadcasters found that they were able to get high rates because they were effectively demonstrating products—and carried their message into practically every home in America. As the potential for profit became clear, some of us realized that the medium was one gigantic money machine. I don't want to suggest that broadcasters were the first government-franchise holders to discover how to make money, but they did develop one new technique to its greatest peak—the Big Promise. It was merely necessary in a competitive hearing for a television licensee to promise bundles of "public service." The biggest promiser got the plum—an exclusive channel. Once obtained, the license became more or less a permanent asset—available for exploitation or sale.

Cultural programs, without commercials, often were relegated to the publicly-owned broadcasting media. These stations, operated by government or non-profit institutions, developed slowly but eventually they established a record of producing worthwhile programs, news and special events. In the United States and Canada it was realized, but little noted, that the two media, public and private, could operate along side each other competitively. In a mixed economy where these enterprises have operated for years, such competition proved good for both.

Television turned out to be a grand economic bonanza. Advertisers jumped aboard. Professional sports exploded. Less profit-minded people saw the social significance of television as a teaching tool in a modern society. The whole educational process was revolutionized. Children and young adults were entranced by the wonders of *Sesame Street* and *The Open University*. TV satellites raised new learning levels throughout the world, especially in the emerging nations like India, Iran, and Brazil, which were hooked into a common world system of mass communication.

Television quickly brought about changes in our institutions, especially the family. The authority and teachings of parents eroded as electronic programmers commanded the attention of youngsters. Schools, peer groups, and churches at first tried to compete with the new creature that brought into the home instantaneous sound and pictures of a wider outside world. No institution was able to ignore the new medium. TV substituted news immediacy for news analysis. Distant wars, industrial and agricultural production, and sports events were "performed" right before our eyes. We became a nation of nonparticipants—watchers. The world became a stage. We called the TV set an idiot box even as it became our principal contact between the home and everything outside our living rooms.

Why hold a brief for the goodness of commercial television? It is irritating, hard sell, and noisy. It plies us with the images of irrational lifestyles and values that breed materialism and greed, and overall, it is probably detrimental to children. If telecasting, private or public, conveyed the evil of a violent society, it also brought us the best of our culture: the symphonies, drama, intelligent talk shows, tours of art museums. For the first time in their lives millions of Americans visited the theater, the music halls, and the world's other centers of culture. Consciously or not, Americans found excitement and interests and new loyalties, views of a larger expanding world. Programs were interrupted by sales pitches for deodorants, hamburgers, beer, and denture cleaners—and subtle social changes crept over our living and eating habits. Station owners sat at their cashiers' windows tabulating the riches of newly discovered markets. Television was in flower.

The private ownership of a radio or television license is unique to the United States. TV stations can be bought or sold easily, though maybe not as quickly as a bag of potatoes, because a bit of delay is required to get the consent of the Federal Communications Commission to secure license transfers. Pick up a telephone and buy yourself a station—your assistants can measure the size of the market, the extent of the listening audience, and its growth possibilities. The value of a telecasting station is determined simply by counting the number of present and potential viewers. The investment in modern broadcasting equipment is sizable, but a buyer can purchase a property by using little cash—he merely acquires it under installment payments spread out over a number of years. I have paid for several television stations in a short period of time—four or five years—right out of the station's own cash flow and profits.

Newspapers have high cost problems of labor and supplies, but profitability of the television stations has skyrocketed. Pure gold. At the time I built my first television station I also operated both newspapers and radio stations. By mid-1940 I had acquired several FM and AM radio stations. No one could foresee that television stations could generate such cash flow or coin so much profit. The fascinating opportunity offered by the blossoming electronic medium of television was there, and in the early 1950s anyone could easily get into the business. Licenses were going begging.

I made a point of learning everything I could about the business, attending trade conferences, equipment shows, and engineering seminars and listening to the experts discuss its possibilities. At one early trade meeting in New York City, I met the advertising manager of the Ford Motor Company. He was flabbergasted about TV's selling possibilities, and his mouth watered when he explained television's capacity to demonstrate his automobiles right in the home. Advertising the new model had been previously the dealer's responsibility. They merely opened showrooms and waited for customers to call on them. Now a TV program would carry its message out far beyond the point of sale.

Taking a plunge into a new venture, taking a chance, can be a chilling experience. People smugly entrenched in their established routines often enjoy seeing the innovator fall on his face. I surveyed most of the cities of the country for places to start TV stations. I wanted medium-sized communities that would welcome the new medium. I picked Grand Rapids, Michigan; Columbus and Toledo, Ohio; Milwaukee, Wisconsin; and Erie, Pennsylvania, where I already operated the newspaper.

I found one thing in common in all the cities: Local banks and local newspaper publishers refused to talk to us. The Mead family in Erie, owners of my competitor newspaper, were at that moment blasting me for my progressive views. George Mead told me in one of his sober moments that the TV stations in New York City, Washington, D.C., Boston, Los Angeles, and Chicago were losing enormous sums of money. And anyway he'd never be able to get his family to join in any venture with me! He kept his family's pride, and I kept 100 percent ownership of a magnificent TV station.

I conferred with Allen B. Dumont and RCA, television manufacturers. They were anxious to sell their equipment to me and volunteered to prepare my license applications. They furnished excellent engineering and legal expertise and more or less financed my early television ventures. With practically no cash down, they permitted me to make long-term payments. Times have changed—credit for television ventures is easier to obtain from banks or insurance companies now.

In 1948 I built at Erie, Pennsylvania, the first building used exclusively for television in the United States. WICU-TV, channel 12, went on the air with great fanfare on March 15, 1949. A few months later we cut the ribbons on my WTVN-TV, channel 6, in Columbus, Ohio. The tiny, cramped headquarters housing our broadcasting equipment and studios were on the fiftieth floor of the LeVeque Tower. We squeezed a lot of activity into those junior-sized studios. We suffered drunken announcers, kooky pitchmen, fundamentalist and commercial religionists. But we developed tremendous national and local excitement in those early TV adventures. Other broadcasters came from around the country to watch us, and newspapers and magazines gave us enormous coverage.

I invested four hundred thousand dollars in the TV

building and equipment at Erie. The first month's operations of the television station produced profits of fifty thousand dollars! At the Columbus television station (where we
already had competition) our first month's profits were
twenty-five thousand dollars. Both stations really took off
when we hooked into the newly formed networks. We
relished getting affiliated with the network schedules. As
broadcasters, we quickly found that it was extremely difficult
to fill eighteen hours of programming. A station in a good
market was eagerly sought out by every network. I made
trips to New York City and Hollywood and met many of
the stars: Milton Berle, Jack Benny, Morey Amsterdam, and
Bob Hope. I enjoyed dinners arranged by agents who often
brought along feminine clients eager to break into the new
television medium.

It seems strange now, but for several years we operated
at Erie and Columbus with only one camera for each station. We broadcast live the first Catholic mass at the cathe-
dral in Columbus, Ohio. Then we rushed the camera and
its two-man crew back to headquarters to carry on the
regular news and interview programs. At the beginning of
television, people watched anything that moved.

It was easy to see the possibilities of combining sight and
sound—the future lay in television. I retained radio station
WTOD (AM), a daytime station, and WTRT (FM), a full-
time news and music station, in Toledo for several years.
Their facilities were limited, but the frequencies couldn't
be changed to another part of the spectrum because I
couldn't get the permission of the bureaucratic FCC. At the
time I was being witch hunted before the Federal Communications Commission—they were trying me on charges
of Communist-party membership and association. Every
move I made was closely scrutinized. There were long,
arbitrary—and frightening—delays in my efforts to build
other television and radio stations. The commission's refusal
for several years to permit me to replace outworn equipment, like TV tubes and camera parts, almost strangled me
right out of the broadcast business. I often wonder how far

I would have gone in the broadcast industry if I had been a respectable member of the Establishment.

There were other obstacles blocking development of new ventures. One factor inhibiting the development of all television was the controversy over the new color TV pictures. The big manufacturers, in trying to get their own systems adopted, were embroiled in a bitter struggle among themselves and couldn't agree upon any common method of using color. As a result, for several years broadcasting was needlessly confined to black-and-white pictures. When the quarrel was settled (in favor of RCA), TV took off. I'm glad that I didn't get bogged down in the engineering conflicts. Today those early techniques seem primitive.

While expanding my interests in television during the early 1950s, I watched my losses on the *Erie Dispatch Herald* newspaper grow. We were unable to increase the circulation of the newspaper, and we couldn't get it to break even in spite of using every promotional gimmick. I recruited professionally competent people, such as Kenneth Tooill of the *Toledo Blade* as editor and Stanley Spear of the *Pittsburgh Post Gazette* as business manager, but we continued to lose enormous amounts of money. New management did not help me against the local competition. I finally sold the newspaper and took a million-dollar capital gain. I had decided that television was more socially effective, more compatible with me personally, and certainly more profitable. Over the long run I've noticed that the big fortunes belong to those who know when to get out—with a capital gain.

In the mid-1950s I decided to sell WTVN-TV in Columbus. I received roughly two million dollars for my investment. The sale produced much-needed capital—and a quick profit of a million and a half dollars. Although I had built a modern building to house the Columbus station, I didn't spend more than a half million dollars building the whole project. Most of my investment merely involved debt. I wrestled with the problem of selling that progressive TV medium in Columbus to reactionary Senator Robert E. Taft because I had found everything about the Columbus operation most cordial. The station was dedicated by my friend Senator Estes Kefauver. We opened the facility to the likes of Senator Hubert Humphrey, Adlai Stevenson, and other prominent liberals of the day. We had a wretched time getting Adlai Stevenson to consent to wear his first blue shirt on television. Then we all tried our hand at applying full makeup powder to his bald head. On the night of our big opening of the new studios we were joined by the popular Frank Lauche, the governor, who later became a U.S. Senator. Our big problem involved keeping his bottle of bourbon safely hidden from the viewing audience. He could really tuck it away—and grow more sentimental and oratorical with every gulp.

Two million dollars was a lot of cash at that time. I bought radio station WIKK in Erie from Keith Kiggens and Don Reynolds. Then I bought Radio Station WHOO from the *Sentinel Star* in Orlando, Florida. Still I had not thoroughly tested my money-making philosophy. I looked outside the broadcasting industry for a major New York Stock Exchange–listed company as a base upon which I could build a publicly owned company. After many conferences with investment bankers, I selected as my target the Seiberling Rubber Company of Akron, Ohio.

With hindsight it was a foolish move. I set out to buy substantial blocks of stock on the New York Stock Exchange. Then I discovered the inherent weakness of one family's control of a publicly owned company. The second generation didn't have the same goals or the same initiative as did the founders, Charles and Frank Seiberling. I discovered that the Seiblerling heirs were more prominent for their social activities than for their managerial skills. Many investors have found out to their sorrow that big sales of a product by a small, inefficient manufacturing company often means that the greater the sales, the greater the losses.

It took several years to make the company viable. It had been saturated with nepotist management. I concentrated on streamlining and modernizing the facilities in the plastics and shoe divisions. The Akron Chamber of Commerce continued its nit-picking at every attempt I made to build a properly located tire-manufacturing facility away from their area. I had my belly full of their antics, and in mid-1965 I finally sold the Seiberling tire division and got my money back many times over. I kept the profitable segments.

I learned a lesson or two from the experience. Antiquated officers couldn't be removed as long as I remained in the forty-nine-percent ownership club. They knew nothing about budgets and controls, and I couldn't shove it down their throats. I remedied all this when I came into control. Seiberling had annual sales of fifty million dollars, and this condemned it as a pygmy fighting the tire-industry giants. I retained the remaining divisions of the company and called the new operation Seilon, Inc. With hindsight I wish I had taken the proceeds of my Columbus TV-station sale and acquired growth-oriented broadcasting or service industries. After all, it takes several years to turn around small, inefficient companies and operate them in this modern and gigantic industrial age, and those years can be used in more fruitful pursuits.

I got out of the losses of tire manufacturing when I sold the tire division to the Firestone Rubber Company by a different technique—I simply delivered a large amount of sales, not necessarily profitable sales. The purchaser knew its cost to convert a pound of rubber into the finished tire product. We revealed to him our own costs in our antiquated plants at Akron. The purchaser couldn't lose. When I received thirty-one million dollars for the sale of the tire division, I immediately reduced the company bank debts. Then I purchased the company's senior securities, including its convertible debentures and preferred stock. I bought a great deal more of the common stock so that I could cement my control once and for all. Whether the stock went up or down, I kept buying. I never sold. (I'm still buying.)

Operating a television station, like any monopoly, is easy and highly profitable. A television license is the exclusive right to operate a broadcasting facility on a particular channel in a defined market area. The larger the number of people covered, the greater the value of the license. The worth of an operation in a particular market can almost be mathematically calculated. About fifty-six percent of the average station's revenue is derived from local and regional sales, and forty-four percent comes from network and national sales. Rates are fixed upon the "delivery" of an audience with the largest premium given for prime time, the period between seven and eleven at night. Prime-time sales account for fifty-two percent of all network revenues. Rates are based upon a cost per thousand of homes delivered, generally about five or six dollars a thousand. Income can easily be projected into the future.

When a rating service, such as A. C. Nielson, estimates an increase in a station's audience, the rates are more or less automatically upped. An increase of a single point in a network's rating can mean as much as twenty-five million dollars a year in increased sales. This produces as much as sixty-five cents a share in additional earnings to a company like the American Broadcasting Company. TV programming and production can become glamorous and spectacular, but the business office deals with massive amounts of money. It is a fertile field, not thoroughly exploited, for scientific management.

It's normal to judge television by its enormous profitability. The industry is woefully uncontrolled, and such a condition does not benefit the public. The abuses of its monopoly position are notorious. For example, the public is denied proper media coverage of our most important events. In June 1978 I urged the presidents of the three networks to interview Paul Newman, the actor, and Marge Benton, delegates to the United Nations Disarmament Conference. Two networks gladly complied, but Richard Salant, then president of CBS News, wrote me that he felt that Newman was more interested in drawing attention of the cameras and microphones to himself than making any real contribution to the disarmament talks. "We at CBS News don't play games," he said. I was infuriated by such blatant censorship and threatened action. He apologized. Millions of people were denied access to one of the most important international conferences in world history—important, but neglected by the world's news media. American newspapers are generally local monopolies, but a television network's blackout of news coverage is a thousandfold more serious. We're in a grave situation when a single television-network executive can play games with the lives of humanity.

The nature of television broadcasting is changing. Direct television from satellites is already producing enormous benefits to both developed and developing nations. Direct broadcasting from satellites does not mean that signals are received directly by conventional television sets. Rather, the signal from the satellite is received by a ground disk antenna directed toward the satellite. Ground receiving stations are proliferating all over the United States. Signals received from satellites are amplified and converted in frequency. The output can be received at the site or may be broadcast using conventional television-broadcast equipment. Reception from the satellites and rebroadcasting makes the present television industry a part of a major new ballgame.

There is an immense potential for satellite instructional television broadcasting. Mass international education is here. Remote sensing of earth signals is already yielding benefits as the new technology grows. We know also that there are few areas of the globe not already under intense military surveillance. Remote sensing is giving access to information on agricultural and even mineral resources. Access to such information has been given to the multinational corporations, disregarding the principle of a country's sovereignty over its territory and natural resources.

Only a few years ago we looked upon the ocean floor as the "last heritage of mankind." Today we look to outer space, that area beyond the concept of air space always regarded as part of a national territory and subject to sovereign national regulation. It will not be easy to control the signals out of New York City, traveling via satellite to remote areas of Asia or Africa. At least we can understand the effect upon cultural patterns. For good or ill, it brings high expectations—and some disillusionment to both rural and urban areas of the world.

Of course, the satellites will bring economic benefits, such as increasing world food output, discovering new minerals, assessing water and energy resources, monitoring pollution of the air and sea, and improving knowledge of climatology. These areas will be best approached under an international organization such as the United Nations Educational Scientific and Cultural Organization (UNESCO). Already the United Nations has set up a program on space applications and developed training programs on remote sensing. Other specialized agencies, particularly the World Meteorological Organization (WMO), Food and Agricultural Organization (FAO), and Center for Natural Resources, Energy, and Transport (CNRET) have been making substantial use of remote sensing.

Once again the United Nations becomes the instrument to harness technology for the common good. It will establish model programs based on the successful experience of many countries or regions. The U.N. through enlargement of existing facilities provides training on collection and processing of data. The very able E. Bradford Morse, director general of the United Nations Development Programme (UNDP), has shown how it could undertake for the benefit of developing nations a major program on space applications with emphasis on remote sensing. Only limited funds are available to carry on these important and exciting programs. I wish that we could shift our priority from useless military weaponry to using this fantastic satellite informational system for the benefit of mankind!

# CHAPTER
# IX

~~~~~~~~~~~~~~~~~~~~~~~~~~~~~~~~~~~~~~~~~

# The Cable

While commercial television is still groping toward its full development, new electronic marvels have been introduced. These innovations startle the imagination, affect our times —and provide opportunities for the enterprising entrepreneur. In the early 1960s a new phenomenon—cable television —began to attract investment dollars. Opportunities were there for mom and pop or for corporate giants. The market was ripe for a combination of pay and subscription television.

Cable TV is a simple technique of capturing electronic signals—a high antenna is raised on a tall building or mountaintop. A great variety of distant TV signals can be picked up and delivered to home sets. "Wiring up" a city and installing cable costs eight thousand dollars or more a mile. When one hundred subscribers per mile sign up and pay a subscription fee of six to twenty dollars a month, the net yield can easily produce an annual return exceeding one hundred percent. Few personnel are required—a handful of employees take care of maintenance; office workers use computerization, and the money rolls in.

Subscribers to such a system get the benefit of a diversity of programs and increased signal clarity. Small city systems are simple to operate. Another goldmine waiting to be opened! At first, no licenses or permits were required from federal regulatory agencies to get into the cable-TV business. Local community governments, such as town councils and boards of county commissioners, gladly passed out the permits to anyone who would furnish the service.

After attending various trade meetings and studying trade publications, I decided to go forward and get my feet wet in the CATV business. I bought a fifty-percent interest in a small, handmade system at Salamanca, New York, for fifty thousand dollars. Joseph Hardy, a local schoolteacher, had raised an antenna on a nearby mountaintop and had run his cable down to approximately seven hundred homes. He charged fifty dollars for a "tap," or installation, fee and made a monthly charge of six dollars.

Then Hardy wanted out. Since he was unable or unwilling to finance the project, I bought the additional fifty-percent interest and invested funds for stringing more cables into more homes. (We heard that Hardy repeated the same venture in several other small communities, whereupon he took his capital gains and retired to a pleasant farm life.) We quickly raised our list of subscribers to more than twelve hundred. In the process we reduced both the monthly charge and the installation charge. Most of the subscribers in the Salamanca area were Indians hard hit by depression. We learned a great deal about the business from that experience. We liked what we saw in cable operations: there would be great possibilities, not just small enterprises in small towns, but in the larger markets. In a year or so I sold the Salamanca system for $350,000 cash.

There is an active and ready market for cable systems. The trade papers were at one time full of for-sale signs. In 1971 we bought the cable system in North Canton, Ohio, from the *Canton Repository*, a Thomson newspaper under the competent guidance of my friend Gordon Strong. We paid seven hundred thousand dollars for its fifteen hundred subscribers. We improved the system and built it up to twenty-three hundred subscribers. We wanted to move into the larger market of Canton, but we found ourselves stymied by another operator, Warner Communications.

After owning the system for only fourteen months, we sold our system to Warner for $1,800,000 cash. While we had it, we collected profits of about $9,000 a month.

In 1966 we bought a rather rundown, money-losing cable system at Hillsdale, Michigan. It leased its lines from Michigan Bell Telephone. The system had many problems operating with the telephone company's cables and connections. We bought as part of the same package the cable system at Jonesville, Michigan, both operations together costing us approximately seventy-five thousand dollars. We had no franchise of any kind from either city. The people of the college town were delighted to have the superior signals our cable brought to them. We brought in some competent engineers to improve signals, and we were able to raise the number of subscribers from about seven hundred to twenty-eight hundred, giving us an operating profit of six thousand dollars a month.

We always found it easy to buy a radio or television station—there are hungry brokers and trade-paper advertisements galore. It's an old routine, but many individuals and corporations have made huge fortunes buying and selling these licenses. Currently the Federal Communications Commission requires the holder to retain a television franchise for three years before selling the property. It's much easier to buy or sell a CATV system; very few consents are required from any regulatory agency. In the days ahead there will undoubtedly be more restrictions.

In cable television, too, the value of a system is measured by the size of the populated area and the number of potential subscribers. Each subscriber is worth between one hundred and one thousand dollars, depending on the size of the monthly fee charged and the number of connections. Modern methods of computing the number of households and the purchasing power per family in a particular market are frequently used to pin down the exact value of an operation. Pay television, an additional charge for the use of a specific channel, increases the owners' take tremendously.

Almost anyone, except foreign citizens, can get into the CATV business by either buying an existing station or starting *de novo* wherever he can get a local franchise. A cable system is almost a complete communications monopoly, which explains why even the small communities can be profitable to CATV owners. As a monopoly, this system easily lends itself to national ownership. Again the old American routine of the big getting bigger is taking over— and now we can see networks of large cable systems in our future.

I tried to get American companies to work on installing cable systems in Moscow and Leningrad, but export of specific purchase orders for electronic equipment was negated by our U.S. State Department. All overtures from authorities in Havana were also turned down by the Washington officials. Similar CATV equipment can be purchased in Great Britain and Switzerland. American companies now stand on the sidelines and watch this business go elsewhere.

In 1972 we purchased three VHF television stations for three million dollars cash. The newspaper-owned stations are in Cheyenne, Wyoming; Sterling, Colorado, and Scottsbluff, Nebraska. With the purchase we also obtained a micro-link system connecting those cities with Denver. We did not invest a dollar of our own money—an insurance company loaned us the entire amount. Tax regulations permit the purchaser of assets to set up an entire new valuation and depreciation schedule. Under this arrangement we were allowed to take twenty-five thousand dollars a month depreciation. We also took another deduction of twenty-five thousand dollars a month for interest on our borrowing. Our profitability and cash flow, therefore, permitted us to pay quickly for the stations out of their own income. The opportunity for big profits was obvious.

We spent the year after we acquired the properties making program and promotional changes. Almost immediately we were offered eight million dollars for the properties. Although the prospect of making a quick profit of five million dollars, without having invested a single

In 1967, Edward Lamb toured South Vietnam via army helicopter.

Time out for C-rations in Vietnam. Note bamboo booby trap
in the center.

A tame monkey perches on Lamb's shoulder.

...amb holds up a plastic bomb charge in his right hand. In his left is a
"safe conduct" pass, dropped by allied forces before bombing a  village.

South Vietnamese soldiers guard suspected Vietcong guerrillas.

Edward Lamb and Martin Luther King at the Lamb home in 1968.

After two days and nights of conferences. Castro is holding fifty-five pages of notes he made, recording suggestions for mechanizing the sugar-cane fields and building various projects.

Priscilla Lamb Guyton, Fidel Castro, and Edward Lamb in 1976.

Two friends, Alger Hiss and Edward Lamb, in 1979.

dollar of our own money, seemed enticing, we found that we liked Cheyenne and the other Western cities in which we operated. The areas served, like so many communities in the Western United States, have fascinating growth possibilities.

In 1966 we also started a cable system in Flint, Michigan, the second largest city in the state. We simply signed a contract with Michigan Bell to lease their cable lines at the rate of thirty-seven dollars a mile, and we opened for business. We needed fifteen subscribers per mile to break even and we targeted one hundred a mile as a possibility. We added subscribers and soon had three thousand hook-ons paying us five dollars a month with an installation fee of ten dollars. Shortly thereafter the little system kicked off a profit of ten thousand dollars a month. We were able to add multiple connections in apartment houses and rapidly raised our number of subscribers. We arranged for the telephone company to block out the city in sections and construct one additional section at a time. While a block was under construction we presold hook-ons until the area was fully connected. We had as many as fifteen hundred advance subscribers signed up with the money deposited in our account even before we made a connection. Over the years we built these systems up to more than twenty-five thousand primary subscribers and ten thousand secondary connections. The system remained extremely profitable, making as much as thirty or forty thousand dollars a month.

In 1974 we bought Michigan Bell's entire CATV plants at Hillsdale and at Flint, Michigan. Since they were not permitted by the FCC to extend their operations in cable TV, they asked us to buy their plants and operations for $650,000, which we paid off with a deferred-payment note. The fact that the telephone company wrote off a couple of million dollars on their investment would have been serious to anyone other than the nation's greatest monopoly. Even the biggest can always use capital losses on their tax returns.

From the outset, we operated the Flint cable system under a legal opinion by the city law department that we didn't need a permit from the city council to carry on that type

of interstate commerce. As various local communities began
to see the tremendous success of cable systems, they naturally
began to look to the new medium as a source of income.
Although the FCC ultimately asserted that local authoriza-
tion would be required to carry various signals, we realized
that a permit from the municipality would be required
sooner or later. The negotiations with the city of Flint
took a year or two, but we agreed that we should pay them
the usual fee of three percent of our gross income. This
was satisfactory all around.

When we had the legal details and the ownership of our
plant set up, we realized that we possessed an extremely
valuable asset. We obtained permits from other nearby
communities, such as Bedford and Burton townships, but we
knew that construction would require tremendous capital
expenditures. Our corporate setup at the time was such that
we did not wish to incur the expense of extending these
lines to various suburbs around the city.

One day it happened. We were sitting in my office in
Toledo and the visitor wanted to buy my cable televsion
systems in Flint and Hillsdale, Michigan. "What will you
take?" he asked. I told him I would take $5.5 million.

He said, "Let's put it bluntly. We will give you five
million."

Even more bluntly I replied, "I'll take five and a half
million, accept it or reject it."

"Five and a half million dollars it is." And we shook
hands.

We agreed that he and his attorneys and financial people
would be in my office next morning to close the deal. We
both knew that we were not selling inventory or other
physical assets. We were selling a market and our position
in that market. We had a potential of almost seventy thousand cable subscribers. We were dealing with people who
knew the cable business and what the profit potentials were.
They had the credit and cash to complete such a deal.

The bigger the deal, the easier it seems to be to make it.
We merely put the lawyers and auditors on the assignment
to work out the details. Although lawyers can ruin almost

any deal, they wrapped up this package without too much fuss and delay. We would be required to pay a capital-gains tax on a profit of $4.8 million—the amount in excess of our cost.

Cable is a type of business that almost anyone can get into, although it is more difficult since the money-making possibilities of the new electronic marvel became clear. The cable business will go the way of all other industries in America: dominance by the few. The big cable operators like Cox take over. Then General Electric takes over Cox. Of course, it is still possible for the alert innovator and the enthusiastic entrepreneur to enter the cable marketplace. Research and close contact with new developments just might allow the individual entrepreneur to initiate a successful project and permit him to take his place in the sun of profitability. I would be the first to admit that the "free" enterprise system still permits a person to get started in new ventures, but it is becoming more difficult. The large expenses of research can be met ony by the giant corporations.

It is probably true that the greatest good to mankind will come from the enormous research centers now developing in the planned societies. Too many of our patents are held in limbo until a private inventor can "get his price"—or royalties. Likely, the consumers will benefit to a much greater extent under a socialized economy. In the meantime consumers in America ought to be adequately protected from the extravagant claims and high pressures of our promotion and commercial advertising campaigns. Again, the television industry is at the center of the problem.

The future of television goes beyond entertainment— already two-way communication is on the horizon. In conjunction with the computer, it's used to send and receive information to and from banks, stores, doctors' offices, and libraries. Simply by pushing buttons on regular television sets, subscribers are able to ask the central office for all sorts of information, including news summaries, sports scores, time check, fund transfers, weather forecasts, and entertainment listings. Signals go out over the air, and telephone lines carry information to the home television set. To the extent that the television home screen is used to exchange information, the role of newspapers and other media is threatened.

Coded signals clog our airways. Vast new industries will appear—and opportunities already abound. We accept these futuristic concepts of shopping, banking, bill payment, check cashing, and message sending. Such is the new technology: we're intrigued and dependent upon gadgetry, and a breakdown of a single tube can knock the whole system out of joint; but computers are programmed to catch and correct most human errors.

Our generation of Americans has been born into a weird society. Americans seem willing to live by the rules of the jungle. Survival in our economy does not always go to the fittest. Our people have tolerated in our monopolistic society the elimination of the small and the new. In spite of my own contraditions and dilemmas, born in this paradise of "free enterprisers" and starting from scratch, I have put together a sizable fortune in the legalized monopoly known as television. The conditions under which I succeeded will continue as long as capitalism survives—which may not be very long. But foreign investors, fearful for their own economies, already hurry to our shores in the belief that America is truly "the last citadel of capitalism." They may be right.

Tremendous progress will be made in the fields of technological development. We are seeing unimaginable discoveries in chemistry and electronics, and aerospace. Unfortunately humanity is not always the full beneficiary of scientific progress. There are many improvements and patents awaiting profitable exploitation. Days, years, or decades from now, under a rational society, our successors will wonder about us. They may wonder how Americans, under an unplanned society, tolerated such enormous rewards to the private owners.

CHAPTER

# X

~~~~~~~~~~~~~~~~~~~~~~~~~~~~~~~~~~~~~~~~~~~~~~~~~~~

# The Boy Wonder

When I completed the sale of the Seiberling tire division to Firestone in 1967, I found myself possessed of several million dollars. About the same time I sold various manufacturing companies in Lamb Industries, including White Products at Middleville, Michigan, and Alumatic Corp., in Milwaukee. Both manufactured routine, unglamorous products, such as bathtubs, water heaters, wash stands, and glass windows. Those industries became so cut-throat and competitive that manufacturers found that the more sales companies made, the bigger their losses. For the most of them it was a race to the bankruptcy courts.

I was glad to get out of such operations; I saw that in our society only a very few of the largest and most mechanized manufacturers in any industry survive. Those in manufacturing or in farming who made fortunes were always the giants. Such is the nature of the free-enterprise system: get big or get out. My manufacturing pygmies didn't disturb the giants.

I decided to forget manufacturing and concentrate on the winners, preferably in broadcasting, leasing, and service

*101*

activities. I recognize that a nation's people cannot survive by taking in each other's washing. But the big profits, the big bucks, were going to those rendering services, including those in the professions: doctors, lawyers, accountants, and architects. The service and financial industries were beginning to be the principal contributors to our gross national product, and such activities were engaging a majority of all American workers. That is where the action will continue to be in any technologically advanced society.

In dozens of speeches around the world I extolled the importance of putting a scientific manager in charge. I wish I had always followed my own advice. There are so many qualities required of such people—good basic education and training, development of the decision-making ability, compatibility with co-workers, imagination, conceptual innovation, and, I like to think, integrity. The perfect scorers in all these areas are rarities, but they do exist. I've hired many, many managers, the good and the bad, the squares and the swingers. I've had the intelligent, competent, and ambitious young men and the bureaucratic, the experienced, the alcoholic, and the alibi artists.

Most of all, I dislike a manager who mouths words about the glories of the free-enterprise system but is unaware of the changing socioeconomic conditions around the world. I've used every gimmick in the world to recruit the exceptional manager-leader: advertising, head-hunting firms, recruiting agents at graduating ceremonies. And I've learned one thing—to do the recruiting myself. The best-qualified manager is top priority, and finding him should not be left to corporate underlings or to a wobbly incumbent. Recruitment of proper management becomes the most important act of ownership.

In March 1968 I was attending an East-West trade conference in New York City sponsored by one of the management associations. Many of America's most prestigious political and industrial leaders were there. Presiding over one of the sessions was an alert, ebullient, outgoing young man named John Hampton Hickman III. After the meeting I congratulated him on his intelligent handling of the rather

controversial trade issues discussed at the seminar. He replied that he knew and respected me. He asked that I have
a drink with him after the meeting, and we went to my
apartment on Sutton Place.

Hickman said that he admired me for what I was doing
in the promotion of trade. He knew that we were unraveling
problems in the operations of Seilon, Inc., the company
that remained after I sold the tire division of Seiberling.
He said that he had spotted the weaknesses and suggested
that he would like to join us and introduce "modern management techniques." He had many ideas for turning the
unprofitable divisions into winners.

I agreed to see him again, and no sooner had I returned
to my office in Toledo the following day, than he called
for an appointment. He said that he had thought of many
programs for the company that required quick decisions.
He wanted to meet in my corporate office or at my home
within hours. His private plane soon landed at the Toledo
airport, and we were meeting on my veranda overlooking
the Maumee River.

Hickman claimed to have studied our situation, and he
outlined what he called our problem areas. He talked my
language, pointing out the need for recruitment of more
"professional" executives. He made a lot of sense. I admitted
my impatience at failing to complete a turnaround situation.
He said that he could point out our objectives, draft programs, adopt budgets, and make the company a major
American enterprise. The upshot was that we met the following week in New York City.

When he arrived at my apartment, he was accompanied
by two attorneys, including the senior member of one of
the nation's most prestigious law firms. Our long conferences
continued into the early hours of the morning.

I had been thoroughly studied and analyzed by the job
applicant. He knew a great deal about me and our operation. He and his counsel assumed that his terms for an employment contract were settled. His one "nonnegotiable
item" seemed to include an option for a sizable block of
stock. He also took care to provide himself with a large

starting bonus, saying that we were saving ourselves recruitment fees. The young executive, whom I guessed to
be under thirty years of age, emphasized that his starting
salary would have to be substantial, something like seventy-
five or one hundred thousand dollars a year.

I am the first to insist that the successful corporate manager is worthy of a big salary, but in this case I had not
made up my mind about his suitability or even his managerial skills; it was all moving too rapidly to be real. I
promised that we would consider the possibilities when I
had checked more thoroughly into his experience, references,
and background. He moved too fast for that. He arranged
for me to meet a group of prominent bankers from Europe,
together with the officers of Norodny, the London branch
of the Moscow bank at dinner the very next evening.

The dinner was an elegant affair, with fine wines and
superb food. He introduced me to each of the guests as
his "partner" in the new adventure he was taking on for rebuilding Seilon.

The following night we had dinner at his country club
out at Tuxedo Park in Westchester County, New York. I
stayed overnight at his home and met his wife, daughter,
and three sons. The house was an enormous old-fashioned
mansion, the former home of J. Pierpont Morgan. Hickman
put on a spectacular show for me and introduced me to
many of his neighbors and big-name country-club friends.
I was impressed and a bit awed by this rising star of the
financial world, a youngster evidently so well connected.

Back in Toledo the following day I began a more thorough check of his background. I was told that he was an
honor graduate of the Yale Law School, a graduate of Brown
University, and an accomplished linguist, proficient in
Mandarin Chinese, Italian, and various European languages.

I noticed that the two or three business associates I interviewed on the telephone did not say much for or against
him. New regulations covering personnel references had
just gone into effect, and employers had to be discreet in
the questions they asked. The credit agencies also left many
details out of their reports. In the executive directories he

was listed as a business executive and an international investor socially active in various clubs and a founder of a little theater in New York City. The deans of his school and university days refused to give us anything but his years of attendance.

I decided to take a chance and hire Hickman as the top executive in the Seilon, Inc. complex. There was, I found, opposition from other company officials. I suspected that they were too quick to sense his flaws and resented interference with their personal precincts and prerogatives. After all, he was a brusque and at times abrasive chap who spoke with finality.

Then we met with all the other officials of the company at its various locations. The atmosphere calmed down a bit. A few days later one of the officials of the company came into my office and insisted that I look more closely at Hickman's background. I still felt, after consultation with others in management, that the local executives were jealous and throwing unnecessary spitballs at him. I admire ambition. I found nothing against him other than that he had a few personal debts. He lived high, as if to the manner born, but I've seen many young high livers building their enterprises, and they have needed only one capital gain to pull them through. I decided to go ahead and employ the young man.

I gave him a substantial salary and options to acquire stock. He started with us the first of April 1968. He promptly reported a profit for the first six months of 1968 of $2,034,000. This profit was mostly the result of capital gains and security transactions, but it contrasted with a loss of $417,000 for the similar period the prior year. Such accomplishments aren't ignored by the market, and our stock rose rapidly. Each favorable tidbit of news was conveyed to the world in elaborate press releases. I have spent my life in communications and sales, but I was soon advised by his newly retained promotion people that it would be necessary "to make the PR message sound newsworthy and profound without saying anything" and that "the more stock prices go up, the more the public jumps in." Evidently Hickman and his advisers were wise to the ways of Wall Street, because the price of the stock continued to rise rapidly on the New York Stock Exchange. Every meeting with security analysts seemed to trigger another three- or four-point rise.

Hickman was flashy. With a new staff of assistants and secretaries, he took over our executive suite. He fired officers right and left. I like men who are decisive leaders, but he tore the whole organization apart.

On April 15, 1968, he presided at our annual stockholders' meeting in Toledo. Reporters who attended thought that I had sold out and moved completely out of the picture. With the aid of his new promotion people, financial circles became curious about this young miracle worker who was about to build a growth conglomerate. "Investors" were told to get in on the ground floor. He stepped to the podium and told me to introduce him briefly as the new president of the company; that he and his assistants would then take charge of the meeting. I refused to permit him to do so; I told him that I would preside as chairman.

It was fascinating to see his imported newsmakers build his image as corporate savior. Here was the modern financial genius in action. Jobs and new business opportunites would be moving into Toledo. His photographers and press people roamed all over the place, with Hickman holding center stage. The resulting personal and corporate newspaper coverage was tremendous. He gave the stockholders a vague hint of what he was going to do, and he made it clear that those who wanted action had better jump aboard if they were going to ride with the "new" Seilon, Inc.

The stock began to move and, after less than a year of Hickman, it had moved from three or four dollars a share to more than twenty-five dollars a share. I owned three-quarters of a million shares of the stock, so I was not unmindful of the benefits. There were times when I made several million dollars in a single day—on paper. But my life-long policy of buying and not selling stock in my companies didn't help my cash bank account.

Hickman jazzed up the corporate executive suite. He hired the prettiest Hollywood-type blonde secretary. She *could* answer the phone; but she didn't have a chance to do much

—he remained mostly in transit or in our New York office. His communication with me fell to near zero.

Our contract with him provided that he immediately move his family to Toledo. Indeed, at one time he looked at several magnificent homes along the Maumee River. But he never could bring himself to leave Wall Street. He spent one day at the Maumee Valley Country Day School, a private academy, and suggested that his children might be entered there. He met with their board of trustees, and the same day they invited him to become a member. On another occasion he stopped in Omaha, near the site of our Lockwood Corporation, a large agriculture-equipment company. The president of the leading bank in town promptly invited him out to his home for dinner. Hickman, the supersalesman, the smooth-talking, brilliant linguist, ended up with a sizable line of credit. His ultracorrect English clothes, his connoisseur appreciation of liquors and Cuban cigars, and his dazzling talk captivated them all.

Hickman's lavish lifestyle made good copy for the *New York Times* and the financial press. He held many press conferences. His annual reports were splendid spectaculars. Usually such reports for companies our size cost between $10,000 and $15,000. The cost of his first report to stockholders exceeded $125,000. The first three pages carried photographs of Hickman in various postures. The multifaceted Hickman—scholar, corporate administrator, financier.

Seilon, Inc., owned a substantial block of stock in a company called Copolymer, Inc., a synthetic-rubber manufacturer at Lake Charles, Louisiana. Our board of directors had tried to sell our interest but had never been able to reach an agreed price. Some of our directors wanted three or four million dollars, and others held out for six or seven million dollars. One morning shortly after he joined us, Hickman telephoned me and said that the day before he had sold us out of Copolymer. I asked him how much we received for the property, and he said five and a half million dollars. I admire decision makers but only after all the facts and all the alternatives are studied. While we debated, he acted. It made little difference to him that he acted without authority.

On another occasion Hickman called and said that he had sold our plastic plant at Newcomerstown, Ohio. He told me that he had received from General Tire three million cash for that operation. Soon afterward he informed me he had disposed of our Batesville Rubber Company in Arkansas, a manufacturer of vinyl shoes. When I heard the loose terms of the sale, I felt dizzy. That deal had been largely consummated in New York City, and our people were soon to learn that the contract was, from our standpoint, a disaster: no substantial down payment and a long pay-out. The money to pay us would come from the sale of our own inventory. We had great difficulty getting our money back after Hickman sold us out of that venture.

Hickman also decided to dispose of our General Wire and Cable Company at Colbourn, Ontario, although it took him a little more time to dump that company. This was another deal that we would like to forget. Considerable litigation was filed around the country resulting from the hasty sale of these manufacturing companies. When I asked Hickman why he was so hell-bent on getting rid of our companies, he said he was just cleaning out the dogs in preparation for adding winners. That seemed logical to me, but it took us a while to realize the extent of the beating we took in getting the dogs out of that kennel. He didn't have to point out that the disposition of so many of our assets put a bundle of cash into the corporate till. I should have known what a temptation a treasury with several millions in it could be.

Hickman asked me to go to Europe to look at two Swiss banks and one Italian bank. We spent a few weeks in Geneva, Zurich, Rome, and Milan. I received a quick education in financial gimmickry. I had heard about the secrecy of Swiss banks. But their operations from the inside were a wonder to behold. Swiss bankers take in millions of dollars and shelter the money from the prying eyes of outsiders. One of the banks we looked at was a haven for the funds of well-known Caribbean, Latin American, and Far Eastern

dictators. It all seemed unbelievable to me, and I soon
realized that I didn't want to get too close to such operations. Escape money and unexplainable fund transfers were
everywhere.

There were so many shenanigans going on inside one
bank that it was difficult for us to learn the true assets, and
we surely couldn't carry on meaningful purchase discussions.
Always we were lavishly entertained but left naked of information. When we mentioned a strange or shady transaction, we were met by a smile or a wink. I finally put my
foot down on these dealings and returned to my office in
Toledo.

Hickman occasionally barged in to corporate headquarters
in Toledo with a retinue of aides. I realized what was happening to a good deal of our huge cash reserve. He lived
high and incurred enormous expenses. He also purchased
blocks of stock in various other companies. At one point he
planned to take over Western Union, and we acquired
many thousands of its shares. With his attorneys he immediately met with their top management to advise them of his
takeover plans. Mention of his acquisition talks were leaked
to the press, and our stock continued to skyrocket. Officials
of Western Union and other companies throughout the
United States and Canada started calling me to ask what
was happening.

We had options on soft-drink manufacturers, jewelers,
real estate investments, and French design firms. Usually I
was as much in the dark as anyone. Hickman and his lawyers, after more conferences with hostile management, found
that we were not particularly welcome in their executive
suites. Instead of raiding Western Union, we scampered out
and sold the stock, fortunately with a slight profit.

We were lucky on the timing—in presidential-election
years the stock markets usually rise as the Federal Reserve
Board increases the supply of money. Along this merry way,
we found that the fees of the New York attorneys, auditors,
advisers, and consultants for these shenanigans were stag-
gering. With all that cash and a swinging corporate president
on the make, we were sitting ducks. Still, there were bankers

in Europe and the Middle East anxious to let us borrow all the cash we wanted. Our corporate-acquisition department, meaning Hickman, looked at more than one hundred possibilities. At least I didn't let him offer our stock, even at an exaggerated price, to snare corporate partners. One of our happy stockholders, seeing the extent of our stock rise, said to me, "This company president may be a reprobate, but remember that he is *our* reprobate!"

His razzle-dazzle technique brought companies into our orbit and more action into our stock. Believe it or not, Wall Street security advisers very seldom appraise management. An acquisition made our stocks go up, period. At that point our Seilon, Inc., provided an example of the difference between a corporation operating under an adventurer or stock market manipulator and one with a skilled scientific manager. It is the difference between building a favorable market quote and producing a bottom-line profit.

Style is not a substitute for substance. Came accounting day, and we were disillusioned and unhappy, picking up the wreckage of Hickman's antics. We were reluctant to fire him, but were not as dazzled by his performance as were the outside stockholders.

He left owing us a considerable sum of money and then entered a variety of new corporate ventures. *Barron's* and other financial papers carried vivid stories about the fallen wonder boy who, after he departed our castle, became entangled with civil and criminal charges. We heard about subpoenas and bench warrants issued for his arrest. If the stock market had been on an upswing, or if he'd been able to complete a couple of capital-gain deals, his story probably would have equaled that of half the conglomerate presidents in the United States.

The lessons provided by such a corporate official are clear. There is a difference between a person who acquires property or achieves ownership and a manager who operates and directs an institution. Anyone can own; it takes talent and skill to manage.

I read of Hickman's corporate activities in such publications as *Who's Who in the World* and *Who's Who in In-*

*dustry and Finance.* It is truly an impressive résumé. So what became of this mysterious high flyer in the international corporate suites? By the late 1970s he was chairman of the Business and Economics Department of Tennessee Wesleyan College and visiting lecturer at the University of Connecticut. He directed courses at other colleges, in North Carolina and elsewhere. His subject? Corporate morality and the social responsibilities of business!

# CHAPTER
# XI

~~~~~~~~~~~~~~~~~~~~~~~~~

# Joining the Money Changers

I was not alone in my strong prejudices against banks and bankers. To me they were a pack of moneychangers and exploiters—and the most potent force in our community. They manipulated the monetary supply, and through the credit system, bankers controlled the politicians, Congress, the judges—and the rest of us.

Before the advent of the modern professional manager, bankers' influence and assets were generally passed on by inheritance from founder to successors. Bankers made a lot of money by taking in other people's money, then lending it out to waiting lines of borrowers. The money they took in worked for the bank's profit, twenty-four hours a day. I noticed one other little detail—people who learn how to secure and use credit always have a better economic and social way of life than those who do hard manual labor.

Alert financial specialists, with the aid of lawyers, accountants, and directors, working under the controls of a maze of regulatory agencies, were running the nation's business. The bankers in effect decreed which factories would be built and which products produced. I'm afraid that I misjudged what financial institutions could and could not do. I thought the banks needed us borrowers as much as we needed them. I was wrong. They had alternatives—they could switch their funds to riskless, interest-bearing, tax-free securities.

My leftist reputation as a labor lawyer was not the best background for gaining the admiration of private commercial bankers. As a member of the progressive movement, I always realized the pressures which could be applied on my real estate loan or home mortgage. Many banks denied credit to unions, neighborhoods, and farmers' cooperatives. In borrowing money, many of us felt that we were cast into an adversary position—be good boys or don't come in here asking favors! After all, the directors of banks are leaders of the corporate world.

I finally seized the opportunity to pull the curtains back from the money temple. It took the precipitous action of a swinging executive bent on acquisition of one more company, any company, to force me into the financial fires. He was on the prowl for operations, and he wouldn't hesitate to pick off the largest corporations around the country.

Perhaps his approach was too blunt—he told the corporate heads right off that we planned their takeover. Today a suitor lines up his finances and makes his tender with as little advance notice as possible. The victim corporation is caught off-guard, with its defenses down. Many tender or takeover attempts now are Friday-night specials—made after the close of the stock market. John Hampton Hickman III, our wonder-boy manager, had the qualities for such quick action. He was slapped down several times, and I was forced to curb his voraciousness—I urged him to take on one assignment at a time.

Hickman started to organize a conglomerate of companies operating in the luxury trade. We looked at and carried on negotiations with Swiss watchmakers, Fifth Avenue novelty shops, jewelers, furriers, and exclusive high-fashion dress shops. He was well along in building a complex of sizable and classy consumer-goods producers. Without telling me, he decided to buy a stake in a national financial institution.

He told me, "We need a home for our money." Only then
did I discover that he had taken the proceeds from the sale
of some of our other companies and purchased several
hundred thousand shares of a registered bank-holding company, the First Bancorporation, headquartered in Reno,
Nevada.

I rushed to look into the western banking operation. It
owned the Nevada National Bank with nineteen branches
throughout the state. Regulatory agencies had required that
the bank-holding company dispose of one of its two banks,
either the Valley Bank of Nevada, a state-chartered bank, or
the Nevada National Bank. E. Parry Thomas and other controlling stockholders decided to retain the Valley Bank of
Nevada and dispose of the bank-holding company with its
Nevada National Bank subsidiary. There were approximately a million and a half shares outstanding in the hands
of about ten thousand shareholders. We went on to purchase
five hundred thousand shares, or thirty-eight percent of the
company's stock. We paid as much as eighteen dollars a
share.

I was nervous about our company's investing nine and
one-half million dollars in the stock of a Nevada bank.
Nevertheless, I decided to acquire additional shares. I was
afraid that Nevada meant only gambling, legalized prostitution—and vast tourism. I had heard little of the state's
other activities—mining, cattle raising, transportation, ware-
housing, and industrial enterprises. Hickman made quick
trips to Europe and borrowed several million dollars from
Michelle Sindona and other Italian and Swiss bankers. He
put up our bank stock as collateral. He hired more new
personnel, especially public-relations people. He flooded the
financial community with announcements of our big plans.
Such sensational activity is music to Wall Street stockbrokers
and caused the stocks of both the bank and its new parent
to rise.

There was no way of keeping track of the flamboyant
Hickman. Chauffeurs and advisers and special consultants
were coming out of our corporate ears. One night when he
drove me out to his country home in Westchester, he ordered

the chauffeur into the back seat of the Mercedes. We rode in the front seat and dashed along between cars and traffic lights. While he drove, he used the auto telephone, calling our various offices in Toledo, New Orleans, Las Vegas, and New York City.

While we careened along on the hazardous trip, he authorized our bank people to make three or four big loans. In between calls to our lending officers he told me of his continuing purchase of stock in other companies. I still couldn't find out much about the millions of dollars we were borrowing and spending to acquire large blocks of securities. He told me about the money we were taking in from the sale of our "dogs," companies he didn't think would fit into our new financial conglomerate. He told me that his eyes were now directed toward cash-rich monetary institutions. He said that such acquisitions would take care of required loan repayments.

We took over control of the Nevada National Bank and at the first meeting elected a majority of the board of directors. Hickman brought in several of his friends, financial people from New York City, Dallas, Los Angeles, and elsewhere, including several stockbrokers. After the fact, he discovered that brokers were barred from being directors of a national bank, so we were immediately in big trouble with the federal banking authorities.

We quickly changed directors. Hickman waited for the second meeting of the board of directors to tell Stewart Webb, the president of the bank, that he was of no further use and that his employment was terminated.

I insisted that we get some Nevada residents as directors. Hickman permitted Floyd Lamb, (no relation to me), long-time employee of the bank and a state senator in Nevada, to become the interim president of the company. The handsome, white-haired Lamb brought to our board several other prominent politicians, mostly state senators. Suddenly our bank had taken on a political hue (far right of center) that I lived to regret. Several other bank officials quickly departed, and Floyd Lamb, to provide continuity, took over additional titles. We were in total turmoil; everyone waited for the youthful "boy wonder from the East" to say where we were headed.

Hickman called a large-scale press conference. He announced that he planned a spectacular future for the bank. First, he would stage a get-acquainted festival, a super shindig in Las Vegas. He invited top state, city, and federal officials, business and media executives from around the country, and management of all the large companies having operations in Nevada. The party at Caesars Palace turned out to be a super spectacular, especially for Hickman and his very special guests. He had four executive suites alongside the swimming pool, one for his family and others for various beautiful people.

I was assigned a cubbyhole room next to the elevator on the second floor overlooking the lobby entrance. The foghorn announcements to waiting autos were made by Joe Louis, the former world heavyweight boxing champion. I didn't mind being upstaged at a party I was paying for, but I was aware that the affair was about as costly as any I had ever attended. Modern jets brought in officials from both coasts, big names from the financial world—a distinguished group indeed. I knew that the showy scheme had one shortcoming—no arrangements were made to take advantage of the goodwill engendered by the party. No one remembered to "make the sale" of our bank services. We stirred up a lot of enthusiasm for our new venture, but somewhere along the line we forgot to tell our bank people that when the pilgrims start singing, "Hallelujah," it's time to pass the collection plate.

We scheduled no work conferences, we made no efforts to promote our facilities, we made no correspondent alliances, and we closed no deals. The guests simply returned to their homes saying, "What a hell of a party!"

We should have had something more to show for the hundred thousand dollars or more that our party cost.

Hickman was being watched by the American banking industry. We had a relatively small bank that boasted just one hundred million dollars in assets. Hickman's big ideas soon shook up the whole state of Nevada. His Wall Street and Fleet Street dress and manner were about as non-Western as one could get. By now we were too involved to back out, and we just hoped that somehow his plans to revolutionize the industry would succeed. He made whopping mistakes—he antagonized people and boasted about what we were going to do to our banking competitors. He brought in more high-powered New York and West Coast promotion people who knew zero about banking.

Important customers, like cattlemen and miners, not to mention the casino operators, resented him. Other financial institutions began to hire away our top executives, and we lost many of our best employees. Our advertising continued to promote the name of Hickman rather than mention the services we could offer. He chose to call it "The Bank with the Heart of Gold"—whatever that means.

It did not take us long to discover the enormity of the loan losses we had inherited from prior management. I wondered how any prudent person, buying a bank, could fail to study its loan portfolio. But who ever said that hasty action is prudent? These "unusual" loans forced us, over the next couple years, to mark off losses of more than seven million dollars. We found that letters of credit had been issued and various commitments made that bound us to come up with hundreds of thousands of dollars in dubious future loans.

We rushed in to make our own bad loans. We took subordinate liens of questionable value on large cattle ranches.

I insisted that we restructure our bond-and-securities portfolio, taking our losses as we found them. We took lumps, big lumps. At the instigation of the federal regulatory agencies, we cleared out several old and doubtful ranch and department-store loans. In the process, I became an enthusiastic booster of the role of a watchdog, the U.S. Comptroller of the Currency. He harassed our banking personnel and made penetrating examinations of the bank and very properly gave us warnings and low scores for bank liquidity and credit extensions. The government regulators merely wanted "to get the facts straight" to safeguard the depositors. Most of all, I wondered what we stockholders had bungled into.

As I took a personal interest and looked into the inner workings of the bank, I was alternately fascinated and flabbergasted by what bankers could do with other people's money. Some of my radical friends had called bankers a gang of bastards and bandits. Now I began to have a view from the inside, appraising applicants for credit and making risk judgments. I had not fully realized what a bank must understand about a borrower if it is to get paid back. I had known vaguely that management of money is a science, a complicated and probably necessary function in any form of political society. There are many ways of tailoring loans, and all of them are structured to make it possible for the bank to get its money back.

I decided to get totally involved and learn a great deal about banks. I visited most of our branch banks around Nevada, first to get a feel for the people and the economy. It wasn't difficult to spot operations needing improvement; the physical condition of many of the branches was deplorable, morale of the staff was low, and record keeping was sloppy.

Some of the conflicts of interest in the institution we found were almost unbelievable; we weren't able to find vital records, but we did find officers indebted to suppliers. Bags of silver and gold coins lay on the floors of skimpy, unprotected vaults. In one Las Vegas branch, bags of cash lay next to a glass window. Nevada National branches were separated from the home office by hundreds of miles, and there was often only minimum communication between them. Local managers in far off cow towns were pretty much on their own. We quickly saw the need for central controls and standard procedures.

There were constant surprises. At an early meeting of the board of directors of the bank-holding company, we found that Hickman had sold, at considerable personal profit, stock he had recently received from us under an option. We assumed that every corporate officer of a publicly held company knew that such a sale by an insider within six months of acquisition was prohibited under Section 16B of the Securities and Exchange Act of 1934. Under the law it was necessary for Hickman to return such short-term profits to the corporation. He raised quite a fuss about it, but the directors insisted.

The curiosity of the directors was aroused, and once alerted, they began to question the legal acumen of the boy wonder. The board forced him to give the corporation a note for more than a hundred thousand dollars to cover his indebtedness. At least in our bank we weren't going to allow huge officer overdrafts, a practice fairly prevalent in certain financial institutions and brought to public attention by the activities of President Jimmy Carter's budget director, Bert Lance.

Obviously, a person can have many admirable qualities and still lack managerial capacity. Innovativeness is admirable, but we like to think that a manager must travel the straight path and maintain his own personal integrity if he is to reach the corporate heavens. Hickman was a decision maker and a colorful, daring plunger—he could have put together a lot of winners. Rather late, we ordered an extensive examination of his background.

We found that previous to joining us, Hickman had incurred enormous personal debts all over the country, that he had been in difficulty with various institutions and lived on an unbelievably lavish scale. He had apartments and chauffeured limousines in New York City, Las Vegas, Reno, and elsewhere. Expenses for maintaining his flamboyant lifestyle cost us tens of thousands of dollars. He created the image of success, and every lavish detail seemed to be picked up by the financial journals. His many press releases describing our future prospects caused the bank stock to go up and up. When the actual bottom-line numbers came out later, the stock dropped.

Having succumbed to the myth that a bank was a mysterious, faraway institution, I began to weigh my own mixture of hostilities. So much of American life is an adversary role, a life of confrontations. I had sought my share of loans over the years, usually working through my sub-ordinates.

When my application for a borrowing was approved, I sensed a victory; after all, I had obtained a loan. I didn't fully understand that a bank prospered when it tailored a sensible package for its customer. I was often at a disadvantage—I took the first terms offered. There were thirteen-thousand other banks in the United States; I had bartered only with my local banker, rather than shopping around. Too often, they were convenience loans. We made deals on our respective reputations rather than the numbers.

As a labor lawyer involved in litigation against the large corporate clients of the Toledo banks, my record as an emerging industrialist was a bit tarnished. Nevertheless, my large compensating balances gave the banks a free ride on my checking (demand) non-interest-paying accounts. They took in my deposits at no cost and invested them in accounts that produced good income for the bank. Often their income was totally tax exempt; they purchased munici-pal bonds. Recently the more sophisticated depositors have received a better deal—short-term deposits, such as certifi-cates of deposit with stipulated maturities. In other words, they receive negotiated interest income.

When one acquires his own bank, one learns a great deal about holding other people's money. The bank, I discovered, has only two functions: obtain funds and lend them at a rate above its costs. A bank places an hourly value on the use of a depositor's checking and demand deposit account. When all accounts, demand and time or savings, cost an average of say four percent, and are loaned out to com-mercial, residential, or installments customers at a rate, for example, of eight percent, there exists a "spread" of four percent, which, after operating expenses for payroll and maintenance, is pure profit.

The competent lender finds it easy to make good loans to credit-worthy customers. The trick then is to get deposits into the bank, promote deposits by advertising and lending, develop new markets, solicit accounts, and put the money to work instantly.

I've had long experience, if not expertise, in various forms of promotion and image building, so I decided not to use premiums or gimmickry to attract new depositors. I would adopt only programs emphasizing the availability of our services and the opening of neighborhood branch banks.

As our deposits grew, large loans were actively solicited from credit-worthy customers. Good compensating balances followed. We decided to loan out our funds to borrowers rather than stack them away in a securities portfolio. We were in a growth area of the country, and there was a great demand for loans.

We needed competent loan officers to show us how to tailor loan packages to meet the needs of our customers. It's an art, and I knew very little about it. A farmer has good and bad years; his lending banker must be able to exercise restraint and wait until a crop comes in and the customer gets in a position to pay off. The fair-weather banker is a short-lived banker. My own father, a commercial fisherman, did his banking business with A. L. Spitzer for sixty years because "the old banker at the Spitzer-Rorick" extended to his friend, "Mr. Clarence Lamb," a hundred-dollar loan to tide him over until the next spring's fishing catch.

I was not a professional banker, and I have the scars to prove it. At the time of my takeover, according to the U.S. comptroller, the operation was a "problem bank." When our management made a wrong decision, we heard simply that "a mistake has been made." We had no budgets or guidelines—in other words, we had inherited bad management.

There was one mistake I didn't make—I didn't run when we took our early losses on a raft of bad loans. With almost ten million dollars now invested in that Nevada bank, I decided to keep on buying the stock, even though the bank's condition looked threatening. As the stock continued to drop in price, I bought more. I followed the same practice throughout my career: buy more and more stock in the companies I control. Read, study, attend trade seminars, and visit the successful people in the industry. I interviewed prospective bank officers, and each new interview opened new vistas to an exciting career. I enjoyed the possibilities even though there were some horrendous problems. Why retire from a fight when one is having so much fun?

My first priority was to get a new bank president. I made a serious mistake. I let an assistant interview and recruit the new official. My deputy LeRoy Sigler interviewed and then hired William Pratt, a senior vice-president of a national bank in San Jose, California. Pratt became a one-man disaster. Attending our first meeting of the board of directors, he indicated his opposition to all my suggestions for modernization. He said it was premature to improve the facilities, open new branches, install twenty-four-hour bank devices, or add drive-up windows. After all, he emphasized, "Mr. Lamb is not a professional banker."

I was especially disappointed when he strenuously opposed building a new main headquarters building in Reno, even though the bank had owned the ideal site for several years. To his credit, Pratt did install some much-needed organizational controls and tried to straighten out and reduce our huge loan losses. But I was to learn that good management requires overall plans, with priorities and timetables.

Probably the most important responsibility ownership can have, besides recruitment of competent management, is an effective board of directors able to set policies. On our new board we were fortunate to recruit Gordon G. Mac-Lean, my long-time skiing friend, recently moved from Tarzana, California, to a new home on Mt. Rose, above Lake Tahoe, Nevada. His family founded and managed the Harris Trust Company of Chicago. He was a student of the West and let us know the full extent of the growth possibilities in the state of Nevada. He assured me one evening, when the bank's status looked pretty bleak, that once we could get the system cleaned up and controls installed, the potentials were tremendous!

I went to a banking school in Chicago to learn some of the skills involved in a bank's operations. Among other things, I learned that offering the services of the bank, whether by making real estate, commercial, or installment loans, or operating a trust department, requires a sense of direction—and a selling program. Persuade the community to trust you. Get the money into the till!

We changed our image by stepping up our messages in the printed and electronic media. We changed advertising agencies. Copy was brightened and given punch.

We let people know that we wanted their accounts and had funds to extend them loans. We dropped silly institutional advertising and started selling specific services. People patronize the most convenient bank and seek out the spot nearest their home or place of employment. In today's world many customers even refuse to get out of their cars to do their banking. We found that friendly service is important and that if the bank could operate around the clock, seven days a week with the aid of the new electronic gadgetry, we could serve a lot of people more quickly. With our automatic tellers we became known as the bank that never closes.

Nevada is a twenty-four-hour community. Tourists at play are almost as busy at seven in the morning as they are at seven in the evening. We made economic studies of the buying and spending habits of tourists and presented the findings to airlines, hotels, and restaurants to help with their own future planning. We installed a research department to help investors in and out of Nevada to understand the advantages within the economic, social, and tax framework of the state.

The bank under previous ownership had suffered more than its share of bad experiences with real estate, installment, cattle, and personal-property loans. The first couple of years after we took over showed that we had to cut our losses quickly and secure a degree of solidity and liquidity if we were to survive. But our new management was conservative and slowed down all phases of expansion and modernization. Changes were put off—modern, efficient new banking techniques were spurned. I even had difficulty in getting the bank's facilities painted or new signs erected. Our management refused to computerize and looked only to cutting costs.

There was a great deal of bickering and childish pouting within the administrative staff. Finally, I insisted that we open one or two more modern branches as quickly as possible. The new technology was here, and I insisted that we take the risk and make new capital expenditures. Our turnaround couldn't take place if we were so conservative that we'd do business only in the old-fashioned way.

The Nevada casino industry deals in cash—and the daily deposit balances of some of the hotel operations run into many millions of dollars. The casino business is legal and normal in the state. We wanted such customers, and we simply had to sell our availability and skill and provide service, and we'd be in business. President Pratt dissented. My efforts to get my bank officials to move forward were unsuccessful. Even I, the nonbanker, could see how we were missing the boat. Argument followed argument.

Decisions were delayed as I argued and tried to persuade our own management to recruit competent people and move forward. It was an unusual situation when ownership had to push management to spend money. Finally, Pratt, after an all-night session with my friend and personal counsel, J. Eugene Farber, and my assistant LeRoy Sigler, gave me an ultimatum: I could either speak to him through Sigler with written and oral communications, or he would put the matter before the full board for decision.

He harped rather obnoxiously on the fact that I was not a "professional banker" and the premise that ownership should stay out of all future operations. Then he gave me a deadline—unless I agreed to his terms by nine o'clock the next morning, he wouldn't even show up at the directors' meeting.

In the morning there he was, standing at the entrance rather expectantly. On the way into the directors' meeting I rather rudely whispered to him, "Go to hell." As the directors assembled, Pratt sat meekly at the head of the table and remained embarrassedly subdued throughout the meeting. After the session I told him that I had had enough of it and that one day he would learn that management could fight everyone except ownership. He soon departed.

I knew I had a winner in this banking property. Nevada was entering a period of enormous growth, something like Arizona had experienced twenty years before. I was in the right place at the right time—and I had the nucleus of a success. Now it was necessary only to get competent financial personnel and build a team to guide its operations. The bank's basic structure was sound. We had purchased a bank with assets of one hundred million dollars and a few strategic branches throughout the state. At the time we were in fifth place among the banks in the state, but I could see a chance to become the best—and maybe the biggest. Fortunately for us, our competitors didn't take us too seriously. The bursting of the promotional bubble of our previous bank president actually helped us to clear the decks and prepare for a fresh start.

The directors of our bank-holding company began to choose sides—several had "friends" who were anxious to buy the bank. It was reassuring during those dark days that so many people wanted to buy my Nevada banking properties. Different companies offered us their stock in exchange. At the repeated insistence of our directors, I met in London with James Michael ("Jimmy") Goldschmidt, the flamboyant, colorful Tory chairman of the Cavenham food empire, and David Metcalfe, the socialite jet-setter. The wine at the party was good, and I enjoyed sitting with Jimmy's close friend, Lady Annabel Birley, the daughter of Lord Londonderry, to whom Jimmy is now married. Their offer to exchange our stock for securities in a British food company didn't appeal to me. After all the mirrors were removed, I could see myself losing several million dollars on the deal after only one or two years of ownership.

When a majority of our bank directors continued to push for the sale and I continued to resist, they resigned. I finally persuaded a majority of the remaining directors of the parent company, Seilon, Inc., to turn the entire matter over to the five-man executive committee, three members of which were my counsel and confidant J. Eugene Farber; my son, Edward Hutchinson Lamb; and myself. That move saved our control of the bank.

After we made the turnabout to great profitability, I was swamped with even more bids to buy the bank at very high prices. English and Arab banks were especially interested. What mattered if our stock went down to three or four dollars a share if at the same time I was being offered twenty-five dollars a share for the controlling block? As I noticed how anxious they were to purchase my control of the bank, I wondered to myself, *If all these foreigners can run this bank, what's wrong with us that we can't do better?* If I could only get the right people! What could be better for one's future than owning a first-class financial institution?

I might have increasing doubts about the stability of the world's economy, but in the meantime I wanted to enjoy putting together a highly profitable money machine.

CHAPTER

# XII

∿∿∿∿∿∿∿∿∿∿∿∿∿∿∿∿∿∿∿∿

# With a Good Manager in Charge

I relished moving into the dream world of banking. The very idea of being paid for holding other people's money intrigued me. I would custom tailor cash-management systems, make real estate, installment, and commercial loans, process credit cards, and finance international and regional trade. I found that the larger the capital account of a bank, the larger the lending limits. How, then, could we clear away the losses and get layers of capital—including what we hoped would be retained earnings—into the till?

We would spruce up the premises inside and out, but we would not tolerate the staid, gray-flannel-suit approach traditional with bankers. Right off I told my bank people that they needed two things: a big sign and a big vault. Banks have never taken full advantage of public-relations expertise to further their promotions. We began to let the community know of our services.

We immediately marked off the sizable bad loans we had inherited and cleaned up our balance sheet. We built several new, modern bank branches and terminals to reach out to where people live and work. Our new twenty-four-hour mechanical tellers and multiple drive-up windows began to serve the auto-oriented, mobile population. Computers were helping to move people rapidly toward a cashless society.

Our electronic fund transfer (EFT), with its capacity for instantly debiting a customer's account was linked to a sophisticated statewide retail-banking-and-merchandising service. Why should a customer waste his lunch hour waiting in line to cash his check and then move over to pay his department store or utility bills, when he could push a couple of buttons and take care of the whole chore?

We began to spend half a million dollars a year on television advertising. In my home town of Toledo, never known as an aggressive banking center, no banker has ever solicited my accounts. This taught me a lesson. When we gained control of the Nevada bank, we sent our representatives out into the marketplace—and our loans and deposits spurted. We aroused the public's interest in our product, and we showed that we were deserving of its trust. We appointed Senator Mary Gojack to head up a consumer-affairs department to handle every complaint.

I saw that I had made many mistakes in my short career as a banker. I sought out my friend Marriner Eccles, former chairman of the Federal Reserve Board and then Chairman of the highly successful First Security Bank of Salt Lake City, as well as other large industrial and financial corporations. We talked for several hours. Off and on I spent several days with my friend listening to his own exciting experiences spanning the days from 1933 to the present. He was wise and generous with his advice. He gave me a few basic points on banking and told me about the many areas, like leasing and mortgage service, underwriting, and credit life insurance, into which we could move.

It became clear that I would have to take on the job of getting together an entirely new team of bank managers. I wanted the best financial specialists money could entice. I wanted only people who would move into Nevada, see the glorious opportunities, and make their careers with our institution. I ran ads in the bankers' magazines, the *Wall Street Journal*, and several newspapers, especially on the

West Coast. I sought out bank personnel and head-hunting and recruiting agencies, not, however, giving any of them an exclusive assignment. Finally, after receiving more than five hundred different résumés, I set out on an interviewing trip. I spent a month in various cities in California, Oregon, Minnestoa, and Illinois, as well as in Boston and in New York City. There were many excellent prospects—real gems —and I learned something about banking from every one of them.

The quality of my bank would be measured by the quality, ingenuity, and integrity of its management. Jimmy Carter may have had the campaign slogan *Why not get the best?* Maybe it indicates the differences between political and commercial terms, but I actually *got* the best. I settled on a young man, age thirty-seven, who had risen to the position of senior vice-president of the Marine National Exchange Bank of Milwaukee, a bank-holding company with several hundred million dollars in assets. George E. Aker had graduated from Saint Olaf's College in Minnesota and the Chicago School of Business Administration. He had attended various banker's institutes and written an excellent book on mortgage banking. We hit it off because he saw the possibilities in Nevada.

Nor did he hesitate to give up the responsibilities and emoluments he had recently assumed with a major bank. But first he took his wife, Mary, and the entire family to survey the Nevada situation. They loved it and decided they wanted to move quickly to the Reno area. His family enjoyed outdoor activities such as skiing and water sports. They found western schools surprisingly satisfactory. He noticed the industrial growth of the free port of Reno as it attracted a large number of research, warehouse, transportation, and other companies then moving into the state. I wanted a leader who could put an end to executive infighting. We agreed that in coming with our bank, he'd report directly and exclusively to me. He would also come to my office in Toledo at least once a month and I'd spend substantial time in Nevada to get our future action plans worked out.

George Aker, all six feet, seven inches of him, quickly made his presence felt in the community. He built one of the best computer centers in the West. He recruited several young, aggressive, solid financial managers to fill vital posts in lending, branch, and trust operations. We reviewed compensation schedules and offered employes stock options, bonuses and pension and profit-sharing plans.

The attitude and enthusiasm of the bank personnel quickly showed improvement. We gave every employe a chance to get ahead by attending training programs and seminars. The staff of five hundred began to share a sense of pride and purpose. I was overjoyed to see Aker and his associates become active in all phases of Nevada community life. We raised salaries so that we were able to retain our employees and induce "competent folks from competition" to join us. Stock-option and employe-stock-purchase plans followed.

We organized new subsidiaries and entered the auto- and equipment-leasing business. Nevada had statewide bank branches, but it became obvious that we needed a great deal of modernization in our country branches, like those in Pioche, Winnemucca, and Elko. We started to open more modern new branches around the state using really up-to-date technology. We sent our salesmen to call house-to-house in the neighborhoods, and we visited every merchant. The names of local residents began to appear on our stockholder lists.

Aker really moved into the community. He was chosen chairman of the local Community Chest, or United Fund. He was given the top spot in the Nevada Bankers Association. Then he brought together twenty-five cultural organizations to organize the Sierra Arts Council. The new group would change an old-time western gambling town into a smart, creative cultural center.

Reno citizens who hadn't spoken in years sat down together to establish a remarkably attractive new complex—art museum, auditorium, music halls, theater for the performing arts. Our bank organized and financed the new civic venture, and we used part of the premises to establish a modern headquarters.

Banks respond quickly to good management. In seven years our bank increased its assets from one hundred million dollars to more than four hundred and fifty million dollars. During 1978 we increased our assets at the rate of nearly ten million dollars a month! Profits zoomed, and the price of our stock quadrupled. Increasing our deposits rapidly, we made solid commercial and construction loans, extending credit to solid borrowers.

We obtained compensating or offsetting balances (usually between ten and twenty percent of the amount of the loan). Large corporations and other big accounts usually maintain their operating accounts where their loans are. Our goal was to build well-established banking relationships with the best possible customers, including major hotel-casinos such as Hilton and Harrah's.

Retail banking zoomed; the whole organization responded to our dramatic programs. Every employe joined the team and helped us to succeed. We cleaned up our balance sheet, eliminating millions of dollars of doubtful loans. We changed securities in our portfolio, upgrading quality and shortening maturities. We followed the suggestion of Marriner Eccles and established a central money-management desk and found that it was one of the best steps we had ever taken.

Robert T. Guyton, who had started his own insurance company in New York City, joined us. He possessed great financial ingenuity, and he and his wife, Priscilla Prudence Lamb (my daughter), were anxious to get out of the Wall Street jungle. In only four years he and his young partners had established successful financial enterprises in New York City. After a short time of fighting the traffic and maneuvering the money markets of Wall Street, he wanted to try out his expertise with our own financial institutions. He took charge of all funds of the bank and organized its securities portfolio. He taught our people how to put our deposits to work within minutes after receipt.

One thing about money—it works and draws interest

twenty-four hours a day, every day. Watching these bond traders operate, buying and selling millions, is an experience to behold. We learned a great deal about making big money in the investment of funds. In 1974 the interest income from our portfolio amounted to three million dollars. In 1975 it went over five million, in 1976 well over six and one-half million, and in 1977 over nine million, and it kept right on rising. We found that by investing in overnight securities and federal funds and upgrading our bonds and shortening the length of the term, we could make added profits.

I may be an enigma in the banking business but I continue to have reservations about this nation's economy, and I insist that we remain loaded with cash. We want, if possible, to be in a position to weather any financial storm. Many big fortunes have been created in times of economic stress, and we want to be around to take advantage of opportunities. If other banks fail, we want ours to be solvent.

I often think back on the big opportunities afforded those who held cash in times of depression. There may come a day, of course, if the crisis of capitalism becomes severe enough, when no bank or other private industry will survive. No prophet can tell us when that will be. Unfortunately, many conservative political or economic leaders seem unwilling to recognize our interdependence with other human beings on earth.

We started to pay cash dividends in 1974, the first in the bank's history. In 1975 we greatly increased dividends, and in each subsequent year we increased the pay-out of regular and extra dividends. We jumped forty-eight places in the national standing of banks throughout the United States in 1975, fifty-four places in 1976, and thirty-nine places in 1977. In 1978 we jumped another forty-five places. More important, from 1975 through 1978 we just about doubled our earnings each year.

Since I seldom if ever sell my stock, it doesn't make any great difference to me what the market quote is. But it was of some comfort to note the comments of one bank-security analyst who said in 1978, probably with some exaggeration, "It's quite possible that no commercial bank in the United

States during the last half dozen years has shown the growth pattern of the Nevada National Bank."

I recognize the importance of making loans in the local community—real estate, installment, commercial and other credit. Harry Green, head of the Federal Reserve Bank, San Francisco, once told me that from his long experience in examining banks, he could go into any city in the country and know what was in a local bank's bond portfolio. If the community appeared to be prospering, if homes were being renovated and buildings and stores constructed, and there was a general appearance of civic forward movement, then the banks were lending their money out in real estate and commercial loans. If the city appeared run-down, decaying, and apathetic, then the bank had put its funds into bonds and other fixed-term securities, including tax-exempt municipal bonds. The money changers in the bank prosper, but the community suffers.

A bank is like any other commercial activity; it must have an alert marketing division. It finds ways to render services at a profit. It develops programs and services for the convenience of its customers—it extends its branches into the neighborhoods and opens twenty-four-hour terminals.

One of the best examples of our management's efforts to tread new paths occurred when in the late 1970s we began to market a new computerized system for processing share drafts of credit unions. In the past, many banks avoided doing business with credit unions, thinking them dangerous competitors. Yet the credit unions and savings-and-loan associations soon became the two most rapidly growing institutions on the American financial scene.

We noted that credit unions in Nevada were having astronomical growth. The group at Nellis airbase had thirty-two thousand members and fifty million dollars in assets. Our bank simply devised drafts in standard check size and format and processed the credit-union drafts automatically through the bank computers. The amounts were posted daily to the credit union's accounts. The cash balances and float became sizable. This new relationship opened our facilities immediately to a hundred thousand potential customers, and we became almost the exclusive bank for credit-union members as we processed their drafts. Our assets and deposits increased by many millions of dollars.

Good credit is like cash in the bank. My personal credit remained perfect—I never have personal debts, nor have my companies ever defaulted on a loan. I may have had extremely low cash balances, and I have often been cash poor, as I buy more and more stock in the companies I control. My money has always worked in some equity. As I become connected with a company, I buy its stock—and the lower the stock goes, the more I buy. If I can buy a stock at a third of its true book value, I figure it's as good as changing one dollar for 3 one-dollar bills. That is not stock-market wizardry—it is using the leverage and the control of assets, often by making small down payments. The object of the game is to increase one's equity in a sound venture. The same rules apply in buying a piece of well-located real estate— small down payment, big long-term debt.

A person who wants to become wealthy can find help from an understanding banker. I like to recall a recent visit to my office by a young man who was a securities broker. He felt that he was working in a dying business, and he wanted advice. I asked him what he wanted to do, and his answer was simply, "Make money, a lot of money."

I asked him if he had ever visited Reno and looked into the opportunities there. His reply was that his father had gone to Las Vegas as a tourist, but he knew nothing else about the state. I told Paul Wolfram that practically any deal in the United States could be put together if one has guts and a million dollars. Wolfram replied, "I have a sister-in-law, Zula, with these qualifications." He was correct. Besides her beauty, imagination, and courage, she had a million dollars in U.S. Treasury notes resting quietly in the Toledo Trust Company.

Wolfram saw for-sale signs on property in Las Vegas next to the Hilton International Hotel. Upon inquiry, he found the price for the four-acre parcel: six million dollars. He returned to my office and reported his discovery. I asked him why he would want to buy raw land and build a hotel-casino, since he had no experience whatever in that line of business. I also told him the Howard Hughes estate's company, Summa Corporation, was eager to sell its Landmark Hotel. On his return to Toledo he secured a partner or two to look into the matter. After tight negotiations my young friends Paul and Ted Wolfram, with their associates, made a tender offer of $12.5 million for the project. Shortly thereafter their offer was accepted and they moved into Las Vegas to operate their new enterprise.

They sought a casino license, and the usual thorough investigation by the Nevada Gaming Commission took several months before granting permission to operate the casino. The occupancy of the hotel was even then running in excess of ninety percent. The hotel under Howard Hughes's management had lost millions of dollars. The losses were due to poor management, skimmed-off gambling funds, and kickbacks in the various purchasing and trading departments. Summa Corporation levied a weekly management fee of thousands of dollars against each of its operating hotels. The total losses in the previous ten years amounted to more than fifteen million dollars. Many persons scoffed at the Wolframs' buying what they called "the worst dog in the Hughes kennel." The buyers moved in April 1978 and made some obvious changes, and within a couple of months they had purchase offers of twenty-five million dollars!

How was this operation financed? Other than Zula's bonds, there were assets involved in the down payment, but one and a half million dollars was borrowed from my bank. Thus they put in a total of two and a half million dollars and had eight years to pay off the balance of the purchase price. In ten months of operation in the first year they claimed a net income before taxes of one million dollars. This profit resulted from their actual cash investment of only one million dollars!

Deals like the Landmark Hotel are available to those who have the vision, who know how to cooperate and put winners together. It is necessary to have creditability with a lending bank. The technique of this money management is simple. There are great assets selling at discount prices. One of the assets in the Landmark Hotel deal was approximately thirty acres of land available for development or sale, and that land has a market value of at least five hundred thousand dollars an acre. In other words, purchasers could sell off assets, maintain profitable operations, pay off all debt, and retain equity control. Another technique available to them is the public offering of stock. They can secure the same result of retaining control and getting their own money out of it completely, even as they operate an extremely profitable entity. As owners and managers, they set salaries, dividend policies, and other matters that count.

Access to a million dollars permits nearly any big deal in the book. It doesn't happen by mirrors; it happens by finding credit with an understanding financial institution.

Corporate use of credit can produce enormous success stories. In one of my operations we started an auto-leasing company, Bancorporation Leasing, in Sacramento, California, with an initial investment of only fifteen thousand dollars. The parent guaranteed its debt to the Bank of America. In five years the leasing company was producing a half-million-dollar tax shelter and three hundred thousand dollars in yearly profit. It was valued at more than three million dollars five years after founding.

In our present booming, uncontrolled society, thousands of Americans have learned how to make big money. The American economy runs on credit, and bankers are in the business of extending credit—hundreds of billions of dollars a year—for everything from housing and factories to autos. Individual use of credit can also produce fantastic results. We bankers see hundreds of examples every month. We extended credit of $250,000 to a man to start an ice-cream parlor in Reno—he sold his cones for one dollar each, and during the first year he showed pre-tax profits in excess of $650,000.

The franchise operations around the country, like the hamburger chains, have given thousands of mom-and-pop franchisees fairly big profits. I know of many that started with small capital and a loan of as little as a hundred thousand dollars and produce twice that amount of income each year. I have always wondered how many hamburgers could be peddled in the American market, but I've also wondered how long we could maintain the momentum of welfare capitalism in the United States. My bets are on the longevity of hamburgers.

For several years it was possible to acquire dividend-paying stock in our bank-holding company at thirty percent of its net worth—and I bought a lot of it. That's being cash poor with a purpose! Control represents advantages far beyond dividends. However, there are disadvantages in continuing to purchase stock in a publicly owned company. After a while the "float," or public ownership in the company, disappears. Then there is very little trading, and the stock price remains dormant. Market values of private companies are generally hard to determine, and only the insiders know all the facts. But as an entrepreneur in the private-enterprise game, I concluded that it was best to own as much as possible of a good company, watch the property carefully, and install top-flight management.

A commercial bank gets many tax preferences and advantages as it handles the depositors' money. As a last resort, it can invest large amounts in tax-exempt securities, such as municipal, state, and county bonds. It's possible for individuals or corporations in the United States to have an income of millions of dollars a year and avoid paying a penny of federal taxes. Many investors, more interested in security than in growth, look at a bank's portfolio to see how little it pays in taxes. Often it's *very* little; indeed, some commercial banks operate on tax refunds.

Although a corporation's charitable giving is limited to five percent of its income, the individual taxpayer is permitted to donate up to fifty percent of his adjusted gross income to nonprofit organizations, such as colleges, foundations, and hospitals. I have always given away more than fifty percent of my income (most years it has exceeded one hundred percent). I try to see that corporations with which I am associated give their full allowance.

Our government gives many shelters, such as tariffs, farm subsidies, special credits, depletion allowances, and other

preferences that permit, even encourage, the legal avoid-
ance of taxes. Leasing companies are among the most
prominent and profitable tax shelters. Income is "deferred"
and depreciation or investment credits can be set off against
profitable activities. We in the corporate suite live by these
tax gimmicks, knowing that under the present system there
is no possibility of meaningful tax reform.

The dodge of shelters and permanent tax deferrals is a
privilege given the rich and large profit maker. Lobbyists
won't let politicians do much about it. The inequity of our
tax systems is nowhere more obvious than in our toleration
of shelters and tax loopholes.

Everyone should learn to read a bank statement. Each
line tells a story. Discover the composition of a bank's assets.
The return-on-assets line is probably the most important
line of all—it reveals the success or failure of management.
Yet another great shelter in a bank revolves around its
setting up "reserves," money put aside, free of tax liability,
to protect against possible future contingencies. That's a
shelter!

A bank-holding company is permitted to acquire only
financially oriented ventures. Leasing operations, although
the least known and possibly the most effective of tax shelters, qualify as bank activities. Under present conditions
of economic uncertainty, the leasing of property is becoming more popular. Our Nevada National Bank complex
operates three leasing enterprises. An auto-leasing division
issues the normal three- or four-year term leases on autos
and trucks. We also started an equipment-leasing company
that leases everything from farm and office equipment to
airplanes and whole factory complexes. Lease payments are
not covered by the usury laws and normally yield a net
profit of twelve to eighteen percent. So-called leverage leases
yield even more. Companies use as many of these shelters as
needed to offset the profits of other operations. In general,
we were convinced that putting funds to work in a rapidly
growing economy like that of Nevada was more profit
productive than any investment could be in tax-exempt or

tax-free deals. As one bank official noted with glee, "Banks have more shelters than a wagonload of umbrellas."

Our tax laws are not equitable. Shelters and private foundations favor only the rich. Even the old single tax would be better than the hodgepodge of our current practices. At least it might close some of these tax loopholes. My own suggestion is that this country adopt an overall gross income tax and a tax on every transaction. Our federal taxing authority can easily be organized to administer such a tax—bank lobbyists notwithstanding.

It seems so elementary—we must raise our nation's income to meet social needs. Sooner or later we'll be compelled to adopt controls—or see the system collapse. My talks to business groups around the country, if not popular, get some attention when I suggest that our tax reforms require such major surgery, not just a continued Band-Aid treatment. Most economists acknowledge that bust follows boom and that our economy cannot sustain itself only by monetary stimulation. We'll need to shape up to realities as we take corrective action.

I believe that inflation is merely a shortage of goods or services. I believe that full employment slows inflation. As we increase production, we achieve a balance between income and outgo. Granted that the prospects of needed reforms through our legislative process are slim, I doubt that inflation or unemployment can be eliminated in a capitalist system. Our political system just doesn't tolerate radical changes affecting established business. While we ponder these issues, it might be well for our affluent citizens to remember that if such peaceful tax-reform solutions aren't adopted, serious consequences, including radical solutions, are sure to follow.

CHAPTER

# XIII

~~~~~~~~~~~~~~~~~~~~~~~~~~~~~~~~~~~~~~~~~~~

# How to Work the Money Game

We all have strong opinions about where society should be going. My modest contributions are directed specifically to making an economy—any economy—work. I'm glad that I am a maverick in such matters as banking, law, labor relations, communications, and the very structure of the economy. Obviously, I am not the spokesman for other industrialists or other progressives; but at least my nonconformist methods have worked. If I speak with authority, it's because I have produced results.

It's only natural that skepticism, doubts, and confusion should cloud capitalist economic tenets—there's been no real planning. However, there are many constructive steps our economy can take to make our society function more effectively. First, and in spite of the protestations of businessmen, we'll have to adopt more controls, adequate taxation, and centralism. Basically, we must have a government able to shape up to its responsibilites.

We need a strong central banking system in the United States. All our lending and thrift institutions should come under the jurisdiction of a single banking authority. The current maze of conflicting jurisdictions and bureaucracy is unbelievable.

It's typical of us American businessmen that we approve of only those monopolies which we control ourselves. We disregard the social consequences of bigness in private enterprise. Pricing can be controlled or administered by the biggest operator in any industry. Prices go up in the auto industry when General Motors wants prices to go up. The "free-market economy" is a fantasy. Most newspapers and television or cable systems start as local and legal monopolies and in due course merge into giant conglomerates. Each bank in local, regional, or money centers has its own monopoly. The monopoly of a bank over credit and money is more or less given to it at birth—the regulatory agencies grant a charter only when there is "room" for another financial institution in the community. Charters generally define geographical territories, even as the regulatary agencies speak of "stimulating competition."

The issuance of credit cards is a clear example of the large institutions' control of the credit market. These profitable bank ventures, such as Visa cards of the Bank of America, are giant monopolies competing with smaller financial ventures. But the race still goes to the big boy. The spokesmen of the Chamber of Commerce may denounce the use of the words *monopolistic capitalism,* but Americans ought to remind themselves that monopolies are still monopolies.

Can we expect major reform of our banking system? Change seems to occur only after the economy suffers a traumatic experience. When the bank holiday closed the banks in 1932, we were forced to accept really drastic reforms of our monetary system. A scared and wobbly banking fraternity could not resist the suggestions of New Deal reformers. Congress, from fright, if not wisdom, adopted rational banking guidelines.

The ingenious Marriner Eccles of Salt Lake City drafted the Federal Reserve Bank Act of 1934 and became the first chairman of the newly established Federal Reserve Board, remaining on the board for seventeen years. I talked to him a dozen times about it, and he always insisted that neither the original nor subsequent legislation gave "the Fed" enough supervisory powers over the banks in the country. When the crisis was over, bankers looked at change only in terms of how their own institutions might be affected. Fear turned to bravado.

The financial lobbies do a year-round snow job on the American people. For years, commercial bankers have successfully stopped the drive for an overall central supervisory authority. Washington lobbyists sponsor many testimonial dinners for members of congress, especially members of the House Banking Committee. Bank trade associations advocate less control, knowing that the confusion they generate keeps them relatively free from serious federal interference.

At least three federal regulatory agencies are charged with supervising thrift institutions, and these agencies are often in conflict with each other. The Federal Deposit Insurance Corporation, among its other duties, regulates state-chartered banks and mutual savings banks. It guarantees depositors against losses and can boast that no depositor during the past several decades has suffered a loss.

The Federal Reserve Board retains control over the bank-holding companies and all banks that are members of the reserve system. The Fed is losing members in large numbers as local banks seek to free themselves from controls. Banks now suggest that they be paid interest on the reserves they keep with the board. This windfall to the banks might run as high as a billion dollars a year!

Savings-and-loan institutions campaign to get on the same footing with national and state banks, but the jealousies and infighting of bitter competitors prevent meaningful federal reform. Credit unions, too, are becoming a strong force in the financial community. Each group has powerful and well-financed spokesmen and lobbyists in Washington. Well-heeled special interests frustrate the most elementary bank-reform legislation. Senator William Proxmire, chairman of the Senate Banking Committee, warns of the danger of this "unsettled situation" among the banks of America, but few heed him. On the other hand, most members of congress listen to their local bankers.

The American banking system now faces an even greater danger. The billions of dollars deposited in American banking institutions by foreigners, especially the oil-rich Middle Eastern nations, are a mixed blessing.

In the mid-1970s Great Britain's deposits in the six largest banks in America exceeded ten and a half billion dollars, Switzerland's six and a half billion, and the Hong Kong area's two billion. But the largest deposits came from the Arab petroleum-producing countries. If these nations should withdraw twenty or thirty billion dollars from American banks, the results would be catastrophic. The whole international financial structure would be shattered—and we would have a liquidity crisis beyond anything we've ever known. Our economic base in America is really that tenuous.

Iran and other nations have shown us that our financial structure may be founded on sand. It survives only at the will of corporations or individuals that make up the Establishment. Banks become the base of the Establishment, and interlocking directorates guide the whole economy, easily securing their collective way in Washington. National officials talk about protecting the national interest, but they espouse causes of the entrenched private sector.

Instead of making bogeymen out of the collectivist states abroad, we would be better off if we agreed to accept a universal financial agency exercising power over all banking and financial institutions. A super world bank.

Concentration of wealth is inevitable in our system of monopolistic capitalism. This trend toward bigness is emphasized when we look at our largest banks in the money centers. The Bank of America has more than seventy billion dollars in assets. Few nations can match the resources of this single private institution. Concentration of assets is increasing in the one hundred largest banks of the country. These giants as "correspondents" obtain much of their strength by rendering services to the smaller financial institutions. Bank-holding companies are annually adding hundreds of banks to their portfolios. Everywhere the trend is to giantism.

The big-city banks speak with great economic muscle; the thirteen thousand smaller banks around the country follow. There is no doubt that depositors and operators of these small independent banks would be greatly strengthened if Congress created a stronger, more centralized banking system authorized to permit bank expansion into larger interstate trading areas. Yet the small independents oppose competition in their bailiwicks; they don't like interference in their own monopolistic preserves.

Politicians, business and labor leaders, and especially we bankers spend our time popping off with disarming platitudes about the nation's economy. Our economic experts give us the last word on unemployment, inflation, and capital formation. They wear a straight face as they scream that the government should lower taxes, lessen expenditures, and balance the budget. They talk about the United States "keeping the peace" as we become the world's biggest arms merchant, supplying weapons to friend and foe alike. Some bankers use double and triple clichés to justify the existence of jobs and profits in a dirty war business that humanity will one day outlaw.

Despite a surplus of weaponry the superpowers build one-half trillion dollars' worth of nonproductive arms a year. We bleed ourselves dry and so are unable to take effective steps to meet the basic needs of half of the world's population. Without global planning, we're floundering. We don't know where we'll be a year or ten years hence. We oppose strong government economic controls. As our economy falters, we must turn to our government—that's the purpose of government. We don't need smaller or less government, we need *effective* government.

I strongly disagree with economists like Milton Friedman and Herbert Stein who suggest that the basic problems of America can be resolved by controlling the supply of money —or by any program of monetary manipulation. The Federal Reserve Board, operating under the shadows of secrecy, has long done that. It increases or decreases the supply of money by turning the printing presses on or off when it decides that the economy is slowing down or heating up. The Fed's purpose is to make funds available by permitting borrowers to have access to credit. As the demand for loans rises or falls, the prime rate rises or falls. For some reason on which economists again don't agree, the Dow-Jones stock market averages gyrate when the money supply goes up or down. I have hired many professional economists in my day and I have little confidence in their soothsaying. Only increased productivity with full employment will control inflation—any economist or prophet to the contrary notwithstanding.

There should be stricter safeguards against the abuse of lending by banks. Insider dealings, discrimination, redlining, and favoritism are rampant. Over the generations Americans have been much tricked, and now we're saturated with scandals in our public and private sectors. It's foolish to deny that there is large-scale personal enrichment—not necessarily crooked—of those on the inside of some banks.

Bank officers once pocketed credit-life premiums that belong to the bank—a raw practice now largely outlawed. Often they personally own real estate leased at high rates to their banks. Bankers like Bert Lance of Atlanta know that large bank deposits in the right places can help personal financing.

The great bank failures, like those of the Franklin National Bank in New York City and others around the country, revealed shocking problems arising from officers' "mistakes" in granting loans. Robberies of banks from the inside continue to be greater than from the outside. In one year in our Nevada bank we had ten bank robberies; yet our net losses amounted to less than two thousand dollars.

Electronic surveillance is becoming quite effective, sometimes in ways not exactly envisaged by the designers of the equipment. On one occasion we installed a TV monitor in the bank lobby at Carson City, Nevada. When the installer first turned on the TV screen, he was surprised to see an actual robbery taking place below him. He fell off his ladder, and the noise was so scary that the robber ran outside and into the arms of the police.

There is still a wide-open field for the young pioneer who looks for career opportunities in international banking and foreign trade. A financially oriented citizen's visit to Washington, D.C., should take in more than the U.S. Treasury and the Federal Reserve Board. Washington is also the home of the International Monetary Fund, central authority for the world's international money system. The IMF is the focal point for the balanced growth of world trade. It helps nations cope with balance-of-payments problems, and its analysis of a nation as a credit risk often determines that nation's whole economic future. Washington is also the home of the International Bank of Reconstruction and Development, the World Bank, the Export-Import Bank, and the Inter-American Bank. All are advancing internationalism.

Aside from the CIA, the U.S. Department of Commerce and the U.S. State Department are probably the principal suppliers of commercial and economic information concerning the Soviet Union, the People's Republic of China and eastern Europe. Action groups from many organizations have banded together into such associations as the Bureau of East-West Trade. We have an elaborate labyrinth of bureaucracy dedicated to carrying out the political decisions of the U.S. government.

# CHAPTER
# XIV

∞∞∞∞∞∞∞∞∞∞∞∞∞∞∞∞∞∞∞∞

# Contrasts

Our species occupies a small planet in the vastness of space. We continue to search to see if perchance other living creatures enjoy other planets. We grew up on a planet we call earth. Now we learn that our experience, though tempestuous, may be leading us toward remarkable horizons. From the fossils of other animals we can see the alternate road humanity might have followed—to extinction.

Now, as so often in the past, the earth's people are split over forms or systems of government. We've hatched conflicts among ourselves not only about the distribution of physical assets, but over such matters as the status of humans who live north or south of the equator. A serious confrontation developed in the twentieth century between the nation-states of the East and the West. Why this crisis between Washington and Moscow or Peking? Why conflicts over such shallow matters as the form of our social systems? Better that we define *capitalism, communism, gradualism,* and *deviationism.* Wars divide us over traditions, gods, and symbols—even as we profess that inevitably we'll reach a society with one common denominator, a society dedicated to the welfare of every human. How many battles will be fought before we come to this happy result?

In the Western industrial nations we work for wages or acquire assets, and these elements more or less set the quality and style of our living. There are so many of us trying to tell others how to pattern their lives. There are sky pilots in the pulpits and pundits galore in the ivory towers. Historians and academicians tell us what we were. We are snowed under by eager advocates. But where can a freethinker or political independent turn for a way to the full life? So many of us at one time or another thought that our problems could be solved by remedial legislation. We remember the days when enthusiastic New Dealers drafted reform legislation for labor, securities, and agriculture. At least they were trying.

I am more skeptical now. Idealistic reformers say that we can undertake novel social experimentation and accumulate data and experience that will one day lead us to a decent, planned, progressive society, and set an example to the entire world. Special interest and economic-political attachments have so far defeated such efforts.

Up to now only the planned socialist economies adjust production to the needs of the community. Work is meaningful and dignified in socialist societies, which successfully distribute the work to be done among all those able to work. Every person is guaranteed a livelihood.

Our mild reformers suggest that a new "educational" approach is required—we need a new sense of responsibility to our fellowmen. These thoughts often seem like vague generalities; yet we must somehow move out and beyond our own glorification of financial power and material success.

For a century or more in our industrialized nations, we were promised paradise within the perimeters of welfare capitalism. But we have no paradise. Millions continue to live in abject poverty and without hope, and we're learning that security and human development under social security and the dole are limited. We've toyed with the possibility of nationalizing the essential food, transportation, housing, and energy industries. This may be inevitable.

Can reasonable people bring into being a nation in which some of our enterprises can be publicly owned and others retained under supervised private ownership? The two systems, public and private, must compete against each other. Such mixed economies have operated on a limited basis in a few countries, though they present many paradoxes.

The principal dilemma remains: Can we secure adequate solutions by peaceful persuasion and the electoral process or will drastic change come only through violent revolution? Nearly half a century ago I wrote, "Soviet Russia's economic planning challenges the rest of the world as an alternative. Its experiments begin to arouse America. It is time to realize that the chart of human destiny justifies the most searching inquiry into the accomplishments of the one existing Socialized State." Now, decades later, I submit that our attention and our studies are still directed to how we can secure meaningful corrections and changes in the rickety capitalist system. The message is still urgent, but now it doesn't seem so radical—or impossible. A majority of humanity now lives under socialist systems.

In those early days we were affected by the writings of several economists. John Maynard Keynes, in his "Essays in Persuasion" and in his "A Treatise On Money," published in 1932, shook the world. Stuart Chase wrote his *Economy of Abundance* in the same year, and it, too, affected economic thinking.

Capitalism was already in deep trouble, and it was clear that someone must think up substantial long-term alternatives. Reformers even then recognized that the New Deal programs would give only a temporary lift. Why, then, didn't we move further to the left and more toward collectivism?

In our present moments of crisis, American national directives haven't really changed. As a nation we are still troubled by the extreme contrasts between wealth and poverty and by enormous deficits, runaway inflation, vast unemployment, and serious crime. We feel uncertainty and helplessness, and we have big doubts about the future. We still accept wars and preparation for wars.

Over the years I have made more than a dozen lengthy visits to the Soviet Union. I have struck up warm friendships with farm and factory workers and with leaders in the government's central offices. I have often felt that the Soviet leadership should permit more citizens to travel abroad. Such exchange and exposure would be mutually beneficial. Undoubtedly our peoples will become better neighbors—we're only humans born on opposite sides of an ocean.

Has the Soviet society introduced a new spirit of equality and sharing?

Would the Soviets return to a capitalist system? I have my doubts that any people anywhere, having acquired ownership of their means of production, would ever permit a return to private ownership.

In World War II the Russians suffered twenty million casualties. Immense areas were destroyed. When hostilities ceased, America, under the prodding of Winston Churchill, renewed its opposition to the Soviet political structure. Once again, "they" were the enemy.

The Soviet nation has known few periods when it was not "contained" or compelled to guard against strong and threatening enemies. The Cold War began. A large share of resources went into their defense establishment. The considerable obstacles the Soviets overcame were convincing evidence of inner strength.

I felt that the Soviets believed they were building a better society than had ever appeared on the face of the globe. They protected themselves from foreign threats and carried out their plans for self-improvement on the domestic front. They warred against ignorance, poverty, hunger, and disease. They wanted to learn, and they freely admitted their shortcomings. As a backward state of peasants and workers, they sought to get themselves organized in a rational way.

I saw the chance to make a slight contribution to their planning. At their request I helped recruit outstanding foreign management specialists to cooperate with Soviet planners. On my trips throughout the country I was invited to visit factory and field installations. I've always taken a camera along and made extensive notes. I have never suffered any type of censorship at any level.

Discussions with their managers, Communist-party leaders, faculty groups, and government officials were informative and fruitful. Right off, the Soviets agreed that the principles of good management are universal. I pointed out that excellent management appears in our own nonprofit organizations, like foundations, welfare organizations, and the Roman Catholic and other churches. The Russians were envious of our private and public institutions, for which we are able to recruit professional managers from graduate schools of business administration. They also wanted to become familiar with the MBA graduate degree. At the time they wanted to be put in touch with the American Management Association.

For several years the Soviet Academy of Sciences and its subsidiary, the Institute of the United States of America, made objective studies directed toward understanding American managment techniques. A competent economist, Yuri I. Bobrakov, who heads up its economic section, is a leading expert on matters pertaining to our own Federal Reserve Bank. The institute disseminated an immense amount of information on the West to Soviet universities and industries. Learned economic theses of American authors, of which five thousand copies might be published in the United States, are translated, and hundreds of thousands of copies appear in the U.S.S.R.

I addressed a major conference in Moscow in the early 1970s and advanced several suggestions for improving their management policies. Directors attended from such principal Soviet industries as aviation, mining, and cement, turbine, and agricultural-equipment manufacturing. I took along materials from our academic world, from various management organizations, and from private consulting and study agencies in the United States. Presiding was Dzhermenn Gvishiani, Deputy Chairman of the U.S.S.R. State Committe for Science and Technology, who is a very able executive. He has extensive industrial experience in the United States and Europe, and he supervised the Soviet importation of many hundreds of millions of dollars' worth of machinery and factories with turnkey operations.

Not many American people understand the tremendous Soviet efforts to become industrialized and systematized. Soviets are hungry for technology and scientific-management information. They seek the most advanced data on the functions of forecasting, structuring, organizing, and coordinating their institutions. I recall their interest in adopting a slogan covering our knowledge of the principles of management, including the Four M's—manufacturing, marketing, materials, and money handling.

I've spoken on Soviet national television networks on different occasions, always without censorship, giving opinions on the status of East-West trade and détente. I continually suggest that our scientific knowhow is America's most exportable product and that our efforts to expand it will continue. I have hoped that our schools of business administration might soon open their doors to Soviet students and technicians.

At one time, we had such a cultural exchange pretty well worked out. Deans of several American business schools agreed to conduct extensive management seminars in the Soviet Union. My friend Dr. Courtney Brown, then dean of the business school of Columbia University, admitted the contribution such seminars could make in bettering Soviet-American relations. He recognized the possibility of upgrading management in the U.S.S.R. I talked with the representatives of many of our leading administrative-training institutions, including those at Harvard, Stanford, and Northwestern Universities. They were all in favor of getting on with such an exchange of men and skills. Unfortunately, the Cold War accelerated and we invaded Vietnam, and all thought of such exchanges was abandoned.

I have continued to visit dozens of Soviet factories and agricultural operations throughout the U.S.S.R. talking to their management and workers. These included observations on their committee control of factory operations. In the shops, representatives of the workers, the trade unions and the Communist party get together and elect a manager, usually an engineer. Making decisions under such conditions is extremely difficult.

The troika structure, with its indecisiveness, will change slowly. All changes in the socialist structure occur slowly. The Soviets, like the rest of us, suffer because of the age of the leaders—there are too many old folks in their bureaucracy. The Communist party insists on retaining control of functions to see that everyone travels the safe ideological path.

I'll always be proud that I had a small role in giving birth to one idea: the initiation of American management projects with Soviet leadership. Many management schools have now been set up. These training schools for thousands of outstanding and important leaders of the economy have now been opened in various cities. Probably the most prominent are at Kiev and Leningrad.

The Soviet countries are labor short, and the leadership knows as well as anyone that most manual activities can be just as efficiently and effectively handled by machines. There is an opportunity for the American business community to offer technology in exchange for Soviet resources. Billions of trade dollars are waiting.

In the meantime, the USSR has become the world's largest producer of many products, such as steel, ships, and oil. They must be doing something right. American blustering and threats won't stop them. While we've dallied and delayed, much of the Soviet market has moved to other industrialized nations.

The United States has barred computer exports to the Soviet Union. We control the sale of our technology for political purposes. In an era of cybernation, such a boycott has not only flopped, but challenges the Soviet Union to use its own native ingenuity to develop its own systems. In the Lenin Hills area of Moscow, reserved for research and technically skilled scientists, are a hundred thousand scientists and management personnel. The center is becoming a birthplace for many of the world's discoveries. Research is varied. I have seen hydraulic equipment developed in the Soviet Union that far outstrips any we produce.

The American corporation does have problems adjusting to the business methods of the Moscow bureaucracy. Our general managers, ultimately accountable for utilizing, protecting, and developing corporation assets, often must delegate responsibility for certain specialized action— and in a foreign country it may be difficult to find certain skills. Our basic concept of the manager's function is to obtain maximum participation in every phase of development and operation.

We put it glibly and say that in its simplest form, we want maximum delegation, maximum flexibility of action, and maximum control—all concurrently. These are flippant phrases to describe scientific management. The Russians have long words too, and they frequently dig them out of the closet to describe similar management processes. Yet in many socialist and developing countries, a great controversy over management function continues to exist.

Lenin originated the term *democratic centralism*. In the American private sector I can look at my own corporate headquarters, where a small staff manages and controls several companies, using but one key control—we handle the purse strings. Publicly, Americans speak of corporate democracy. I don't think there is such a thing as a democracy in a profit corporation with one share of stock with one vote, any more than there is a corporate soul. Possibly the Soviet system presents a much more useful and advanced form of social responsiveness. Their self-criticism is democracy in action, designed to satisfy the social needs of the people. There is but one objective of a corporation in capitalism— *profit*—and we never make any bones about it. Goods and service move in our marketplace only under the motivation of private gain.

Do Soviet workers have a greater personal dedication to the success of their venture than one finds in capitalist enterprises? They show great enthusiasm. But enthusiasm can never be a substitute for the professionalism of the American manager. The manager is the key link between the corporation and all areas of responsibility. We give managers the authority to: (1) hire, fire, and adjust the compensation of his division's human resources; (2) determine product-line makeup; (3) establish marketing, pricing, distribution, and promotion, including advertising strategy; (4) acquire or dispose of assets; (5) control inventory levels and content; (6) execute contracts, leases, and joint-venture agreements; and (7) retain professional and other specialized services. That's a lot of authority!

Americans do feel that they, as consumers, can participate in decisions affecting their lifestyles. Marketing in the United States is not only consumer oriented, but in many cases, it is market or consumer directed. If the consumer wants whitewall or radial tires, the tire builder, if he wants to survive, had better produce whitewall or radial tires. The Soviet leadership is beginning to conduct popularity polls to determine the preferences of their people. Defective, shoddy products are increasingly left on the shelves.

What, then, is the difference, since both the Soviet Union and the United States have diverted such vast amounts of their resources to producing defense and military weaponry? Consumers in both countries have suffered. In the socialist countries—other than the Soviet Union, where such a large proportion of assets is spent for "defense"—the supply of consumer goods available to the people has been increasing as productivity is stepped up. In the last analysis, American productivity is higher primarily because in addition to our backlog of technology, we have developed the art of scientific management.

Russian leaders ask about our wage and incentive programs. They should be told that we generally break down compensation into four categories: (1) money; (2) authority; (3) prestige; and (4) security. Our management people also seek to move up the ladder of responsibility for reasons other than the premium of extra compensation. In the fierce competitive battles for leadership, we closely audit mangement performance along the way. Improving the caliber of supervisory people doesn't appear in five-year plans and isn't emphasized enough as an objective of Soviet forward planning. We in American businesses are required to give warranties or guarantees of quality in all fields of man-

ufacturing or processing. Regulations are imposed to see
that products meet specifications. We guarantee a workable
life of certain appliances for as many as fifteen to twenty
years. One manager in a Moscow factory told me, "Oh,
how I could improve quality if I had the authority to fire
a few indolent or sloppy workers!"

Today we live in a thermonuclear-balanced world, and
we have begun to share some sophisticated space ventures
with the Soviet Union. We'll learn sooner or later to exchange our natural resources, such as gas and minerals, for
commodities. The America that inherited and developed so
many resources is suddenly becoming a have-not nation with
surpluses of only grains, coal, and weapons. An interdependent America finds that it must buy or acquire many of
its resources from other nations. Why isolate ourselves from
the U.S.S.R.?

Threats and boycotts can one day lead to serious confrontation—or war. We must get big, proud, and jealous
nations to organize a common, friendly interchange of peoples and goods. It's ridiculous to suggest that our societies
will develop side by side without improvement in the living
conditions for the peoples of all nations.

A vast exchange of trade between the two countries could
herald the elimination of artificial and outworn political
barriers. The tenuous boundaries among the first, second,
third, and fourth worlds will be cut, and we can all come
together in one world. Our old policy of hemming in the
economies of North Vietnam, Cuba, the People's Republic
of China, Angola, or Soviet Russia has caused each to suffer,
but none to fall on its face. Americans must recognize the
political facts of life: that all nations are moving toward
industrialization, that our modern closeness to each other
requires an exchange of trade and people—and that all nations must accept the common denominator of an international governing body. Alliances and treaties among nations
are not sufficient to feed peoples.

Recently I had a pleasant chat with the deputy mayor
of Leningrad. He gave me an attractive medal, which they

award visitors. In our conversation he asked me to help
him prepare a talk for a visiting group of Americans. He
said, "Tell me—what are some of the reasons, other than
profit making, that motivate American corporations and
individuals?" He also asked, "To what do you ascribe the
increasing crime rates in the United States?" My answer,
probably too simplistic, was that American corporations exist
only to make profits. The failure to share jobs, profits or the
fruits of production equitably among individuals constitutes
a principal reason for the existence of such widespread crime
in the United States.

In 1977 I was a guest of the Soviet government at the
celebration of the sixtieth anniversary of their revolution.
As an American proud of our revolution for independence
more than two hundred years ago, I noted one difference.
We established only political perimeters to safeguard citizen
liberties. In the Soviet Union they celebrated a people's
success in getting their economic liberty and security back
into their own hands—in a world with diminishing national
borders.

We'll continue to have poverty, unemployment, no gun
controls, discriminatory taxation, inflation, and other social
evils, as long as we continue our race for profits. The big
danger in America is in the smugness of our ruling elements
(the owners). Many of us have enjoyed unbelievable affluence,
and yet our countrymen still can't believe that the life of the
capitalist system is so limited. We may think that our printing presses and sloganeering will save us. The need for jobs,
shelter, and energy must be solved even in a well-intentioned
welfare state. If we continue to ignore all the trouble signs,
we'd better be prepared for an internal explosion. At this
time we can say that America still has its real revolution
ahead of it.

•   Although there are contrasts between living standards in
capitalist and socialist societies, it's rather fun to see the
squirming contradictions among the industrialized "free
enterprise" nations. The United States defeated Germany
and Japan in World War II, then, to protect private busi-

ness, furnished each with our military umbrella. Both prospered mightily, flooding the American market with their technology. Japan quickly raised restrictive tariff walls against American manufactured goods. Our businessmen may well wonder which side Emperor Hirohito will be on during the next crisis.

CHAPTER
# XV

~~~~~~~~~~~~~~~~~~~~~~~~~~~~~~~~

# An American
# Planned
# Society

America has had a glorious place in the sun. Are its fortunes
now turning sour?

We emerged from a severe depression in the 1930s, only
to travel through a whole new series of crisis-ridden boom-
and-bust administrations, forcing us to understand more
about economic planning. Frightened by what might happen to this country, in the face of oil shortages and of rising
expectations abroad, we see ourselves stranded. Practically
every natural resource, except grain and coal, is held by
others.

Naturally we've lost confidence in our role. Public-opinion
polls show that Americans suffer a general disillusionment
with their political and economic systems. One day these
same people will have to accept the need for a rational
allocation of the world's resources. Whether we can move
into such a position without trying to smother others in a
war becomes the dominant challenge of our times.

We have wasted our assets on escalating military production. We have intervened throughout the world to impose
our own brand of "democracy" on other countries. We have

found that we cannot rely on our military bases in Iran, Israel, and Taiwan. Our choice is between certain annihilation and a system of rational humanitarianism.

We worry that the cartel nations, possessed of vast resources in petroleum, coffee, minerals, and so on, gang up on the United States. We bluff and we scream as we admit our helplessness. The emergence and unity of third- and fourth-world countries serves to emphasize our fall from leadership. Among nuclear powers, we're but one of many. Each possesses the capacity to eliminate all mankind. Nevertheless, our secretaries of state continue their unilateral deals, trying to put together powerful blocs to confront other blocs. We're bankrupt if we think that our survival can continue by building a continuing confrontation between the United States and the Soviet Union.

We hold unilateral conferences at Camp David and shun multinational conferences in Geneva. Traditional treaties become meaningless. We remember that before the ink was dry, American leaders announced that we would not be bound by the 1975 Helsinki Security Agreements. But we criticize human-rights violations in selected other countries, charging our adversaries with violations of the very same Helsinki Agreement.

The rich United States, the epitome of capitalism, tentatively carries its "surplus" unemployed citizens on the dole. And the welfare roles continue to expand. Prosperous industrialized nations, even in their periods of domestic upheaval, grow richer. The less-developed nations, mostly south of the equator, grow poorer. After the scandals involving Watergate, South Korea, and corporate bribing of public officials, we try publicity campaigns to revive enthusiasm for the free-enterprise system. We try to build confidence by using mirrors.

National deficits grow larger. Who among us expects that our national debt, almost a trillion dollars, will ever be repaid? Deferred perhaps, but not repaid. There is even some doubt that a balanced budget, a rational plan for the nation, can ever be devised.

Can we develop a planned society under our present

American Constitution? It protects private property of corporations as much as it does individual rights.

For several years I have urged, as an industrialist, a banker, a broadcaster, an attorney or in any of the other roles under which I function in my effort to gain a hearing, that industries serving the social and national needs should come under more complete public ownership and control. All institutions should be governed by the paramount needs of society. It is clearly vital for the survival of this country that our defense industry be among the first to come under government ownership. Popular demand may force nationalization of the oil industry even sooner.

In 1944 we believed that Franklin D. Roosevelt's economic bill of rights, treated in conservative quarters as a political publicity stunt, could become genuinely effective in alleviating violations of individual rights. It declared the right of everyone to a decent-paying job, to adequate housing, to education, to medical care, and to a secure old age. Roosevelt's advocacy of the Four Freedoms—freedom to worship, freedom of speech, freedom from want, and freedom from fear—sparked our hopes. He suggested that the people have another right, that of participation in decision making, especially in those matters which affect their own social and economic welfare.

Realizing that our goal must be the satisfaction of human needs, we ask, How do we get from here to there? Answer: We must shape up and make a few hard decisions. We must accept a sane, ecological framework of society and operate under an educated management team able to guide workers in operating a rational, equitable system. We must admit the shortcomings of our free-enterprise system and prepare to move into a rational international community.

CHAPTER
# XVI

~~~~~~~~~~~~~~~~~~~~~~~~~~~~~~~~~~~~~

# Live Dangerously

We all have only a few years of life on this small planet. They can be interesting, helpful, even dangerous. I've found that life is like running down a ski slope: meaningful, hazardous—and fun. As we stretch ourselves into our mature years, somewhat like the orchid's blooming, we can be grateful to our ancestors for the development of such good, inherited genes. We can make our own lives more exhilarating by adding a touch of danger.

We enjoy nature's wonders, the fresh air, healthful exercise, and the will to survive. We accept our good luck blithely. Good luck? Isn't that just a residue of design? But why philosophize so long as we have it? Whether we live phlegmatically or dangerously, we're what we are in this environment—physically not much more than what we consume. We're glad that the human animal has come such a long way. We're going further. We'll go right on looking for new goals and new worlds. We're marvelous and we're beautiful, so let's relax. Humanity's struggles have been fierce and exciting, but we can still smile; we've found increasing time for recreation and play. Laughing at our own personal predicaments and escapades is therapeutic.

My mind is full of vivid memories. A skiing companion standing only a dozen feet away from me at Davos, Switzerland, was buried by an avalanche. I couldn't anticipate his death, and there was no apparent reason for my escape. It's impossible to rationalize or find a reason for such a tragedy. Nor can I explain that tragic day at Portillo, Chile, when six ski instructors were killed in a series of snow slides. My friend Mike Hughes of Sun Valley, Idaho, a ski instructor in the Andes, miraculously escaped burial. He was the only one able to get back to the rest of us at the lodge. There we waited twelve long days before we could be helicoptered out.

From my standpoint, such accidents were merely a coincidental set of circumstances. In 1974 when I was snowed in at Rustler's Lodge at Alta, Utah, the days grew increasingly depressive and boring. Doors were locked, and travel between lodges was forbidden. Long confinement caused everyone to get itchy and stir crazy.

The whirling snowstorm finally abated, but the visibility continued to be bad. I dashed down to the lower slope, taking my downhill skis. During the prior week, the popular trails had been easily traveled by the beginning Alpine (downhill) and cross-country (Nordic) skiers, but on this gloomy day the trails were empty. I took the Albion (formerly called Never Sweat) lift to the mountaintop, where I found that a heavy, blinding haze had set in. Starting off on a down trail I had traveled many times before, I was sure that it must take me back to the base of the lift. I skied for a few minutes without identifying a marker. Suddenly I realized that I was off course and lost.

Nervously, I changed direction and continued to slide down-slope, but still I couldn't see a single guidepost. I skied for at least an hour trying to pick up my location. Trees and signs were blanketed with heavy snow. I usually travel in the woods with a compass. For some unexplainable reason I didn't carry one on this occasion. I was alone in violent weather nine thousand feet up a mountainside.

The storm intensified. I wondered, was this to be my fate —to be lost in a popular ski spot in the Wasatch Mountains in an area where I supposedly knew every rock and tree? I've met other men who had become lost in the snows—it is a harrowing experience. I remembered reading about one fellow in Maine who sat down on a rock and froze to death. His body was found only a hundred yards from his cabin. I resolved not to sit down until I dropped.

My fog-bound path for part of the way was down-mountain, but I now found myself among unfamiliar heavy timber. I'd been confident that I could recognize a river or trail somewhere along the way. Alone in blinding conditions, dark as midnight, I couldn't even see my gloved hand. I realized that there was no chance of a ski patrolman discovering or stumbling over me now. I had enjoyed down-hill skiing for five decades; but in new, deep-powder snow, five or six feet deep, I had never possessed adequate maneuverability. This was no time to regret my ineptitude—I couldn't even proceed through the giant pines. I was more disgusted than scared—only a dummy would have permitted himself to get into such a situation.

By now, I had been wallowing through the forestry lands for more than three hours—and evidently not two miles from the lodge. All the time the storm worsened. I knew only one thing for certain: I was getting into deeper trouble as I moved aimlessly about, probably traveling in a circle.

Almost an hour later I stumbled into a caution sign indicating a trail off Sugarloaf Mountain. At first I felt that it was the dangerous "Snakepit" cliff area, where a skier had recently been buried by an avalanche. He, too, had been reckless, skiing alone in a forbidden area. I pushed cautiously along, step by step. After what I thought was eternity, I had an enormous break. Out from a ridge of trees, I saw a familiar trail marker pointed toward the Alpen Glow Cabin. That sign only a couple of feet square, on the side of a mountain into which I stumbled totally exhausted, was just about the most welcome sight I ever experienced.

I was dog tired and frightened. My actions had been dangerously foolish. I reached a telephone and called the ski patrol. Within half an hour a snow tractor arrived, and I was packed off and delivered safely at the lodge. Friends who had been concerned for my safety were too polite to mention that I had violated just about every rule in the book. Instead they offered me a hot toddy. I was shaken but too embarrassed to admit my stupidity in going out alone into the stormy mountainside. Disaster strikes fast when the snow slides.

This hectic world tolerates a great deal from each of us. Members of the animal kingdom live dangerously—all the time. Modern people get hit by a truck or get drafted by a nation anxious to fight a "holy" or "patriotic" war or to grab land. My life has been endangered beyond the normal hazards by watching my government explain various strange experiences I have undergone at home and abroad.

I'm not antigovernment nor do I believe that my government is anti–Ted Lamb. However, I've had many close escapes that involved my government and its agencies, like the CIA and FBI. I never claimed that the conniving of our covert operators overseas ever quite equaled the gyrations of the Federal Bureau of Investigation in hiring professional witnesses as the government attempted to frame me in the witch-hunt days of Senator Joseph McCarthy. Whether in the field or in the courtroom, such governmental activities as wire tapping and break-ins against a private citizen are naturally abhorrent. The most fundamental right of every American citizen is to be protected against the follies of his own government. In America we call such protection the Jeffersonian heritage.

My mind goes to so many other areas of the world. No war zone could possibly compare with that of Vietnam, where America itself was brought to its knees. Our attempts to fortify and police the world were doomed to failure. We foolishly tried to maintain military bases and authoritarian, corrupt dictatorships in Iran, Chile and Cambodia. It represented sheer stupidity. Our policy of encirclement or economic strangulation can produce only catastrophe. Our

technological arrogance led us to believe that we could
conduct a push-button war, preferably between the hours of
nine and five. At the height of the war I went to Vietnam
as a reporter. An outspoken critic of our Vietnam meddling,
I was nevertheless given a helicopter and crew. I traveled
throughout the country. Just thirty-five miles out of the
Saigon airport, the helicopter next to mine was shot down.

I cannot prove that the CIA or the American military
caused my personal dfficulties in Vietnam. But I did have an
appointment to be picked up in a rendezvous in the woods
outside Lai Kai—and the helicopter never showed up. Ultimately I was lucky to hitch a ride back to the base with a
Philippine intelligence operator—maybe he should have been
called a mercenary. We went through the Vietcong countryside—fortunately to safety. It was a strange way to treat a
visiting critic of the war.

I attended military briefing sessions and met with leaders
like Ambassador Henry Cabot Lodge. I visited rehabilitation
centers. But one of the most ridiculous war exercises occurred
when I accompanied our troops on the early-morning capture of a central village. They staged a "county fair" operation. Then two American doctors gave local volunteers
medical treatment. Women and children received candy and
food. A jazz band tooted away. Men were herded into the
village compound and waited in the broiling sun while each
individual was vigorously cross-examined. Finally, after the
sugar supplies of the village were confiscated, the captured
men were hauled away in helicopters for imprisonment in
a concentration camp. I watched our army murder one
Vietnamese youngster who tried to escape. The U. S army
left him in the road, his body to be recovered at night when
the villagers could again come out into the open.

I took dozens of pictures of the operation. My newspaper
and magazine articles may have contributed to an understanding of the American operations in Vietnam—a disgrace-
ful episode in our imperialist adventurism. I was disgusted,
but I began to feel that somehow this war would help the
leaders of the United States to realize that we did not rule
the world. Indeed, we could not militarily defeat a single

nation. The alternative was beginning to show up on the global horizon—not unilateral domination, but multilateral negotiations of human affairs. When one considers the enormous stakes in our society, individual interests and rights are important, but so many millions of people on this earth are denied so much by the actions of the affluent superpowers. The globe is crowded, but our task is now to make it equitable and safe.

An attempt to assassinate Fidel Castro was made while I was visiting him in Camagüey province in March 1969. It was my first formal meeting with him. The bullet would have had to go through me to hit him. Possibly it was all planned to be a double murder but that's idle speculation.

Photographers took many pictures, and I made extensive notes shortly after the shooting. As a guest of the Cuban government, I did not wish to say anything about the as-sassination attempt at the time. I did not release the story until later, when the CIA was denying that it had had any connection with attempts to assassinate Castro.

Reports that the CIA had hired Mafia characters to kill Castro surfaced at Senator Frank Church's Intelligence Com-mittee hearings in 1975. At that point I felt a moral obliga-tion to tell my story. I wrote to Senator Church about my exposure to the assassination attempt. I wrote articles for *The Nation* (June 28, 1975), *New World Review* (September 1975), and *The Churchman* (May 1976). I appeared on sev-eral radio and television programs. To refute the CIA denials, I dug out the photos and the notes of my eyewitness account of the assassination attempt. Whatever the intent of the assassins, we escaped.

Maybe I'm idealistic, but I never wanted to think that an agency of my own government would shoot at me.

This is what happened. After several hours of conversation at Castro's Camagüey retreat, we got into the jeep. Fidel was at the wheel. I sat in the front seat at his right. Dr. René Vallejo, his friend and personal physician, sat in the back right seat with a security guard at his left. We were in the first vehicle of a seven-jeep caravan.

We drove for an hour or so, stopping to visit various

farms. Then we went to an experimental dairy farm where our entourage talked to several of the workers and again many pictures were taken. The Cubans were excited about their newly developed breeds of cattle. Castro was particularly pleased by the progress with what they call the F-s2 breed, the second generation. They're beautiful black cattle, and the Cubans are proud of them. A whole nation's meat supply was being revolutionized.

When we left the farm, Castro moved to the rear left seat. I remained in the front right seat next to a burly military driver. Soviet machine guns were in both front and back seats. I rested my feet up on the dashboard next to one weapon. We drove for another twenty minutes along the very dusty roads. I felt sorry for the occupants of the five or six jeeps following us—I knew that they were eating a lot of dust. We then came to a place where a military jeep was parked on the right side of the road. As we slowed down, we could see that two men were standing near the front right side of their jeep. I assumed that they were security people.

The one in front wore a white shirt, the second, a greenish fatigue shirt. The first man moved rapidly beyond the front of the jeep carrying his automatic weapon. Suddenly, we heard four or five quick shots. It happened fast. I could hardly understand or believe what was happening. It appeared that the second guard knocked the gun of the first soldier upward so that the shots went into the air. The whole episode took place in a matter of seconds. Our car continued to move forward, and possibly it wasn't more than thirty feet before we came up to the parked vehicle. By this time at least three of the jeeps following us surrounded the assassin's jeep.

The guards reacted quickly. Machine gunners sprang to the ground and overwhelmed the white-shirted man. The commander shouted not to shoot the white-shirted fellow and ordered, "Hold him!"

I continued talking to Castro. He first seemed to duck, then rose in his seat slightly. Then he, too, looked back as we sped off. He said without interrupting our conversation, "I'm glad anyway that they didn't kill the man. Now we can find out about his background." I was too startled to be nervous.

Disregarding the turmoil about us, Castro kept on talking about a new strain of grass they were introducing into arid Camagüey province. There were big sweat drops under his fatigue cap.

I had been in the direct line between Fidel Castro and the assassin. At least he must have realized that I couldn't have had anything to do with planning the crime.

We continued along the country road for eight or ten miles, then visited another experimental farm where they were building new milking barns. Castro said, "The land is very dry in this section and must be irrigated often. Outside of growing food for the cattle, we won't give first priority for building Camagüey into a modern, productive province. We'll do the best we can—our engineers are trying many things." He added, "There are only a few thousand people in the whole province. Other areas are so much more fertile and available for development that Camagüey may be the very last province to be tackled."

By now the security guard seemed to huddle closer, and I understood why. I never wanted to become a *cause célèbre* in that fashion!

Later that evening, while we were having dinner, various members of the group reported to Castro that the assassin was a member of the Communist party. He had achieved a position of trust, but I was told that the Cuban leaders had already begun to have doubts about his loyalty and connections with outsiders.

Since that time I have often recalled the assassin and his attempt to kill the Cuban leader. How much mercy should be shown to a hired assassin? Dr. Vallejo later told me that the man admitted to being an agent of the CIA. I thought about many things as I lay on my bed that night at Castro's back-country headquarters. I wondered about individual liberty in a socialist state. The counterrevolutionaries, supported by my own government, were trying to destroy the economic and social security of a whole people. Did my own government have a contract with the Mafia to eliminate me at the same time it was trying to kill Castro? I couldn't sleep. I admired the cool way in which Castro handled himself. He had lived under Yankee threats and assassination attempts for long years.

When I returned home I didn't tell even my wife about the assassination attempt because I felt that there was no reason to scare her. Nor did I want the American government to have reason to raise a phony rumpus over the danger to an industrialist who visits Cuba.

I greatly admire Fidel Castro and what he and the Cuban people have done and are doing to achieve their social revolution. When the history of Cuban-American relations is written, we may well wish that we had acted as friend and good neighbor to the first socialist society in the Western Hemisphere.

I was nervous at the moment of the attempt on Castro's life, and it raised the question of my own mortality—I had suffered too many narrow escapes recently. It encouraged me to bring my last will and testament up to date.

Later that night I kidded Castro that he seemed to be the executive department and a one-man planning commission. Mindful of recent events, I talked to him about what would happen after his death. We talked about the method of making decisions. We talked more extensively about how budgets were put together in the American federal and state governments. I told him how much more thoroughly we prepare the so-called variable budget in private corporations. We talked for hours about the possibilities of modern planning.

Another attempt to assassinate Castro and his guest had failed.

I have made many subsequent trips to Cuba, and I've seen the development of recent programs for schools, farms, and industries. I've seen the improvement in human relationships under their new constitution. I've seen the influence and movement of Cuba into the world. In the Caribbean, in countries like Jamaica, one can see the new work-study high schools and hospitals contributed by the Cuban government. Visitors are beginning to pour into the country, political prisoners have been freed, and more than ten thousand Africans are attending the Cuban technical schools. Cuba represents one of the best examples of building a democratic socialist society in all history. The cost was high, but the results are remarkable.

# CHAPTER
# XVII

~~~~~~~~~~~~~~~~~~~~~~~~~~~~~~~~~~~~~~~~

# My Life Under the CIA and the FBI

It was apparent that my career was not typical of that of other American industrialists when I received a letter from the Federal Communications Commission on March 11, 1954: "We have information in our files containing charges that for a period of years, particularly the period 1944–1948, you were a member of the Communist Party in Lucas County, Ohio."

Two decades later, during a meeting of our bank's board of directors in Reno, Nevada, one of my lawyers told me of the amendments to the Freedom of Information Act adopted by Congress in 1974.

I asked, "How does one now go about getting the information about himself from the files of the Federal Bureau of Investigation and the Central Intelligence Agency?"

We decided to send urgent telegrams to both the CIA and the FBI asking for surrender of all papers concerning me. We knew that the files must be extensive. Those agencies had considered many of my activties since the 1930s "subversive." Yet I was surprised when William Colby, director of the CIA, immediately responded to our demand.

He said that it would take the CIA "at least forty-five full working days" to comply with my request. As it turned out, he underestimated the voluminous amount of paperwork required or, more likely, the way bureaucracy drags. It took five months of preparation and screening before we received documents.

The "declassified" information first released to me was innocuous. One of the reports listed my name and address —nearly everything else was "deleted for national security." I was short-changed—the survival and security of the nation could hardly have been endangered by any of the activities they listed. I went through the roof—the bureau was flagrantly flouting the law covering my right to access of security files. I appealed their refusal rather noisily. The agency reversed its first decision. I began to get fuller records and reports which ulitmately came to several thousand pages.

Two government agencies, the Federal Bureau of Investigation and the Central Intelligence Agency, peppered my labor lawyer days in the 1930s and 1940s with violations of my rights: They broke into my files, intercepted my mail, and tapped my phone. Clumsy and departmentalized, the supersleuths seemed to try everything the hard way. I could and would gladly have given them more information. The professionals in the intelligence agencies could have spent their time in better pursuits than clipping published newspaper and magazine articles. They could at least have visited the research department of the local library. Surely, catching spies must involve more sophisticated techniques. I rather regretted their stupidity in overlooking the obvious; instead they reviewed their own files covering my business activities. Their résumés failed to report even a five-page spread in the May 1956 issue of *Fortune* magazine entitled "The Squire of Sentinel Point."

Bureaucratic searching for subversives must cost the taxpayers a pretty penny. At least a dozen agents reported on me. I used to see them around my hometown at cocktail bars and restaurants; occasionally I told them where I was going next. J. Edgar Hoover had taken a special delight in

gathering personal intelligence about his suspects, especially
those with a tinge of red. They could have obtained a few
tidbits about my private activities that would have proved
much more spicy.

The FBI furnished extensive reports to the prosecution
in my Washington witch-hunt trial during the early 1950s.
At the time the Federal Communications Commission was
trying me for perjury over my denials of Communist-party
membership. One interviewer claimed a scoop: "Lamb testified that he was very glad and proud that he helped organize
the National Lawyers Guild in the 1930s when he became
its executive vice president. 'I make no bones about it,' the
Toledo millionaire told us. 'I am proud of it; you had a
New Deal and a Fair Deal because of fellows like myself.' "

The FBI agent said that the allegations against me were
that I "knowingly associated with communists." "While
Lamb denies the charges," the agent said smugly, "The National Lawyers Guild, of which he was a leader, has been
cited as a Communist front." The supersleuths listed at least
a dozen other organizations in which I was active, some
dedicated to developing friendship with the Soviet Union.
Most were well-known, such as the American League Against
War and Fascism, with which I served in one capacity or
another for two decades.

My raw FBI biographical data covered dozens of pages;
it was much more thorough than an exhaustive Dun &
Bradstreet financial report. The CIA discovered that I had
been in *Who's Who in America* for more than thirty-five
years. The FBI pointed out that as head of a law firm in
Toledo, I developed a wide practice representing many
labor and leftist causes.

"Lamb has practiced little law since the early 1950s, and
for the most part, his occupation has been that of a self-
employed business executive," it said, and continued, "The
subject, Lamb, has considerable personal wealth estimated
at over $50,000,000 and since 1964 has been chairman of
the Seiberling Rubber Company."

An entry in their interagency report for August 21, 1961,

reads, "Mr. Lamb is notoriously reticent. about his companies' affairs. A direct approach to Lamb has not yet been
attempted, but this will be done if it is desired."

The CIA began to prepare for an all-out, in-depth interview. However, they didn't want it to take place on CIA
premises. A report advised: "Try to get him into a hotel
room—if not in Washington, then in Toledo." At long last
they tried the easier way to make an appointment: investigators called me on the phone. At my invitation three of
them came directly to my corporate suite in Toledo.

The exhaustive report for September 22, 1961, recounted
the information they obtained in their interview and stated,
"Mr. Lamb proved to be a cordial individual, not at all
reticent about discussing his extensive business operations."
One report continued,

> Mr. Lamb impressed this interviewer as an interesting
> personality in that his attitude toward the world of
> business contains a large measure of idealism.
>
> At the conclusion of the two and a half hour session,
> Lamb pulled a very interesting rabbit out of his hat.
> He confided to [blacked out] that a meeting is being
> organized to take place at the United Nations in
> February, 1965 and invitations have been extended
> to President Lyndon Johnson, Soviet leader Khrush-
> chev and Pope Paul, among other world leaders. The
> New York meeting will be under the sponsorship of
> the Center for the Study of Democratic Institutions and
> the purpose of the meeting will be to get world-wide
> acceptance of Pope John XXIII's encyclical, *"Pacem
> in Terris."* The agenda will include efforts to gain
> agreement of the (1) principles of peaceful coexistence,
> (2) disarmament and (3) creation of a UN police force
> to cope with the task of keeping the peace."

The CIA representatives were especially anxious to discuss the reasons for our inviting Khrushchev. They should
have read the newspapers—widespread publicity about the
Peace on Earth meeting had appeared in the world press a
month earlier. But that's the way bureaucracies work.

The CIA wrote long reports about my extensive travels in the U.S.S.R. and Yugoslavia. The latter country asked me to give technological assistance for rebuilding their tire factories. The intelligence files contained several newspaper and television interviews and magazine articles about my visits to the socialist countries. I was amazed to see a Xeroxed collection of my private letters and cables written to private citizens and public officials in the Soviet Union.

The CIA said in a handwritten, confidential note that I must be "competely examined" about my real purposes. I must be "debriefed." They scheduled a session in Toledo for October 6, 1964. According to a memorandum, they reported on that occasion that I was, in some supposedly subversive way, "attempting to organize groups of high school and college students to tour the United Nations"!

Another CIA report said that "Lamb has visited the Soviet Union several times. He has been characterized in the past as very close to the Communist Party in the early 1930s and actually a member of the Party in the early 1940s. He is given to the espousal of liberal causes." Later, after more trips to my offices, the investigators seemed to drop the idea that I was ever a member of the Communist party. When they toured my offices, I assured them that despite the various investigations of me, I felt that in the future I would be moving further to the left and that the times would inevitably bring about drastic changes in the distribution of the nation's wealth. Time after time I reiterated my dedication to progressive social-welfare programs and my contention that what this country needs is a better-planned economy. I don't think they understood.

I may have been a victim, but I am not expert on clandestine operations of secret organizations. In the so-called open society of the United States we spend hundreds of millions of dollars piling up information on our fellow citizens. I can only characterize the CIA studies of me as stupid and bungling. They spent large sums to discover the obvious. It would be foolish to say that we don't need an adequate intelligence or defense system. But what are we defending? Against whom? I asked myself whether our concern with human rights or social justice is merely an. effort to impose our ideology on the socialist countries.

The CIA representatives reported that they were "shocked at seeing Lamb's art museum containing original Old Masters, like Tintoretto, Rubens, Van Dyke and Gainsborough." They noted that on my walls were "autograph [*sic*] letters from George Washington, Thomas Jefferson, Cardinal Richelieu, Napoleon and King Henry VII." They had asked me to identify "various items given me from foreigners." For good measure I proudly identified gifts from Soviet, Chinese, and Cuban friends.

The CIA files are filled with notes on correspondence I have had with government officials, including letters to President Richard M. Nixon and members of his cabinet. I was surprised to see that my memos to our presidents ended up in such strange places. In one letter to Nixon I urged "that we accept a brotherly spirit among our hemispheric neighbors in an attempt to accomplish the peace of the world. It is in this spirit that I urge you, Mr. President, to decide in favor of free trade and free travel between the United States and Cuba. I do not seek to be an amateur diplomat—I merely hope, for humanitarian and economic reasons, that we establish friendship among men."

A CIA report for May 1, 1969, said that it "had received a call from [*name blacked out*] telling us that [*name blacked out*] had been informed by a source that Fidel Castro was interested in making overtures to the United States for closer ties. The source of this information is Edward Lamb, Toledo, Ohio. Since this information could be of considerable interest, we suggest that your office re-establish contact with Mr. Lamb immediately."

Other censored notes suggest that my telephone lines were frequently tapped. Microfilm reports indicated that the CIA was being furnished newspaper articles from a [*deleted name*] stating "that Mr. Lamb was making two or three trips a year to Cuba." One report was made within a month's time after my visit with Castro. (This was the occasion when the assassination attempt was made by a person who identified himself later as an agent of the CIA.)

Several memoranda offering copies of my letters and magazine writings went from the CIA to various other government offices. The CIA was especially interested in reviewing my trips to Cuba in August 1968 and March 1969. One CIA report told of my supplying Cuba with "twenty U.S. original sugar harvesters costing $45,000 each." Another charged that I had evaded U.S. export-control regulations and that I exported duty-free component parts from our plants in Mexico and Louisiana. Such allegations were totally false. Later on, the CIA agents frankly admitted to me that they knew that such sales to Cuba never materialized. Such is the flimsiness of the news-gathering service of the CIA.

Another CIA source disclosed copies of my article "Of Men, Cane and Cows in Cuba," in *The Center* magazine, July 1969. The investigators wrapped up their bulky report by enclosing anonymous letters with an enormous bundle of newspaper and magazine articles. Their informants were paid on a piecework basis.

The CIA intensified its inquiries about my activities when my *Trial by Battle* appeared in 1964, published by the Center for the Study of Democratic Institutions. They put a twenty-four-hour vigil on my movements. Agents followed me in New York City and Toledo; they interviewed my neighbors and associates. On April 17, 1964, Hoover gave orders to all FBI divisions to secure "any information regarding travel plans of Edward Oliver Lamb. In reviewing these records it's requested that they be carefully examined for any information, including travel agencies from the Toledo area in order that consideration may be given to developing local sources regarding the travel plans of the subject."

On June 4, 1964, the bureau alerted all agencies around the country reminding them that my passport was not valid for travel to Albania, Cuba, and portions of China, Korea, and Vietnam. On June 11, 1964, the bureau said that I was on the list of individuals being closely watched and asked the New York office to contact Pan American World Airways and attempt, if feasible, to ascertain points of travel as indicated by tickets I purchased. "These tickets should be specifically reviewed, if available, to determine if his travel included a visit to the Soviet Union," a report said.

On August 8 the FBI discovered that I had been on a Pan Am flight to Europe and then submitted its information to SAC, the top security agency. The harassed chief legal officer of Pan Am objected to such thorough checks. He asked that the date of travel and flight number be known before the airline was forced to furnish the government with copies of my ticket and itinerary. At the time computers had not been programmed to furnish such information.

The FBI became engrossed in getting copies of my speeches made in Moscow in early July 1964. I had often urged the installation of management techniques in the Soviet system and indicated that "the principles of management are applicable and can function under private or under social ownership." FBI memos reported that I would continue on a speaking tour in the Soviet Union for an additional two weeks and said that I would then be returning to the United States. All possible information should be obtained about my itinerary and intentions. Emergency messages were sent about my travels to CIA offices in London, Paris, Berne, Rome, and Madrid, as well as to unnamed foreign "liaison" units.

The bureau was particuarly concerned in its memo of August 11, 1964, that I might "speak with a degree of authority" since I was president of Seiberling Rubber Company and various other corporate enterprises. Their report pointed out that "Lamb Industries sells 90 percent of all the mechanical sugar cane harvesting equipment in the world. Lamb himself is described as being one of the richest men in the world."

When I sold the tire division of Seiberling Rubber Company to Firestone, the FBI was given a hurry-up task: "Investigate that 'multi-millionaire,' prominent Toledo lawyer, television executive and businessman reportedly of the 'Cyrus Eaton type' and a friend of the Soviets. He has been the subject of intense security examinations and is currently on the reserved index Section A." Section A classified as an individual with a communist background, no substantial subversive activities in the past five years, in a position to influence others by reason of wealth or connections. The agency memo was also sent to the department charged with antitrust matters and to the Internal Revenue Service.

Going through the wild Washington witch hunt during the Joseph McCarthy years of 1946–52 hardened me to the reality of redbaiting. Economic as well as political issues were involved. Had I been convicted I would have lost my right to practice law, not to mention ownership of television and radio properties worth millions of dollars. The ordeal extended over a period of three years, and I like to repeat that my defense expenses ran in excess of nine hundred thousand dollars.

The legal battle settled on the simple point that I had lied in signing my applications for broadcasting licenses when I denied membership in the Communist party. Not everyone is fortunate enough to be able to spend nearly a million dollars defending his veracity and property.

I had the benefit of the skills of J. Howard McGrath, just then retiring as attorney general of the United States. During his incumbency, he was, of course, the boss of FBI Director J. Edgar Hoover. Shortly after I retained McGrath, he arranged that we should fly to Saratoga, New York, and attend horse races with his friend, Hoover. For three days we watched races and attended small but glamorous parties.

I found the FBI director an extremely easy person to talk with, and we got along pleasantly enough. On one subject he hardened—he became livid and paranoid when he talked about communism. His objections were mostly on religious and ideological grounds, and he often cited the threat to our "free-market system."

I appraised the man as not so much a fascist fraud as an ambitious cop. He knew a great deal about my own liberal past and said that he could understand how a labor attorney could get "tarred by association." He was considerate enough not to pursue my knowledge of Communist-party officials and radical activists.

As an attorney I was often given information in confidence, and I knew that the attorney-client privilege is sometimes used as a shield for fraud and deceit. As the weekend progressed, Hoover, the bulldog-faced bachelor, seemed much more interested in his two lady secretaries. He said he liked beautiful horses and beautiful women—in that order.

Certainly, the person who adopts a cause, the partisan who is smothered in controversy, enjoys the full and meaningful life. But we should never forget the victims of political opportunists. My good friend Alger Hiss is one. At one time Richard Nixon caused Hiss's name to become a synonym for traitor. As the head of the Carnegie Foundation, Hiss entered the nation's service in the U.S. State Department. Adviser to President Roosevelt at Yalta, he became the secretary general at the United Nations organization conference at San Francisco. In the early 1950s Nixon and Joseph McCarthy began their reign of terror that would end by paralyzing our government and suspending the fundamental civil liberties of all Americans. The victims went to jail—and the politicians into high office. The stresses unloosed against progressive people tested the courage of citizens at all levels. In the confusion, many liberals and radicals turned tail.

We have the renegade informers. There was Whittaker Chambers, who invented the pumpkin evidence against Alger Hiss. With Richard Nixon's help, the red hunters discovered tapes and films that purportedly linked Hiss with the communists. They produced a battered typewriter, the famous Woodstock No. 230099, which they claimed had been used in 1938 to copy State Department papers. Ten years later, in 1948, the grand jury indicted Hiss for perjury. (Prosecution for espionage was not covered by the statute of limitations).

The hysteria of the times sealed the fate of Hiss and sent him to the penitentiary for many long years. Having achieved such a victory, Senator Joseph McCarthy went on to scare the nation by claiming that the State Department itself was completely riddled with "known Communists." The CIA, the FBI, and the State Department competed with each other to ferret out victims for the witch hunters.

I used to talk to Alger Hiss about his ordeal. Never, for

a moment, did I believe him disloyal. Eighty FBI agents had at one time scoured the country looking for evidence against him. But in May 1949 the Philadelphia office of the FBI actually said that "there is a definite possibility" that the Woodstock typewriter was not the one owned by Hiss. When such informaion helping to clear him was uncovered, it was withheld from his trial! The documents released in 1976 under the amended Freedom of Information Act clearly proved that the FBI withheld evidence that might have kept Hiss from going to prison.

A dedicated group of friends continue to work for his vindication. Alger Hiss and I now smile, bitterly perhaps, about the outcome of our separate trials on Communist-related issues. We were both defending ourselves against politically and economically inspired witch hunters. I lost millions of dollars as a result of my ordeal, but I doubt that anyone cares one iota. Hiss lost his personal freedom.

Most of all, for many years Alger Hiss suffered harassment and ostracism—and disbarment. He remained front-page news for three decades, all the while hardly able to eke out the barest existence. After my own ordeal I was able to go on to other industrial, legal, and banking activities. I had been graced with the financial ability to hire the right lawyer, a close friend and drinking partner of Senator Joseph McCarthy, no less!

I learned that investigation by our secret governmental organizations can be manipulated and neutralized. Money— and lawyers—talk. Intelligence agencies of every government are often in the business of purchasing information from paid tipsters and informers. There are double agents and double-crossers. Our government infiltrated left-wing organizations and recruited indigenous agents and collaborators. Almost two dozen of the leading professional turncoats, or paid informers like Louis Budenz and Marie Natvig, testified against me. For fees they moved from campground to campground bearing false witness. For more money, many of them would change sides. We turned down the offers of Harvey Matusow many times when he offered to contradict his own testimony.

Howard McGrath and I once attended a dinner with Senator McCarthy sponsored by White House correspondents. All attention was centered on the senator from Wisconsin, in spite of the presence of President Dwight Eisenhower. During an intermission Senator McCarthy and I stood at adjacent urinals conversing while almost a hundred reporters crowded around trying to question him. It was an anomaly. I was in prestigious company. It gave me status—a "Communist sympathizer" in the company of the greatest witch hunter of them all!

Richard Nixon's pursuit of alleged communist activities skyrocketed him to fame and into the White House. After his criminal acts were uncovered he received from his appointed successor, Gerald Ford, a pardon of every crime, known or unknown. Equal justice under law? The same favors were never shown by our law-enforcement agencies as they railroaded political dissenters and war resisters to jail.

In the early 1960s the State Department refused to renew my passport. The reason was unclear: It may have been my past connections with civil-liberties cases, my overseas travels to socialist countries, or my participation in various antiwar demonstrations and activities at home. I considered my course of action. About the same time I received telephone calls from Washington lawyers who offered to help get my passport renewed. Instead, I managed to get an appointment with Frances Knight, longtime director of the U.S. Passport Division. She was cordial enough but didn't seem disturbed when I threatened to file suit to get my passport. The U.S. Supreme Court had recently issued decisions affirming the right of Americans to travel abroad. When sometime later I received my passport, it was marked, "Not valid for travel in Cuba, China, or Albania."

A couple of months later I returned to the United States from abroad with the first visa entry on my gold-emblazoned passport marked "Cuba." I had been compelled to return to New York's Kennedy Airport "the long way around" via Madrid, Spain. My Cuban friends had loaded me down with lovely gifts, including several boxes of Havana cigars, which I placed at the very top of my luggage.

The horrified customs inspectors took me into a "special interrogation room"—of all things, marked with a red star! One of the officers (his name, incidentally, was Kennedy) started the examination with sharp criticism of my trip to Cuba. He questioned me about the reasons for my making a "prohibited trip." I smilingly told him how much I had enjoyed the experience and that I could hardly wait to get back and restudy Cuba's remarkable social accomplishments. "What about these cigars?" he asked. "I don't use them myself," I replied. "I'm giving them to my friends; will you take some?" He refused my offer but then, turning away from the others, whispered into my ear, "I agree with what you say, Mr. Lamb!" He helped me repack my bags and then actually carried them to the exit.

I am among the Americans who have learned the hard way that the CIA has been involved in murder of foreign leaders and has financed "front" organizations in other countries. They have set up secret armies in Vietnam and subsidized American newsmen at home and abroad. It sometimes seems funny that our national leaders hypocritically criticize the loss of human freedoms abroad. It tends to make us all suspicious of each other.

We're not a nation of stool pigeons; we're a land of people trying to find our way to an equitable society.

# XVIII

~~~~~~~~~~~~~~~~~~~~~~~~~~~~~~~~

# How the CIA Sabotaged Our Technical Equipment

On one of my visits with Fidel Castro, I told him of an experience we had with our Thomson mechanical sugar-cane harvesters back in 1966. A New York City machinery dealer, personally unknown to me or my organization, had telephoned our manufacturing plant in Thibodaux, Louisiana. He wanted to buy one of our giant cane harvesters.

Our manager asked, "Where do you want to use it?"

He replied, "In Texas."

The manager said, "But there is no sugar cane presently grown in Texas."

The man replied, "We're going to develop it there."

Our manager said: "Well, we'll be glad to talk to you about it."

The visitor arrived on the next plane. Seeing one of our large Golden Thomson sugar-cane harvesters on the Louisiana loading dock, he said, "I'll take that. How much?"

When told the price, about forty thousand dollars, he counted out the money in one-hundred-dollar bills. Such an on-the-spot cash sale is highly unusual. A cane harvester must be tailored to the particular terrain on which it is to be used. Since our manager wanted to make the sale, the harvester was immediately loaded on a flatcar and sent off to El Paso, Texas. We heard nothing further about the matter for nearly three weeks. Then early one morning several men from the Central Intelligence Agency in Washington, D.C., and New Orleans called at our plant in Thibodaux, Louisiana. They asked if one of our harvesters had been sold to people in Mexico, and they described the particular machine. Our people recognized that it was the machine sold to the recent visitor "for use in Texas."

The CIA agents said that the harvester was now in a warehouse at Veracruz, Mexico, awaiting shipment to Cuba. Flashing their identification badges they told our manager they wanted to have engineers come into our Louisiana factory and study the construction of the harvester. The next day three industrial engineers descended upon our plant and told our workers that they were new members of our factory force. They spent several weeks studying the mechanics and construction of our equipment. Using our material they published in Spanish an "operating manual" with the details of construction—totally rearranged and distorted. The engineers returned to Veracruz. The gears were reversed so that the machine became totally ineffective. The CIA then released the harvester from the customs house.

The Mexican officials obligingly permitted shipment of the equipment to Cuba. Shortly thereafter the Cubans shipped the machine to the Soviet's Rostov-on-Don tractor plant for mass production. A couple of years later I was making a management survey in the Rostov plant and I saw one or two of these machines. Pictures of this "newly developed mechanized suger-cane harvester," which they claimed had been developed by Russian engineers, were widely published throughout the Soviet Union. Sometime later twenty-six of those machines were shipped to Cuba. The machines did not work and remained rusting in the fields of Cuba for several years. Shipping this damaged machinery to Cuba was a costly bit of American sabotage; it scuttled an emerging nation's efforts to get on its feet.

The CIA's dirty trick bothered my conscience. It re-

minded me that American spy agencies were hiring saboteurs to set fire to the Cuban sugar fields. I told Fidel
Castro I had known nothing about the earlier episode of
sabotage at the time the CIA moved into the Thomson
plant. Our local management, through fear and intimida-
tion, agreed not to tell anyone, including the owners, about
the presence of the CIA engineers.

Because of the despicable CIA practice, I decided that
I'd like to make amends. Like many other Americans, I
wanted to see modern technology get into the hands of
Cubans and other emerging nations. I hoped that in spite
of terror and boycotts imposed by my country, these developing countries would somehow survive.

After I began to obtain copious CIA files covering my
private and business life, I looked for my government's
own account of the destruction of our sugar-cane-harvesting
machinery. Even though our intelligence agency had made
a long and complicated attempt to sabotage Cuba's sugar-
cane production, neither I nor the American public would
read a single word involving the machinery-destruction episode. Our government shrugged off responsibility. To this
day clandestine activity in Cuba remains "classified information pertinent to our national security."

The refusal to sell American equipment and know-how
has had quite the opposite effect from that intended by our
American State Department. French, Australian, and West
German industries promptly sold the Cubans many thousands of advanced agricultural machines, including tractors
and combines. I was glad to help by furnishing sources. By
1977 the Spanish, English, Argentines, Rumanians, Canadians, and Italians were annually shipping to Cuba more than
two billion dollars' worth of sugar-refining, petroleum-
processing, fertilizer, plastics, and industrial equipment. The
Soviet Union continued to ship more than a million dollars'
worth of goods each day; the port of Havana became a de-
lightfully bustling trading center!

The CIA continued their surveillance. In early 1978 I
received an additional two thousand pages of information
from the FBI and the Naval Investigative Service, for a

total in excess of fifteen thousand pages. The Service moved into the act because I lived on Lake Erie and Canada lay north of the lake. The FBI files indicated special interest in my finances. One memo suggested that no matter how the FBI pursued me, my net worth seemed to increase. They concluded that I must be receiving income from foreign sources, not bothering to note that at the time I owned several Canadian companies. To the FBI my wealth came from "abroad." But there was one even greater danger—the danger that my broadcasting facilities in Erie, Pennsylvania, would subvert foreign viewers!

I've tried for years to convert Canadians to a regional alliance with the United States—and I told the CIA that my television stations were anxious to build bridges of friendship at every opportunity! I could tell the CIA about my warm friendship for Pierre Trudeau, prime minister of Canada—and they would be surprised to learn of his great interest in the world community.

Among the FBI memos was one from Henry Kissinger's National Security Council. He had been alerted to the meetings of our Center for the Study of Democratic Institutions in Mexico City. He was especially concerned about our dialogues and the possibility that we might accept the invitation I brought from Fidel Castro, for the Center's trustees to visit Cuba. He noted that the prominent jurist, William O. Douglas, the "prominent industrialist, a supporter of Communist causes, Edward Lamb of Ohio," and a prominent educator, Robert Maynard Hutchins, were to participate in the discussions.

Voluminous files from the government intelligence agencies make me question the meaning of the words *national security, democracy,* and *human rights.* I see copies of my letters to others that were intercepted, opened, and photocopied before delivery. My files reveal my government's campaign plans and contracts to get me, to strangle my economic and political activities—all because I want to build bridges.

I suppose that I should take pride in the prominence of my prosecutors. The FBI efforts to convict me as a communist had involved the top government officials, including

President Dwight Eisenhower. The CIA files contained a memo to the attorney general dated May 6, 1954, from the Republican member of the Federal Communications Commission, Robert E. Lee, who said that the group would "get a jump on obtaining pertinent information; that they felt very good over developments in the E. O. Lamb case," but "they needed a certain amount of buttressing"; that the White House was very much interested in the project" and "was pushing to get their show on the road." They wanted to "give as much information to the Criminal Division of the Department of Justice as possible."

The departments of government were cooperating in their campaign to frame me. In one memo the FBI emphasized that an informant, a former convict, "is now under *contract* with the FCC to locate witnesses who can testify re the highly controversial Lamb's subversive activities (my italics). They continued that "public disclosure of the fact that this informant was also being paid by the FBI for information furnished regarding the Lamb case would no doubt result in much embarrassment to the Bureau."

A private citizen can be harassed on many fronts by a multitude of agencies—all at the same time. They enlist the support of private groups, like the veterans' organizations. Memos disclose that on May 4, 1954, thirty bidders sought to buy the municipally owned WSUN-TV at St. Petersburg, Florida. Ted Mack (producer of a show called "The Original Amateur Hour") bid $1,154,000. Edward Lamb Enterprises, Inc., of Toledo bid $2,265,000.

All hell broke loose. The American Legion, at the behest of the FBI, led a campaign to bar the grant to "the radical Lamb." Congressman Edward Hebert of Louisiana called his Un-American Activities Committee together. He was hardly unbiased. He once made a speech about Lamb, "who is saturated and drenched in communist writings, associations and affiliations, given five radio permits in a period of two weeks by the FCC which keeps red-blooded Americans cooling their heels outside in the corridors." His speech, with many others, was reproduced in a right-wing magazine, *The Firing Line*, and then forwarded to "patriotic" groups in

St. Petersburg. Local city, county, and state officials, as well as local newspapers, were flooded with hate mail.

The TV sale was blocked. The city subsequently lost many millions of dollars on its TV operations. The white elephant was later sold for what the city agency said was "peanuts."

Will America ever bring these intelligence agencies under effective control, making them responsible to Congress and holding them strictly accountable for their actions? As a result of development growing out of our Vietnam nightmare, we discovered that the CIA had armed forces and secret armies in southeast Asia and elsewhere. Its paid informers included prominent newsmen. America refused to remove its troops from South Korea under the very same congressional resolution that demanded that Cuba remove its troops from Angola!

The CIA, often referred to as the political police of American capitalism, faces its biggest battle—can it ever win hearts and minds, even the trust, of the American people? Or will it be the agent of greedy corporations working against the emerging demands for a better life of the great mass of the world's peoples? We know that the CIA hires secret armies in Indochina, makes assassination attempts on the lives of foreign leaders, controls corporate empires, recruits mercenaries in Africa, and funnels millions of dollars to social-democratic parties in Portugal, Puerto Rico, and Italy.

There was collusion between the CIA and the American ITT corporation to bring down the Allende government. CIA manuals on sabotage were distributed to Chilean technicians and businesspeople. The CIA has manipulated the trade-union movement in various countries, finding a special and enthusiastic ally in the AFL-CIO hierarchy. Testimony of CIA murders and expenditures are now slowly coming into the open as former insiders make their electrifying disclosures.

Americans have enjoyed so many years of growth and progress that complacency has hardened us. Now we face drastic changes in our programs dealing with energy, population, nuclear weaponry, and technology. We need more dissenters from routine life patterns, more grass-roots movements toward internationalism. We can hope that intelligence agencies will concentrate less on snooping and more on bringing to our attention economic and social developments around the globe.

The American people, getting their knowledge of subversion brought to them largely by defectors, have been disillusioned and disgusted with the clumsy, clandestine efforts of the CIA. A government intelligence organization's duty is to protect and help its own citizens. In the United States police organizations should have the affirmative obligation to respect and defend the constitutional rights and freedoms of every American.

CHAPTER

# XIX

~~~~~~~~~~~~~~~~~~~~~~~~~~~~~~~~~~~~~~~~~~~~~~~~~

# Cuba and Fidel

Just as in the 1930s I yearned to visit the first planned collectivist society of the Soviet Union, in the early 1960s I developed a burning curiosity about the Cuban revolution. Cuba's revolution just didn't seem like any other Latin American uprising. We had read conflicting reports in the American press about the new regime's social intentions. Would the heroic attempts of the Cubans to build a more equitable social system in the Caribbean, whatever it was called, succeed? Cubans, we were told, were directing their attention to developing and sharing in the nation's resources. From the very outset our newspapers played up Castro's rough handling of saboteurs and counterrevolutionaries. They played down or ignored Cuba's strong efforts to improve the standard of living among all Cubans.

We saw plenty of pictures of traitors being executed. We saw nothing of the building of new schools and homes or the effort to modernize sugar refineries, irrigate and cultivate fields, or nationalize food supplies so that all people could eat.

The Bay of Pigs invasion in 1961 was a tragic fiasco.

Americans from the outset suspected that we were being lied to by our own representatives. Still, we didn't think it possible that the glamorous John F. Kennedy would lie to us. I was a friend and supporter of the U.S. ambassador to the United Nations, Adlai Stevenson, and I shuddered when he falsified the facts about the armed involvement of the United States.

American liberals were confused, upset and disillusioned. The United States soon compounded its mistake when it placed cruisers outside Cuban ports to invoke an embargo. I watched those vessels offshore—the action galvanized Cuban resistance. It also provided our trading competitors around the world with access to the Cuban market.

We paid Cuba a ransom of several shiploads of food and drug supplies and obtained the return of our Bay of Pigs invaders. Cuba settled in to build its economy. Fortunately, at the time of the Cuban missile crisis, the United States made a secret deal with the Soviet Union pledging that we would not try another military invasion of the island. That was a tremendous victory for Cuba, because it gave the island a respite. It saved face all around and gave folks in the Pentagon and the Kremlin one less reason for confrontation.

After the missile crisis there were more incongruities in our Cuban relations. We continued to send American surveillance planes over Cuba. We brought back to Miami thousands of Cubans who wanted to leave. We extended the Cuban arrivals substantial housing and loans. Castro claimed that Cuba was getting rid of its malcontents, misfits, and counterrevolutionaries. He insisted that those who remained were the energetic, beautiful, and happy people who would build a new society. Castro's reformist campaign had great appeal for the young, healthy, and socially minded. The old and the affluent preferred to get out. Cuba became the experimental laboratory for building socialism in the Western hemisphere.

In order to know something about its background, I researched all the books and periodicals covering past and present Cuba. On December 2, 1823, President James Monroe advised Congress and European powers that the Western hemisphere was off-limits to European attention or influence. He also promised that the U.S.A. would not interfere with the existing colonies or dependencies and presumably that meant Spain's control of Cuba.

Since Monroe's day we've had the Good Neighbor Policy, the Alliance for Progress, the "mature partnership" designed to assert the control of affairs in our sphere of influence. But we've also had the Bay of Pigs and many military interventions and economic boycotts.

It's not easy to understand the strategy of U.S. policymakers. Were we trying to contain a Cuban revolutionary movement, seize Cuba as a colony using our Guantánamo base, or just limit foreign influence in this hemisphere? Whatever our purpose, our actions helped Cuba become a significant world power.

At the turn of the century President Theodore Roosevelt negotiated a deal for the American naval base, Guantánamo, taking permanent control of some thirty-six thousand acres overlooking the Windward Passage—and we agreed to pay the picayune sum of two thousand gold dollars as annual rental.

*Fortune* magazine once said that Toledo's Edward Lamb Building was called the Little Kremlin. Possibly my business competitors were responsible and my associates a bit embarrassed by the identificaton, but everyone at least admitted that we have plenty of action in my headquarters. I ask my managers to go wherever the action—and the problem—is. Therefore, no one should have been surprised when I took off without any advance notice for a trip to what was in the early days called Communist Cuba.

I was working as a reporter for my television stations at the Republican National Convention in Miami in late August 1968. Frankly, I was bored by the drabness of the process by which an American political party selects its candidates for the presidency. Then, upon the nomination of Richard M. Nixon as president and Spiro Agnew as vice-

president, and while the balloting dragged on, I decided
that I had had enough. The time was ripe to slip away
from the convention hoopla and travel to Cuba.

There were two schools of thought about going to Cuba.
As a matter of constitutional law, I was opposed to asking
for permission of the U.S. State Department to travel
abroad. The State Department had long been active in
restraining my trips around the world. I flew to Mexico,
which at the time was the only nation in the Western
hemisphere formally recognizing Cuba. At the large, tightly
guarded Cuban embassy in Mexico City, I was received
courteously and quickly given a visa. The consulate officials.
were most helpful, possibly because I owned a sugar-harvester-
manufacturing company with plants in Veracruz and in
Louisiana. They lost no time in helping me get on the
Cubana Airlines flight that left at noon three times a week.
At the airport the Mexican customs officials insisted on
taking my picture again and again. They had to have
retakes, one official admitted to me, because the first photos
"might not be satisfactory to the U.S. State Department."

Customs officials in Mexico often receive tips for exit
permits. I gave them, for good measure, a broad laugh.
Cuban friends gave me packs of drugs to deliver, all sorely
needed by a Havana hosital. My suit bulged, and my pants
were stuffed out of size. My contraband weighed at least
fifty pounds and grew heavier every mile of the trip.

Many buildings in the United States were being bombed
by anti-Castro terrorists. We didn't know then that their
explosive came directly from the vaults of the American
Central Intelligence Agency. Such hostility only intensified
my desire to travel to Cuba, especially since it was so totally
boycotted by U.S. diplomatic and economic forces. What
could be happening inside Cuba that should arouse so
much frenzied opposition in Washington? Was it our continued failure to bring that little island to its knees?

I have spent a good part of my business life in the sugar
industry. I had a special interest in Cuba's economy, since
Cuba is the largest producer of sugar in the world. A few
liberal newspapermen like Herbert L. Matthews of the

*New York Times* and several militant radicals throughout the world were pointing out that Castro's revolution was something meaningful and different. Under Colonel Batista, American tourists knew only that Havana was a fun place: girls, gambling and life in the sun. American corporations knew Cuba as a place for cheap labor.

As a newspaper publisher and television- and radio-station owner, I had interviewed my share of political leaders on the right and left of the political spectrum. They included Franklin D. Roosevelt, Joseph Stalin, Harry Truman, Juan Perón, Pope Pius XII, Chiang Kai-shek, Dwight Eisenhower, John F. Kennedy, Adlai Stevenson, Lyndon B. Johnson, Richard M. Nixon, and Gerald Ford. I developed a personal, if not a professional, interest in big names.

I preferred the cordial, intimate friendships of American politicians of the intellectual liberal fringe, such as Estes Kefauver and Adlai Stevenson. The exciting people of our time were found among the leaders of various progressive causes, whether in industry, education, trade unions, or politics—especially those backing civil or constitutional rights: the muckrakers and the radical elements.

Any cause worthwhile to me has but one aim—the liberation of men. Because of man's long history of intolerance and racism, it is necessary to keep our eyes on the basic problems of our time—the liberation of *all* humans. I wondered if in Cuba one would find the perfect testing ground to prove that human freedoms can be preserved even while building a more equitable society.

The seeds of a revolution are always present. Terrorism is an adjunct of revolution. I have never been convinced that revolution can be nonviolent. I was a great admirer of the nonviolent Dr. Martin Luther King, and for several years I've been a Trustee of the Martin Luther King, Jr., Center for Peaceful Change. Yet we remember that he, like Mahatma Gandhi and other nonviolent leaders, died at the hands of violent assassins. I have been impressed by the fact that Fidel Castro continued in office because he used force to put down the counterrevolutionaries. Doesn't every regime stay in power through force?

I was very anxious to meet Fidel Castro personally. Was he communist, demagogue, or modern Robin Hood? He had become the one Latin American leader who aroused the curiosity of an entire world. He was not a Marxist when he came into power. He would tell me later that he hadn't thought his way into communism; he had been forced into it, largely as a result of the actions of the "Yankee imperialists." When we threatened the Revolution's survival, we forced Castro to the East.

I wanted to know from Castro whether, after becoming a communist, he was receptive to utilizing the fruits of science and technology of the West to build his agrarian economy. When political power is achieved after a successful revolution, I wondered if he knew that there would come the time when someone must be able to operate and make the system work.

There were broader questions. What was his concept of society—the role of the state, the planning of the economy? How would he reach the Cuban mentality, protect customs, and promote aspirations? What about individual freedoms? Would his revolution continue to be maintained by force? Was there really a "new man" aborning? I have been in nearly every socialist nation in the world, and I know some of their problem areas. I have seen the difficulties they face in adopting planning programs and utilizing modern management. In Cuba, as well as in other emerging nations, the managerial and scientific revolution was still a long way off.

When I arrived in Havana in late August 1968, I was met by Abe Maciques, the director of the Cuban television network. Milling around the airport lounge was also a large, obviously curious staff, including a pretty, very business-like young woman, Angela Rico. I was told that she would serve as my interpreter. They gave me the red-carpet welcome when I checked into a suite on the top floor of the Habana Libre Hotel, formerly the Havana Hilton. The air-conditioned rooms were stocked with fruit, food, and liquor.

I was asked what I wanted to do during my visit, and I told them I wanted to do a great deal of investigative work, often, if possible, on my own. It seemed superfluous, but I told my hosts that I was not an agent for anyone, that I had no financial interest in any project, and that I had come to find answers.

They assured me that I could go anywhere, take my cameras, and see and talk to anyone. They told me that there were several people in Cuba who wanted to see me. For the next ten days from early morning until late at night I moved around the island. I met dozens of farm workers and industrial leaders.

I first met Fidel Castro as he and his entourage in three jeeps bounded along the dusty road twenty miles outside Havana. I was visiting an experimental-farm project in the so-called Cordon de Habana, or Green Belt, a growing and recreational area 15 to 20 miles wide and 150 miles long. The prime minister, surrounded by several peasants and security personnel, wandered from one farm project to another. He seemed to know many of the peasants personally, often shouting out their names. He put his arms on their shoulders as he asked questions about the family, crops, buildings, roads, and sanitary conditions. He made copious notes and inquired about the living conditions of the youngsters in the schools and nurseries.

He moved to my side of the road but stopped to talk to another group of workers. He asked them about their evening literacy classes. He seemed to be kidding and telling stories, and everyone quickly became involved in a lively dialogue. Then he grew serious. He said that he had heard that the village farm training classes didn't seem to be going too well. Was the problem the teachers, the equipment? He moved rapidly. On his short-wave radio he called one of the departments in Havana. Then he looked at his notes and talked to his aides and asked that they follow through and be sure to take care of all inquiries. Like a politician at a country fair, he handled dozens of complaints. The crowds looked at "our Fidel" with compassionate approval.

Castro's chief aide, Dr. René Vallejo, a white-bearded, English-speaking medical doctor and a constant companion, spotted me. He came over to the newly painted white fence when I was visiting with the Green Belt project manager and introduced himself. Vallejo had heard of my presence and my background as an American industrialist. Castro was bidding the peasants farewell when Vallejo asked if I would like an introduction to the prime minister. About the same time the tall Cuban leader waved in my direction. He and his companions wore their sidearms attached to their fatigue uniforms. He dismounted from his jeep, clasped my right hand, and placed his other on my shoulder. No wasted protocol, just a friendly conversation. He asked if we couldn't get together for a long visit sometime, "the sooner the better."

I was pleasantly surprised by his modesty, twinkling eyes, and softness. The informality of this world-famous revolutionist, there along a country road, made my welcome seem so much more impressive. He had good reason to be on guard—especially with any guest from the United States. This was the man our own State Department, our CIA, and other intelligence agencies were trying to assassinate. (But this was also the man whom even "Operation Mongoose," for which the Mafia was recruited in 1962, had not been able to kill. The mighty United States under President Kennedy just couldn't murder this single national leader.)

That trip through Cuba was filled with interviews. I kept abundant notes and took hundreds of pictures of sugar-cane fields, factories, housing construction, hospitals, and schools for young and old students. I proposed to gather up all the facts I could about this exciting new world. I wanted information about day-to-day living conditions so that I could tell the truth to my friends back in the States.

I wandered through the cities and towns alone during the days and occasionally at night. I would be the last to say that the eyes of security guards were not on me at all times. After all, they, too, were curious—an American strolling freely around Cuba was unusual at that time.

If I had any eerie feelings, it was because there were no guards, no policemen anywhere in sight. However, every Cuban building of importance was heavily guarded, usually by the civilian militia. My hosts had given me a car, an interpreter, a specialist—and carte blanche to visit around the islands. No one ever had a better opportunity to see first-hand what the new Cuba was all about.

We spent lots of time in the television studios, engineering and medical facilities, and factories and refineries. Everything I wanted to see, I saw.

On a subsequent visit to Cuba I received a call from Abe Maciques at my hotel in Havana. This was about 11:00 P.M. March 18, 1969. Maciques was excited as he said, "Get ready to take off at six in the morning!"

I knew what he meant, since I had spent the early evening with him. He had whispered to me that he was sure that the decks had been cleared for our conferences, but whether we would be meeting early or late, north or south, no one could know.

Exactly at 6:00 A.M. we were picked up by two cars, one of which contained Dr. José Miyar, president of Havana University, whom I had met on a previous visit. In the semidarkness we went to the military airport outside Havana. There we were met by several other leaders, including the ministers of agriculture and labor, several armed guards, and a couple of members of the central committee of the Communist party. After we left the ground in Castro's personal plane, I was told we were going to Camagüey province. The plane was splendidly furnished and paneled with accommodations for twenty-five passengers. Half a dozen heavily armed guards sat ahead of and behind us. Machine guns peered out from every corner—even in the restroom. It was all very exciting, but I wondered what I was getting into.

At Camagüey military airport we were met by another group in a civilian car and two army jeeps. Our tour through the city was rapid—one jeep went ahead and one behind us. The jeeps each had four military occupants, all of whom were heavily armed with machine guns. Maybe they weren't trying to confuse me as we drove around the city of Camagüey seeing the sights. Ten minutes later we headed out into the back roads. It was lucky that we had moved into the lead-car position and made, rather than caught, dust during that forty-five-minute drive. When we finally came to a complex of white buildings and pulled up at the gate, I was met by the handsome, white-bearded Dr. René Vallejo. We chatted for a minute or two, and then Prime Minister Fidel Castro came out on the porch. He smiled pleasantly. He was interested in my trip and asked if he could make my visit more meaningful. He said that everyone hoped I would remain as long as possible.

Although his headquarters is located in hot, arid country-side, there were colorful gardens surrounding the compound. Cut tropical flowers graced the center table. We sat down on the porch and talked for an hour, enjoying orange juice.

Castro said, "We're very glad that you accepted our invitation. Maybe your trip will persuade other American businessmen to visit us." He wanted to get my reactions to what I had seen. "What would you like to see? You name it, and we'll see that you are accommodated!"

I told him that my interests were generally economic rather than ideological. I had observed the management of many of the Cuban operations, and I was impressed with the energy shown by so many people in building their economy.

He pointed out that Cuban techniques were crude by our standards but that the country was making progress. "There is such a long way to go," he said.

I asked, "What actually is your socialist government's receptivity to technological advances—what are the limits?"

He laughed. "We prefer to think we are communists. We accept every scientific fact, every technological advance."

We agreed that the main thing was to get results and not bother about semantics. Castro said, "We have enough troubles without worrying about the labels or names we are called by others."

After a lunch of fruit and seafood we sat for a while swinging in the rocking chairs on the porch of the little white house in the back country of Camagüey. I noticed that a dozen guards moved inconspicuously in the background. We told stories, and I tried to evaluate the man.

Even after a light lunch he munched oranges. He said this was one way of keeping his weight down. "We all have to resist too many temptations to add to the flesh. It's a problem," he laughed.

I kidded him about there being fewer bearded men in Cuba now than in American colleges.

"There are so few of us left," he quipped. He reported that even his brother Raul, vice prime minister, had shaved —and as a result looked much younger. "Maybe we're getting like the girls who want to keep looking young."

We were joined in the conferences by Armando Hart, member of the politburo in charge of organization of the Communist party; José Miyar, head of Havana University; Minister of Labor Risquet, who seemed to be the only other person at that session with a beard; and attractive Ophelia Hernandez, a faculty member at Havana University who, with the everpresent Dr. René Vallejo, acted as my interpreter.

We moved quickly into a discussion of the Cuban social revolution. I suggested that the nature of each nation's political or social system was its own business and that I had come as one interested principally in the economic functioning of a society. I was not so versed in dialectics or in class struggles between workers and their "exploiters" as I was in obtaining social justice and human freedom for all men everywhere. He nodded in agreement. At that time he was himself picking his way through various phases of Marxist ideology.

Castro said that he was convinced that I would see in the Cuban economy a "new mentality developing among our citizens." Everyone, young and old, was "involved in the work of planting and harvesting and making our developing society succeed." He said, "We give emphasis to making work a dignified, desirable activity for every person, that the whole concept of our educational process is involved in the preparation of all members of the community to become socially useful citizens."

We talked about the traditional concepts of Marxist class war and where society would go from here. It didn't take us long to get into my favorite subject, the "third force," that of the new emerging class of scientific managers. I repeated that after the seizure of political power comes the need for the management cadres.

He said, "In this, I heartily agree. No society can function with only the presence of human resources and natural resources. There must be the other element, the skill which harnesses these resources, the science of making the economy function."

I pointed out that in the United States we already have more than a thousand schools of business administration and that we are graduating more than sixty-five thousand professionally trained managers, able to utilize computers and other sophisticated tools, each year.

Castro was surprised to hear that these MBAs command starting salaries of as much as fifty thousand dollars a year. I didn't think that he'd like the term *business,* with its connotation of private profit, or even *manager,* with its connotation of control of human activities, but I told him that I had been working on a new title for such academic institutions. If he ever decided to accept my suggestion that we work on such administrative schools in Cuba, we'd all come up with a new "grass roots" name that would make it more palatable to all. Whether public or private ownership prevails in a nation, the need for such managerial skills is critical.

Our conference was held at a time when Cuba was enjoying relative calm. The Bay of Pigs was half a dozen years behind us, and the missile crisis had receded into history.

There was still some harassment of Cuba from our Guantánamo naval base. Émigrés were attacking Cuban ports from small ships. Provocations, such as the burning of cane fields, had slowed down because our armed forces were needed in the increasingly bitter war in Vietnam. I had seen hijacked American planes land in Cuba. Soon we would plead that our hijacked aircraft not be received by Cuba. It was at least some recognition of Cuba's existence.

We discussed various American political figures. Castro said that he felt the greatest man in America's modern history was Franklin D. Roosevelt, who, though born into wealth, had an understanding of basic human needs. He recognized the affirmative obligation of the state to provide the human requirements, such as housing, jobs, education, food, and health care for all.

Castro declared that John F. Kennedy and Robert Kennedy both had been "rank opportunists" and, born in wealth, had done only those things which would capture the popular fancy and "obtain a political plurality."

He admired Senator Eugene McCarthy for his success in pointing out the inadequacies of the American political system.

"Senator William Fulbright of the Senate Foreign Relations Committee," he said, "has been your greatest realist. Senator George McGovern is clearing away the myths which separate us. Most of your American political leaders, like Lyndon Johnson, Richard Nixon, and Hubert Humphrey, do not seem to recognize the fundamental ethics of revolution in forcing change and improvements."

After every discussion of an ideology or a personality, he returned to his number-one priority: Cuba's need for technological help. I was impressed with his practicality—he wanted the Cuban economy to work. He said that Cuba already had "over two hundred foreign technicians, some from England, others from France, the Soviet Union, and Bulgaria and in spite of boycotts and threats, a few from the United States." He said, "We have many American volunteers helping us in the fields. We're just beginning to attack the bigger problems, but we realize that we need thousands of technicians to teach us and help us build our economy."

We talked at great length about the possibility of introducing management-training courses or seminars in Havana. I told him of my own lectures and recruitment of lecturers in socialist countries. Castro wondered if such a program for Cuba could attract a teacher from the American schools of business administration. I felt that management authorities would be available, including possibly members of the American Management Assocation. We were uncomfortably aware that all such programs might be vetoed by the politicians in the U.S. State Department. The American boycott against goods and services, enforced with cruisers and sky surveillance, was hurting, no doubt about it.

Castro is hardworking and has a large curiosity. Just as though he were a student in a lecture course, he took voluminous notes. At the conclusion of our two days of conferences he had fifty or sixty closely written pages. The first night we talked until 2:00 A.M. We were back in session at 7:00. He repeated, after sleeping on the question, that they had decided to concentrate on agriculture rather than industrialization for the next few years. Most of all, we talked about modern planting, cultivation, and harvesting techniques and the possibility of mechanizing different crops.

I told him about our potato-harvesting equipment used in the northern states and about our sugar-cane equipment operating in the South. He was downright excited about such developments—he had not known at the time that technicians had also developed mechanical harvesters for citrus fruits and various vegetables.

I hoped that some of our current politicians, like Senators Eugene McCarthy, William Fulbright, Frank Church, and Jacob Javits and Justice William O. Douglas, all of whom had indicated interest in visiting Cuba, could see for themselves what was happening.

But Castro indicated that although he didn't wish to be inhospitable, it would be better if American politicians didn't come to Cuba for a while, "because they are then going to be in for quite a surprise."

Of all the American politicians, he most wanted to see Senators George McGovern and Wayne Morse.

I talked about my friend Drew Pearson, the columnist, and his desire to go to Cuba. Castro pulled out of his files several anti-Castro articles Pearson had written and said, "What do you think?"

It was pretty clear that Drew Pearson and his assistant, Jack Anderson, had written a great deal of bitter anti-Castro stuff. I told him I would talk to Drew about the matter when I arrived back in the States, since I was sure that he had great integrity. I said, "If he is permitted to come to Cuba, he would surely call the shots as he sees them." (I conveyed these messages to Pearson, but only a month later, he died.)

We talked of many subjects—the hijacking of planes, broadcasting frequencies, Cuba's expropriation of American plants. Always, we came back to the subject of socialism, technology, and the planned economy. Castro wanted to know how we managed our giant corporations, especially the vast multinational companies and conglomerates.

"At least in that area," I replied, "I have the scars to prove my exposure to such problems. No matter how you cut it, I've found that any human institution is as good or as bad as its administrators—and that includes management skills in directing communication and the correlation of resources. To me, scientific management has become the dominant issue of our times. Management of transnational activities is an emerging science that may one day help us reach and operate the world community."

We talked for a couple of hours on the role of the manager, how he actually functions in the group process. He was interested in the whole concept of management by objectives and in the delegation of responsibilities down through the organization. He rather relished the idea that every problem shouldn't be passed up to him.

When would the door be opened for visitors? I told Castro that a group from the Center for the Study of Democratic Institutions, a think tank based in Santa Barbara, California, wanted to visit Cuba. I would appreciate it if they were given visas and every courtesy.

He replied, "We would be delighted to have them here; are they economists?"

I said, "Several are businessmen, and the others are sociologists, philosophers, economists, and teachers."

He emphasized, "We're pleading for help from such people—we want to talk to technicians and especially businessmen. We don't want hippies. We want people who can help us. We're like other emerging nations—we can't spend all our time talking ideology; we need technology. We'd probably welcome the whole U.S. Chamber of Commerce!"

We talked about the question of burning sugar cane in the fields before it is harvested, as is practiced in several countries. Castro said, "We haven't done that here, but why shouldn't we look into it and do it?" I told him that I would get agrarian experts together with them and see that available literature on the matter was forwarded to them. I had arranged for delivery of several bushels of seeds, including carrots, soybeans, hybrid field corn, and other high-quality crops.

There had also been included in the packages a new brand of sweet corn. Castro didn't seem to understand. He thought that we were teasing him. He asked Dr. Miyar, "Sweet corn; what's that? Do people eat it?"

I said, "Yes. It's very popular in the United States. We put salt and butter on it."

He said, "Do you can it or freeze it?"

"Both," I said. "It is among our most stable, delicious table items."

He urged Dr. José Miyar to see if he could get some fast-growing sweet corn into the fields and try it out. "A modern maize might help our Cuban gourmets." He added, "Cuba has to do so many things from scratch. At least, when we develop new foodstuffs, we'll see that it is the best quality and fairly shared among all our people. We know that we can't concentrate on our own satisfactions. We'll have to continue to export a great deal just to get currency to buy foreign mechanical equipment."

His eyes were twinkling. "We studied how to make ice cream in our *cabellas*, or ice-cream parlors. We tried to copy the Howard Johnson formula, but it didn't work. Then we found that we had a man in Cuba who knew how to make the best ice cream. Indeed, he knew how to make fifty-four varieties. I had him come to see me. I told him that if he would teach the Cubans how to make ice cream, he could leave the country and go whenever he wanted to. He was most cooperative. He didn't really want to leave Cuba. Instead, he set up ice-cream-making classes. Our people are now well taught in the art. We are now serving thousands of gallons of good ice cream to our people every day." He was aglow as he added, "With our new herds, think how our milk and ice-cream production will skyrocket!"

At Castro's table I tried several types of locally produced cheese. He said, "Our problem for export is to get a name that is catchy, and yet, since people do not associate cheese with Cuba but only with the Dutch, we have to adopt some fancy Dutch and French handles for our cheese. We're starting contests to choose our name brands. Actually, it's a pretty good product. The Russians think so now; others will follow."

We discussed the film and television industries. He liked Saul Landau's new film, *Fidel*. He said he did not wish to have it shown in Cuba until after it had been exhibited in the United States and Europe, simply because he did not wish "to give the wrong impression. There is already too much personality cult around the world." Cuban law does not permit the erection of any building or monument bearing the name of a living person.

He was pleased that the work of Ché Guevara was being so favorably received by the young people around the world, especially on the American campuses. We talked a great deal about the ill-fated activities of Guevara in Bolivia, and he showed the deepest affection for the brilliant young revolutionist. I had just read Ché Guevara's diary, and many items in it made me know a bit of the perfidy of the Bolivian Communist-party leaders—and I've since learned how they operated under the direction of our CIA.

We discussed developments in the Cuban television stations and their satisfactory operation even with the most outmoded equipment imaginable. He pointed out that they were able to produce their own cartoons and some films but that they wanted very much to import educational and worthwhile films, especially those illustrating productive processes used in the industrial nations.

We discussed the remarkable possibilities of educational

television. Castro said that they didn't want "a lot of the soap-opera trash and the commercials being shown on American television."

I told him that we'd see that Cuba received a large number of cartoons immediately. I told him of my former film shipments destined for Cuba that had gone astray in Canada. "Tough," he said. "Our children would have enjoyed them." In later years I solved the problem of shipping film material into Cuba. I was also helpful in getting new, modern TV equipment into the country from Japan, France, and the Soviet Union.

My enthusiasm for the Cuban experiment may have been surpassed by that of my son, Edward Hutchinson Lamb, who devotes more attention to the field of electronic journalism. I told Castro an anecdote about "Hutch," who has inherited considerable assets. He was making out his last will and testament, and the lawyers were listing various schools, colleges, and hospitals which they suggested should receive bequests. These included his own alma mater, Western Colorado University, and mine, Dartmouth College and Harvard University, as well as his mother's, Smith College.

Hutch said that he wanted to make bequests to Wilberforce and Havana Universities, where his gifts would be "meaningful."

"Meaningful, perhaps," said the lawyers, "but in the case of Havana University, probably illegal." They persisted in their recommendations against a Cuban gift.

Finally Hutch replied, "To hell with all of you; it's my money, and I'm leaving it to Havana University, where I know that it will be used to help a lot of people get on their feet. I expect that the United States, before I die, will again be a good friend to Cuba. If the United States continues in its foolish policy toward its neighbors, then the United States will be on its way to hell too!"

When I told this story to Castro, tears came to his eyes. He said, "There's a man. Please let me meet Hutch!"

I discussed CATV cable television, then emerging in the United States. Castro was anxious to hear all the details. He said, "Couldn't we put this into Havana and other cities utilizing our present telephone lines?" I gave the technical requirements, including the need for head-end equipment and a high TV antenna. He saw that the system could be easily adapted throughout Cuba. I had previously outlined the potentials of CATV in the Soviet Union, but we knew that the U.S. State Department had vetoed sending any such equipment to the U.S.S.R.

At present radar and other signals are received in Cuba via nominal or very low towers. Castro wanted to know the price of a fifteen-hundred- or two-thousand-foot tower, for both broadcasting and receiving, plus the various coaxial-cable items necessary to wire up a city. They broadcast on three channels: 2, 6, and 8. He asked one of his TV specialists to determine the possibility of receiving various programs from the States, Mexico, and other Caribbean nations. I told him how cable television functions, and I left considerable product literature with him. Cuba later acquired a great deal of such equipment and modernized its facilities.

Castro dreamed of the possibility of utilizing their new, high tower to broadcast powerful signals to the Caribbean and to the southeastern United States. Cuba, as a bit of an outcast, was not limited by international agreements that assign channels among nations. I reminded him how the broadcasting of TV signals on various channels by Cuba would affect the allocation of most broadcasting stations in the United States.

Abe Maciques, head of the television network, was present during our discussions of television. He left for Moscow with the Cuban trade delegation the following day. They hoped to pick up some modern broadcasting equipment from a list I gave him, even though they had problems adapting to the Soviet product. Russian television has adopted the French system of 820 lines per scan, whereas the American system, which Cuba uses, has only 525 lines per scan. Castro said that "maybe in due course the American boycott against the import of technical equipment may be lifted and then we will be a very large customer. All we need is a five-year financing plan from the United States. We have been getting six to ten years of credit from the

French, English, Swedish—and much better than that from the Soviet bloc. Our credit, I repeat, as the world knows, is absolutely okay."

We sat around discussing various technological developments in America. I told him about our plastic shoes, which are produced at the rate of a pair every twenty seconds. Castro could hardly believe that the technology in the plastic business was so far advanced. I told him of various items we were producing in plastics, including ball bearings. Cuba now has three plastics plants. He wanted to know all about the vinyl shoes. I took his size (9½B) and the sizes of other guests and promised that I would let him try out a sample. The shoes retain their color, and the cost of producing them is very low. Although vinyl is warmer than leather, vinyl shoes just might be an ideal consumer's item for Cuba. He said that they had "spent three million dollars in cash with the Italians to get a turn-key spaghetti factory," but for half that amount they could get a first-class vinyl-shoe plant. They could sell their large production of leather hides abroad at fancy prices!

It's almost grotesque, the political fumbling of American business issues. I talked to Fidel about those vinyl shoes we manufactured at our plant in Arkansas. I gave him samples and brochures describing the equipment. Two weeks later he had engineers visiting the headquarters of shoe equipment manufacturers in West Germany and Italy. In another three weeks the presidents of those same companies were in Cuba bidding for the equipment business. Contracts were given an Italian company. The machines were installed on December 5, 1969. The machines were operating by the time Fidel Castro made a major speech on July 26, 1970.

I was on the platform as he used the modern shoe equipment to demonstrate the labor-saving features of modern technology. Each machine turned out between 150 and 200 pairs of shoes an hour—some 3,500 pairs every twenty-four hours, using only thirty workers. By 1970 every woman in Cuba had a pair of the new vinyl shoes. Although such shoes often overheat, in wearability and in styling they compare favorably with the older leather shoes. Castro said that nineteen thousand workers produced eighteen million pairs of leather shoes a year but that only twelve hundred workers could produce thirty million pairs of vinyl shoes annually.

We also discussed mechanized bean, citrus, and potato harvesting. I reported what I had seen at the town of Guira, where enormous irrigated fields are planted. I described America's production with modern equipment and contrasted that with what was being done with raw handpower in Cuba. He was as excited as a schoolboy as he talked about "the electronic possibilities of this new age." He was writing down in longhand practically every word I said. He has a remarkable, retentive mind, and he repeats statistics on the most diverse subjects. He must have dozens of filing cases filled with notes. But then, I never saw Castro in an administrator's office, although I know that he has several.

At the same time, he scribbled off a note to Arturo Delgato to be sure to get in touch with him and discuss modern methods of potato cultivation and harvesting. When I told him our harvester cleans potatoes and separates out the stones, he said, "Think how this will save the time of our workers—and even the oxen in the fields."

I told him I had seen six thousand volunteer workers in the potato fields working late into the evening and had been dumbfounded that people, however enthusiastic, could work so hard. He saw that with the modern cultivation practices and the introduction of mechanization even into the warehouses, they could easily be able to triple production by using only a few machines.

"These machines will free our people for more recreation, leisure, and educatonal activities. It's our hope and our salvation; the machine will free all mankind!"

Later when we were again discussing the sugar industry, he asked me how many mechanical harvesters I thought they could use, and I told him the details of our advanced machines. Each will easily do the work of three hundred men. I thought that probably a thousand machines would do all their harvesting. He said, "We have been studying this matter, and we believe that we will be able to utilize three thousand mechanical harvesters as soon as we can get them." I gave Castro the names of manufacturers of such equipment in Australia and West Germany. On subsequent trips to Cuba I saw dozens of these modern harvesters at work in the Cuban fields.

We talked a great deal about the harvesters, or combines, the Cubans had been developing by themselves. He, of course, had known and studied our Thomson cane harvester, and he knew of the Soviet attempts to copy our Thomson machine in the past. I told him that I had seen the Soviet prototypes of our combines and loaders in the Soviet plants and also in the fields of Cuba. We both agreed that the quality of the Soviet harvesters was not adequate, and we referred to twenty-six of them that were sitting idle in the Cuban warehouse. I also told him that in downtown Havana I had seen twenty-five or fifty Soviet cotton pickers and that I had seen the same machines in the same lots the year before. The machines had not been moved out into the fields because they just wouldn't work.

Castro said, "I would like to have you go out with our minister of agriculture and look at our mechanical harvester. We just brought it out of our own technical-equipment center. We have two of them already built, and another twenty-five will be completed in another month. We have put in a tremendous amount of engineering and research work on this cane harvester. Would you give me in confidence your appraisal of this harvester?"

The following day, a Sunday, I went out to a farm near Cardenas with agricultural officials. They picked me up at the Josone Estate, where I was staying near Varadero Beach. This Josone Estate is the compound where important guests stay and some international conferences are held.

Castro said, "A group of your friends, those guests at the conference on Latin America you are soon holding in Mexico City, sponsored by the Center for the Study of Democratic Institutions, will be housed here, if they'll accept our invitation. I would be delighted to spend a lot of time with them under most pleasant conditions. There will be no perimeters on our talks." Unfortunately, the center's trustees did not accept the invitation to visit Cuba. As the result of a dreary controversy among themselves, the trustees missed an early invitation to study the truth about Cuba.

I went out into Cardenas' sugar cane fields and watched their harvester perform. At least seventy-five specialists attended. They told me that I had carte blanche to go into any part of the machine and that they would put it to any test I ordered. They also urged me to take any pictures I wanted. I did take dozens of pictures, including some showing the cutting and loading phases of the operation. The Cubans ran the machine up and down the field a couple of times, and I studied it very closely, making many notes on its operation.

I told the chief technician that the operation was an excellent job and that they should be proud of their efforts. It was obvious that they had spent untold thousands of engineering hours in the design and construction of that harvester. I later wrote articles and produced pictures of the status of Cuban sugar-cane production. But the editors of the *Sugar Journal* and other publications in the United States refused to carry the stories. Censorship accompanied the American trade boycott.

The day arrived when Castro took me out to the airport at Camagüey. We gossiped for a half hour. President Dorticos was leaving but stopped by for a short chat. Then Castro and I talked for a few moments inside his private plane, and he said, "In thinking over this matter, I do not believe that Cuba should undertake any broadcasting activities at this time that would disturb the possibility of any negotiations we can have with the United States We can continue our studies about broadcasting and receiving, but we do not wish to do anything of an aggressive nature in any way. We'll hold up the building of such broadcasting towers for the time being." He said that they would, however, continue their engineering and other studies covering the construction of an enormous tower to receive signals. He said that they could build towers in their own shops with steel and advanced techniques from the U.S.S.R. Later they would get giant steel and even nuclear plants from their eastern neighbors. The American boycott of Cuba continued.

The subsequent history of mechanization of the Cuban sugar fields proved the correctness of their decision to scuttle their cane harvesters and start all over again or to import from other countries. Although their engineers couldn't at first get visas to visit our plant in Veracruz, Mexico, I took our own experts to Cuba on various occasions. Sometime later, the Cubans, after flying into New Orleans, weren't allowed to visit the World Sugar Conference. They were compelled by our State Department to hole up at a motel in New Orleans. I assembled every piece of literature, every speech delivered, every item at that convention and sent it off to Havana. It arrived before the Cuban delegates landed back at their own homes. I never felt that technology could be confined behind national boundaries. Much better that food technology, like the production of spaghetti, be efficient, so that more people have an adequate supply at lower cost.

I'm glad that so many people have now interviewed Fidel Castro and that every visitor reports it as an exhilarating event. He may drop into a university or take his guest on a jeep ride through the countryside. On July 4, 1974, our Independence Day, my daughter and I, with several friends, were enjoying the occasion out at Havana's beautiful Tropicana nightclub. About 11:30 P.M. a member of his staff whispered in my ear, "The prime minister is coming to your hotel right away." We hastily departed. The streets in both directions were already blocked off. When the prime minister stepped out of his jeep, he gave us both a warm hug and apologized for visiting us so late in the evening—he had had to attend a ribbon-cutting ceremony at the opening of the Argentina Trade Fair.

He was accompanied by Vice Premier and Foreign Minister Carlos Rafael Rodriguez, and they asked if we'd like to take a ride. My daughter climbed in the back seat first and quickly let out a howl. She was astride a machine gun and hadn't straddled it four-square. I was in the middle, and Castro squeezed in beside me, with Rodriguez in front. For three hours we traveled around the countryside. My daughter, studying Cuban social institutions like nursery and elementary schools, was completely enraptured by the prime minister. Any visitor sees in this one man a leader of his own countrymen and a man who is shaping the course of emerging humanity.

I am not above criticizing Castro's Cuba. Yet I choose not to nitpick every detail of Cuban efforts to build a satisfactory social order. I don't like authoritarianism from the right or the left. Even more, I dislike repressive morality.

Cuba will be judged as an early battleground for the birth of the new society. The comments of smug critics, like Maurice Halperin, in *The Rise and Decline of Fidel Castro,* are readily available. Almost a million Cuban émigrés are in the United States. But the fact is that an oppressed colony has overthrown its imperialist shackles. The people are freely building a wholesome new homeland. A new society is blossoming.

I love the people of Cuba, so friendly and courageous. I love the island, with its mountains and running streams, its seashores and recreational areas. Most of all, I admire Fidel Castro and all the other dedicated and spirited Cuban men and women who are leading mankind into the future.

The Cuban Revolution created more than 1.5 million new work assignments, and there are not enough people to fill the available jobs. The revolution permitted more than seven hundred thousand adults to learn to read and write. Twenty-three million copies of textbooks were published. The participation of the Cuban worker is a stimulating example of how input is contributed by every citizen. I was encouraged to see the vast majority of people at every level participate in drafting the new Cuban constitution. More than 650,000 meetings were held to discuss this proposed constitution. This remarkable document is the result of grass-roots citizen participation. Men and women sixteen and older have the franchise. Seventy modifications came out of these popular debates. When the constitution went into effect on February 15, 1976, it had been created by a referendum under a free, universal, and secret vote. 5,472,876 citizens voted in this referendum, 97.7 percent voting to ratify their new charter of government. It is not too much to suggest that this historic document is among the most widely discussed, most democratically accepted instruments in the history of mankind. It recognizes, among basic rights, the economic and social and political obligations of an organized society to its members. To me, that's an important ingredient of a democratic society.

Fair-minded Americans are curious, possibly a little bit envious, of the accomplishments of this first planned economy in the Western hemisphere. The plain facts indicate that the Cuban people have achieved a wholesome sharing of the nation's assets, and its people have reason to hope for a better tomorrow. The demonstrated success of this small nation is watched with equal pride by many nations. American labor, industrial, and agricultural interests should be leading the parade to extend a congratulatory handshake to this fascinating emerging nation.

Through their foreign subsidiaries, American corporations do a large trade with Cuba. The foreign trade of Cuba doubled in just the four years between 1971 and 1975. Cuba wants our technology, agriculture, manufacturing equipment, fertilizers, chemicals, and drugs. They need industrial plants, such as steel, paper, medical and hospital supplies, and shipping. The Soviet Union is aiding Cuba in building a steel complex and nuclear plant. Other nations have trade delegations signing up for large enterprises. But notice an anomaly: American corporations store rice grown in Louisiana in surplus-storage bins while the same corporations sell rice grown in other countries to Cuba through their foreign subsidiaries. What could we import from Cuba? Sugar, molasses, nickel, copper, chrome, tobacco, coffee, and fruit.

Trade is a two-way street. Mexico, England, France, Canada, Japan, and other nations have extended eight billion dollars' credit to buy needed industrial goods. Cuba will pay with hard dollars—or Cuban products. The credit of socialist countries is excellent.

I am very proud of the Cuban people and proud, indeed, of my warm personal friendship with President Fidel Castro. He is a world revolutionary leader and he is affecting the future of the human race. On the inside of a gift package he gave me on March 22, 1969 (shortly after the assassination attempt on us) he wrote "A maestro magnifico amigo Lamb, muy fraternalmente, Fidel Castro." I have carried on a correspondence with him and one letter he wrote me in 1975 graces my office wall. I put it atop a letter from our disgraced President Richard Nixon. It reads in part,

> My Esteemed Friend Lamb:
>
> In the efforts toward development of our economy and what we are doing, at least so it seems to me, and I remember discussing in our conversations, is the problem of scientific direction. This you so enthusiastically have tried to introduce into our activities and this has great importance. I had occasion to express to you something of what we have done in this respect and I thank you very much for the initiatives that you have taken in this direction. We have instructed our comrades in charge of the development of mechanization of agriculture to give all the necessary attention to the conferences that will take place in Mexico. I hope that our experts and specialists draw from these conferences every possible good result and benefits.
>
> I would like to reiterate to you and to Priscilla that you have our invitation to visit our country more frequently. You know the weather and climate and you are also familiar with the friendly spirit of our people towards those friends who are able to understand our historic efforts.

The story of such a friendship doesn't end—it blossoms with each new day's problems, failures and triumphs.

Castro spoke in the Karl Marx Theater in Havana on April 19, 1976—fifteen years after the Bay of Pigs. He reviewed the new constitution and other accomplishments and said, "There is no perfect human work, including, of course, revolutions, which are made by men with all their limitations. Humanity's march toward the future must necessarily include sorrowful experiences, but the future belongs to principles, to revolutionary solidarity among peoples, to socialism, to Marxism-Leninism, and to internationalism."

# CHAPTER
# XX

~~~~~~~~~~~~~~~~~~~~~~~~~~~~~~~~~~

# Toward the Sharing Society

I am a part of nature, and therefore, my best friends are naturalists. They are brutally frank in telling me what I am. A sobering thought: When I lift my boot from the forest floor, I may have uncovered as many as a million other living things. Maybe I have stamped the life out of a few thousand of them, perhaps depriving others, like the larger insects, of their food supply. I, man, a predator, affect the spiders, the lizards, the birds, right up to myself—man.

With ingenuity and gun, man has bested all other animals. Having reached such a pinnacle, he now can tame or destroy his own species. The task is made easier when he invents an ideology. He can even talk about the "dignity of man" and shout his affirmative pro-humanist approach. Arabs fight Jews, Muslims battle Christians—wars of the ages continue. Protestants and Catholics murder each other in Northern Ireland—over philosophical differences. Decent instincts die, and man's posture wanes in the cycle of nature.

When we travel into the woods, we notice our similarities to other creatures—the same need for food and shelter and attunement to the environment. It is a refreshing, rewarding experience for a human. Lungs and thought patterns are cleared in this relationship with Nature. America's largest rodent, the beaver, is the only mammal, other than man, able to alter its environment to suit its needs. It builds dams and canals, mostly while predators are off-guard, at dusk and dawn. It pursues fish and goodies for its family. But the earth's master predator steps in and destroys even the beaver's habitat. As the entire beaver species becomes endangered, man develops another condominium or golf course and sings praises to his own accomplishments. He may claim it as a progressive step forward. But is it progress or retrogression? Man's technological skill in deveolping nuclear weaponry permits him to lay waste the crust of our entire planet. Is this the ultimate in human progress? Is it too late in history to get back on course and make human life truly constructive and meaningful?

Thanks to nutrition, medicine, and gathering knowledge, our modern generation is several inches taller than our ancestors of colonial days. Our surrounding neighbors of the planet haven't had such a chance to survive. Trees and flowers from the lowlands of Georgia to Nevada's high Sierras have given way to man's industrialized and polluted urban centers. People continue to pour into the cities; we cling to the frontier mentality that considers land to exist only for human exploitation.

We argue in Congress and environmental circles whether we'll permit "clear cutting" in forests, without much consideration of the devastating consequences. Strip mining continues to be one of our national disgraces, while mining companies lobby to pursue profits. We can almost compute what's left on the planet—each leaf in the forest, each grain of sand on the beach.

Now we realize that uncontrolled bulldozer development is not a sign of growth but a mark of a decaying society. How fortunate that Barry Commoner, Buckminister Fuller, Barbara Ward, Linus Pauling, René Dubois, Maurice Strong of Canada, and other environmentalists came along and gave us pause to take stock of our dwindling resources.

It's comforting that Americans are returning to the out-doors. To me, life in the open is almost the ultimate joy. People are hiking, boating, golfing, jogging, swimming, tour-ing, and playing more in groups. On the other hand, it is sad to see so many of us who merely watch the best of each class, the professionals, on television. Our organized recreational activities become less participation and more observation. I'd like nothing better than to inspire mankind in the plain art of walking.

The unplanned nature of our growth produces problems. Farmers become part of the suburban sprawl and land speculators grow rich in dollars. We're frightened of the future. People around the world find it desirable to invest in a piece of real estate just in case, but they've sold the old homestead and taken their capital gains. We suspect that our periods of boom will be followed by bust, so we live for today, knowing well enough that our lives may be headed for a really rugged, painful future.

Man discovered a new haven by flying away from this biospheric arena, the planet earth. He can run, but he can't hide. Our astronauts blazed a trail and found they must return to face the limits of this existence that mortal man has enjoyed for hundreds of millennia. As man has de-stroyed other living things, he has fouled and corrupted his own nest with pollutants. We're all in it with our philosophy of "Live it up and let tomorrow's generations deal with our mistakes." We've used up the resources, and we'll leave a heritage of gas fumes and waste.

What can possibly hold back all these prosperous modern people who "seek only happiness" for themselves and their families? As Barbara Ward and René Dubois suggest in *Only One Earth,* man enjoys the experience of comfort, security, joyful participation, mental vigor, intellectual dis-covery, poetic insights, bodily and mental rest, and most of all, hope. He may have hopes and dreams, but in actual life he is burdened with backbreaking labor, a prey to wars and famines and deadly disease.

It is normal to long for joy, comfort, and security. At the

end stands death, a termination of all his known activities on earth. He reacts violently against fear of the unknown. He suffers anguish about a life hereafter—such is his uncertain condition. How much better if he could spend his efforts on building a responsive and caring society.

Henry Thoreau escaped from his fellows and returned to his Walden Pond. In our time Scott Nearing, ousted from the faculties of the University of Pennsylvania and the University of Toledo for "communist" teaching, returned to the natural life in the Maine woods. (I campaigned against his being fired in the hysterical times of the Depression.) The "patriotic" fringe of Toledo's academic and industrial society ostracized him and barred his efforts to speak out. Efforts were made to keep his manuscripts from being accepted by publishers. He was considered a dangerous radical in the 1930s, but we who knew him loved him. In 1932 he and his wife, Helen, bought a woefully rundown farm in the Green Mountains of New England for a couple of hundred dollars. They chose to stay in the United States and right wrongs rather than emigrate to friendlier countries.

The Nearings had doubts about the rickety social order, as did many of their confused fellow professionals. But they decided to do something about it. They accepted life in the natural setting of the back woods for "economic, hygienic, and social reasons," as Scott Nearing puts it. They have liberated and disassociated themselves from what they felt was an era of exploitation and enslavement. They have not sought the accumulation of profit nor the plunder of the planet. A half century ago they were among the very first of America's practicing environmentalists. They built with their own hands sturdy houses, barns, and gardens of vegetables, fruits, and flowers. They resolved to replace worry, fear, and hate with "serenity, purpose, and at-one-ness." Today thousands of curious visitors stop to see for themselves the Nearings' simple, healthful existence.

The retirement of the Nearings—the abandonment of the grime and violence of the cities—is not an option available to most of us. Millions of urban dwellers would like to forget the overcrowded ghettoes. Conditions have worsened. The rich have grown richer; vast fortunes in oil and autos have become larger. We are also conscious that in the capitalist world hundreds of millions of our fellow human beings go to bed hungry every night. Social programs decrease and military expenses escalate. Employment difficulties and uncertainties have grown despite technological improvements and the welfare programs of the capitalist state. In our nation technology is not made a servant of the state.

Imperialist nations have lost their colonies. Through violent or peaceful techniques, vast segments of the world's population have achieved planned socialist economies. Yet in our profit-oriented society we cling to our hostilities and our confusions. Americans, fragmented into many conflicting social segments and political jurisdictions, may be slow to recognize that environmental issues transcend man-made political boundaries. Every clean-up effort, even stopping the dumping of waste into the lakes, has been fought by some powerful trade association claiming that reform meant "the loss of jobs." In the battles between the giant corporate oil drillers and those who would conserve resources, free enterprisers chalked up their victories. They worked their ways with congressmen who listened.

Our preaching generalizations about human rights and spiritual values seldom take into account certain inherent dangers. The economics of nationalism block our path to the future. Yet commonality and equality of men everywhere are sufficient goals as we approach a new century. Naturally, we will become quite a different breed than exists in our current society.

We can be sure that unless the blacks and the other oppressed people of the world secure actual social and economic justice, there will be bloody, effective change. Equality and sharing are the two big issues of the coming years. We're sophisticated, experienced, and knowledgeable enough to know that change there will be—maybe communist, maybe socialist, maybe a mixture with capitalism. Major problems will not be corrected by any system of voluntarism or by the whim of the privileged. The people of the world do not want a handout. Those nations which plan and effectively control will obtain a degree of social justice. The pace of change in the promised land quickens. We're headed toward the Sharing Society.

# CHAPTER
# XXI

∿∿∿∿∿∿∿∿∿∿∿∿∿∿∿∿∿∿∿∿∿∿

# Outreach

Why would anyone ever want to leave Sentinel Point, my pleasant home and garden overlooking the Maumee River, twelve miles outside Toledo, Ohio? Locks of the Miami and Erie Canal, completed in 1835, lie below us, their gates no longer emptying water and barge traffic into the historic Maumee. Giant oaks, cedars, and maples shelter the restful retreat. Imagine such a homesite for enjoying life and rest in the out-of-doors.

There is delightful beauty in the antiques, art collections, and library within. It is from this vantage point that I observe the world. Days on this planet are always too short to have really discovered myself or my surroundings. While here on this planet I may not have found the light, but I have certainly emerged from the dark. I discovered growth —that the beauty of the budding flower of life is surpassed only by its full blossom.

Over the ages men established their habitat on ridges, preferring to live on the sides of lakes and streams. So it must have been when we moved to Sentinel Point. Exhumed ashes show that Indians, the Native Americans, had their residence here for more than eight thousand years. Local historians say that the French, under the explorer, LaSalle, settled at Fort Miami, now Maumee City, as early as 1680. Local boastful boosters claim that our predecessors antedated the settlement of Detroit by three years.

Later the Indian tribes, especially the Ottawas and Miamis, were induced to join the British in our Revolutionary war. The Indians were glad to square off against the expansionist American colonists. Thus it was that the English troopers with the enthusiastic support of the natives faced Commander William Henry Harrison's soldiers at Fort Meigs. Hundreds of the participants were slaughtered near our doorstep in a battle known as Dudley's Massacre. Cannons on our homesite killed the American defenders of the fort across the river. The Americans were called "defenders" because for the moment they had possession. Indians had been dispossessed from their lands by firearms and fire water.

French, British, and Americans were impartial in one aspect—they all wanted to strip the Indians of their land. The fight over their loot would come later. As for William Henry Harrison, he went on to become president of the United States. We excavate today and we find Indian skulls, British skulls, and American skulls piled in common pits. It is to this ground, hallowed or sullied by warriors, that my ashes will return to the eternal cycle of nature.

Our town of Maumee, now a bedroom suburb of Toledo, is a beautiful community, in spite of housing developments and shopping-center modernity. Wolcott House, a local history museum, houses Indian lore such as bows, arrows, and the invaders' flintlock guns. It demands the almost constant attention and vigilance of Prudence Lamb. It attracts visitors from the world over, as well as busloads of the local school gentry. On the north side of our home lies the House of Six Pillars, where the American novelist Theodore Dreiser lived while he was a reporter for the *Toledo Blade*. Here in 1900 he wrote *Sister Carrie*.

We've had unusual as well as unexciting neighbors. To our south, at 622 River Road, lived Bill and Betty Warren.

He sold insurance for Northwestern Mutual Life Insurance Company. After a stormy five years of marriage they were divorced in 1943. She then married a plodding politician from Grand Rapids, Michigan, named Gerald R. Ford, who in due course was appointed president of the United States by a disgraced Richard M. Nixon. In an earlier day Morrison R. Waite, the seventh (and probably the worst) Chief Justice of the United States Supreme Court, lived in our town during his lackluster career as a local lawyer. He was the seventh person asked to take the post. Today his descendants are proud of his occupancy of the prestigious position. The Toledo enthusiasts have dedicated a high school and other institutions to his sacred memory—such is our hunger for identification with fame.

The telephone rings. I am asked to appear on Bill Walker's TV program, "Confrontation," in Toronto—and face cross-examination by Quebec separatists, tariff protectionists, and others unhappy with Canadian-American relations.

"After all, you were on Pierre Burton's program advocating a merger of the two countries—do you still push for joining the two peoples?" There will be more telephone calls—and more challenging, exhausting trips.

Off to the office. First to arrive, last to leave. I have a dozen more active American corporations in banking, broadcasting, and manufacturing. All require attention. First things first: I must concentrate on recruiting competent management people able to reorganize and simplify the corporate structure. I love the out-of-doors, but I admit that a successful business deal is also fun—good management offers big rewards. How to make the role of administrator more creative and challenging? After all, it is in the industrial-financial world that we find the real action. It is, of course, paradoxical, this pursuit of private profits while working for a more rational and sharing society. The social activist always faces this bitter choice as long as he lives in the private-profit world.

It's curious how we work, travel, and even endure tensions and hardships so that we may enjoy recreation. I'm no workaholic, and I like to delegate responsibility. But it's hard for me to see the difference between work and play. Labor and activity become the gist of life. I like to look back on thousands of experiences, amusing or serious, as so many footnotes in life.

We live in times when society is being revolutionized through technology—television, computers, and satellites. National and state lines, those symbols of antiquity, still get in the way, raising man-made barriers against worldwide interchange. Nationalism protects the *status quo*. Against such a backdrop those who are dedicated to bringing about a change to internationalism become the true heroes of our time. A century or two from now historians may laugh that we should have taken ourselves so seriously, even that we should have expected the survival of an unjust, unresponsive political-social system as that in twentieth-century America. How will the story be told—what will our libraries record, and how will our successors look upon our current mores? Let us campaign to get Americans to recognize the need for amendment or abandonment of our weird efforts to impose our economic or social will upon the rest of the globe.

The further the human race retreats from social planning and control and the tighter we cling to the unrestrained national action, the closer we approach collapse. We fool ourselves about our individual freedoms. Freedoms exist only within the perimeters of a secure social order. As we know too well, voluntarism, whether of wages, prices, or compliance with standards of conduct, just isn't enough.

I have been accused of being a communist throughout my life. I didn't mind, because the word became almost a synonym for a more idealistic society. As a matter of record, I have never been a member of that party. However, I am glad to state that I am totally in favor of the creation of a sharing and participating society.

Societal forms come and go. In the days ahead we will have a more crowded planet, and we'll require more restrictions upon our individual actions. We may even be able to achieve a partially planned, that is, a mixed, economy by political rather than military means. But violence will become the necessary way if we who live in the United States fail to give up a few elements of our individual and collective status. At this stage of history a foreign policy limited to anti-Russianism is obviously short-sighted, shallow, and self-defeating. Better that we recognize our interdependence and open the gates to trade and exchange with everyone.

One snowy day, November 1, 1977, in Moscow, I sat in the Kremlin listening to the report of President Leonid Brezhnev. An enthusiastic audience had traveled from 132 nations to celebrate the sixtieth anniversary of the October Revolution. Sixty years that changed the world! These were the people who brought to mankind its first planned society.

The communist leaders spoke of détente and peaceful coexistence and healthy competition among nations, irrespective of political systems. Enthusiastic speakers boasted of their accomplishments and pleaded for an easing of tensions, limitation of nuclear arms, and increased trade. While I wondered about actual developments, my mind went back over those sixty years, years of turmoil and war. Soviet Russia had been invaded and boycotted, but it had never been beaten. Here was the leadership, still talking about peace and détente.

Over the last several decades I have made almost a score of trips to the Soviet Union. Now I look around the Kremlin's Great Hall at the cheering delegates. Clearly, tremendous progress has been made during the eighteen months since my last visit. But mere growth isn't all good—Soviet highways are becoming polluted and cluttered with autos and trucks as the nation becomes industrialized.

Consumer goods are more abundant, new stores are opening, and social services and housing are all expanding at a remarkable pace. Jobs are available, and adequate health care and schooling are guaranteed. I'll admit, too, that as a banker, I find it a strange experience to watch a society where inflation and unemployment are no longer crushing problems. Like every American, I ask myself if our political systems are compatible with each other.

My own America has done so much by way of military manipulation, boycott, and discriminatory restriction, all designed to prevent the Soviet society from getting on its feet.

Yet in the recent past the Soviet economy has displaced that of the United States in so many ways. It has unexploited resources, and it is introducing the technological advances to achieve leadership in mining and manufacturing.

It's not easy for Americans to admit that our resources are vanishing or that we are now almost totally dependent upon other nations for these essentials. It becomes important that we in America make a solemn self-appraisal. It is time to be concerned over our own dilemmas or embarrassed by the confusions that exist among our capitalist economists.

Each day we ask ourselves, will the United States lower taxes to make business and jobs, impose taxes to expand social services, increase or lower the money supply, adopt controls of wages and prices, or will our Congress merely talk nonsense about the inviolability of our unplanned free-enterprise system? Will those wretched oil lobbies continue to govern our country?

As an official guest of the Soviet Union, I attended many receptions, toured nearby farms, visited the faculty and students at the universities, and interviewed several of the top Soviet leaders. A long-time friend of mine, Yuri Bobrakov, head of the economics section of the Institute for U.S.A–Canadian Affairs, has frequently entertained me at dinner in his home. He told me that the Soviet Union had just made a decision. They were going to buy enormous amounts of grain from the United States—not from Canada, Australia, or the Argentine, but from the United States.

Although Soviet crops had been reasonably good, they had recently installed additional grain-storage bins around the country, and they could lay in a larger supply of wheat and corn for the future. He told me frankly that an element of political motivation lay behind the decision. They believed that purchase of surplus American grain would improve the atmosphere, strengthen the willingness of the American wheat growers to understand the possibilities of the Soviet market, and ease the general tensions between our countries.

On my return to the United States I made the announcement to the various wire services, and although the secretary of commerce denied my report, the price of American grain within the next few days went up more than twenty-five cents a bushel and added hundreds of millions of dollars to the depressed income of the American farmers.

Ten days later the Soviet Union announced officially that it would purchase in excess of eighteen million additional tons of corn and wheat in the United States. The American farmers were elated: their prices had risen and national surpluses had been eliminated. What did it matter that when the Soviets have surpluses, they will be shipped to the Third World?

CHAPTER

# XXII

~~~~~~~~~~~~~~~~~~~~~~~~~~~~~~~~~~~~~~~~~~~

# Conference or Confrontation

That maverick Robert Maynard Hutchins influenced many lives. He showed us the significance of dialogue. From the time I was one of his students and he the dean of the Yale Law School, we had outrageously noisy arguments. Through our long, more subdued but argumentative association we enjoyed at the Center for the Study of Democratic Institutions at Santa Barbara, California, my respect for the innovative educator grew.

Hutchins was always the obstreperous, witty, and charming university chancellor and the classic advocate of free thought. He looked on the university and its development, not as a collection of books or students, but as a "community of scholars"—a place where free men could think and speak freely. He relished the quarrel itself. He was always questioning; there were no final answers. Even as he probed the system, he could shake the blue-ribbon tycoons, like the John Rockefellers, Cyrus Eatons, Chester Carlsons, William Bentons, and others, out of their money. He pursued studies and projects that examined and often criticized the preferred status of the wealthy.

242 THE SHARING SOCIETY

Hutchins and I did not agree on many matters, especially physical exercise. His beautiful classic features suffered no ill effects from his disdain of outdoor activities. The eternal doubter, he took many forward-looking positive steps as he produced highly constructive studies to further a rule of law for a distraught world. He supervised dozens of drafts of a new American constitution. His studies of a new world constitution seemed to have been undertaken amid a wilderness of disinterest.

We had many discussions on the true meaning of democracy. He emphasized its political base; I, its economic base. Although I recognized the basic urge for individual freedoms, we seemed to disagree on the need for the preeminence of the state, at least during the transitional stage to collectivism—the basic need of the state to retain its dominance against the counterrevolutionists. Hutchins, like our mutual friend Justice William O. Douglas, felt that the U.S. Constitution existed for the primary purpose of protecting the individual from the excesses of the state. I emphasized the affirmative obligations of the state to meet the basic needs of its people. We envied his witty speeches and provocative writings. He frequently summed up his own lust for life and the pursuit of the free spirit as he quoted Walt Whitman's lines: "Solitarily, singing in the West, I strike up for a new world." In 1951 he pushed that very statement as the motto for the University of Chicago.

The pace of our civilization is not confined to our educational system, or to the learning programs practiced or preached by pedagogues. I have always had a passionate respect for the libraries of the world. I cherish the parks and the open spaces, but I agree with Hutchins that the great books, the custodians of human knowledge, are a principal way for anyone to make life fuller.

There are many radical changes scheduled for our future. It's good that women are coming more prepared to take their place in the job market of our transitional society. Our young accept the dignity of their work contribution. Work-study programs are becoming a part of the educational process. No matter whether the means of production are

publicly or privately owned, the well-informed builder and
the imaginative doer will become society's heroes. The educational halls are charged with developing these qualities.

We all spend too much time trying to be number one.
But not everyone wants to be or can become the champion.
Abraham Lincoln ran unsuccessfully for political office
many times. I find it a wholesome and humbling experience
to think of the many areas where I failed to reach the peak.
Unlike Lincoln, I never desired to cling to any political
career long enough to win the big one. I won election statewide only when I ran for Ohio delegate-at-large to the Democratic National Convention. I had the help of the local
political machine, so my victory was not much of an achievement. I was a successful, but obviously not the nation's
greatest, civil-liberties, corporation, and labor lawyer. I had
acquired a sizable fortune but had never aspired to or come
close to achieving the distinction of being the richest American. Come to think of it, I even get second billing when my
name is perpetuated among my progeny. Ten nephews and
grandchildren have been stuck with the name *Edward,* but
each tucks my name away in the middle, and it never quite
makes first place.

Even though it's the only career open in many communities, political job-seeking isn't particularly appetizing to
many of us.

Too slowly I realized that service to others could become
the supreme career. I wanted to build bridges among men
and among nations. Possibly the only "first" that I have
ever earned in this world may be my devotion to the international world organization. I really hope that each of us
can be "first" in his dedication to building a unified and
organized world community.

My contribution to the permanent display in the United
Nations building honoring the International Women's Year
was strangely important to me—it was said to be the first
time the UN accepted such a gift from a private citizen.
All the medals, all the razzle-dazzle, all the prestige and
honors can go to the politicians out front so long as we gain
support for the world organization. What greater glory can

each of us have than to lay a brick in the foundation of the home of mankind?

People who write letters to the editors live longer. They are vital and interested. In their local efforts they participate in life. So do the noisy ones at town and legislative meetings, and so do those who march and demonstrate. It's inspiring to see young protestors at the nuclear plants. They are raising questions about our homeland's environment. They are the freedom fighters of our times. When all is said and done, there is a place in the battle lines for everyone. Among the greatest contributors to the welfare of mankind are the unsung heroes in the background who build the support organizations, the organizers of the rallies, the toilers in the fields, and yes, even the fundraisers for the causes.

From my earliest days I cast my lot with the reformers, radicals, and muckrakers. Other men may say that if they had their lives to live over, they would do things differently. Not I. This worldly adventure, the controversy, the self-improvement are plain fun. But they are productive only when one moves beyond self and becomes a part of one's society.

How do we get personally involved in affairs of government, especially matters of international or foreign concern? Interests of local importance, such as paving the street near our front porch or building the local sewage system usually absorb our attention. We tend to leave participation in worldly affairs to a small elitist group of foreign-policy "experts." Yet our daily lives are saturated with the failures of national governments to settle global problems.

Martin Luther King gave a sermon on April 3, 1968. He had gone to the mountaintop, he said. "I have looked over and I have seen the promised land."

I've seen the birth of the League of Nations, as well as that of the United Nations. These vital institutions and systems were steps forward. Mankind, interdependent, ever more sophisticated and less jingoistic, is headed toward a better world. Tomorrow there will be stronger and more effective international structures. Finally, we'll look out the window and see the exchange and interplay and the realization of our dreams. We will move to the promised land of brotherhood and common sense.

We have learned that whatever we do affects the other occupants of this globe. We are discovering our planet's place in the universe, and we're discovering mankind's role within the earthly orbit. Already remarkable in so many ways, the human being will learn how to live in a rational and responsive community. As national and social borders wane, our future will move on the upbeat into a society in which we treat each member in fairness.

One day, though I know not when that will be, our narrow nationalism, our religious biogtry, our emphasis upon selfish personal success, as opposed to pride in communal achievement, our social and nationalistic prejudices, will seem as primitive and outdated as cave-dwellers.

# CHAPTER
# XXIII

~~~~~~~~~~~~~~~~~~~~~~~~~~~~~~~~~~~~

# Tomorrow

Our forefathers pictured the universe as an enormous cage with mankind as its center. Cage or no cage, man's species proliferated. He managed to control about everything on this planet—except his relationship with his fellowmen. Yet for a variety of reasons, many felt that war and self-destruction were built into animal-man's future. There were war heroes galore, but there were also men and women who walked a different pathway—beautiful people who looked for ways to an orderly world government. The footnotes of history will duly record these worthy humans. The builders of bridges of friendship may never be honored like the kings, generals, and presidents who led invasions and directed mass slaughters. In sum, isn't the central theme of man's existence founded upon the individual's adaptability and responsibility to his community?

Early Americans put their new society together and swore their commitment to freedom and a humane social order. Our revolutionary forebears adopted guidelines of conduct and philosophically sought to establish ethical and moral standards. In today's "free society" we claim not only the right to believe, but the right to disbelieve. Our freedoms are provincial. The "freedoms" we talk about today are largely confined within the borders of the United States. We say we have "rights" and freedoms because we have a U.S. Constitution. Yet the rights of persons outside our borders are equally basic—indeed, they are the universal rights of mankind. Now we also recognize our interdependence with others. Irrespective of our differing beliefs or structures and after eons of fighting, we have finally begun a pragmatic search for a sane and safe society—an organized world institution.

Today we find ourselves members of the club of humanity four billion strong and growing. But we're fragmented into many cliques and nation-states. A great many of us started our lives by waving the flag of our country, right or wrong. Shortly, we discovered that nationality itself might be our biggest problem. So we asked ourselves bigger and more basic questions—what can we do personally to work for a rational society, possibly help build a house for humanity, an organized headquarters to govern and serve *all* the peoples of the world?

We, the mighty and the meek, will continue to hope for peace and stability. Sometimes optimistic and sometimes desperate, our confidence rises and falls in the manner of the Dow-Jones stock averages. Gyrations in the scales only measure problems; they don't solve the issues revolving around our daily frustrations and disillusionments. The reality of existence and even our perspective is often blurred because we are inclined to focus attention on local rather than global affairs. We see disparities of wealth and poverty so close to home and we notice the litter in our ghettoes. We need more than our leaders' lofty speeches and pious pleas for peace. When we hear our president screaming for "national security," the record sounds dull, repetitious, and ridiculous. We ask ourselves a thousand times if there isn't a better way, a constructive method of helping to organize an orderly and responsive world government.

We social activists wear out our lungs shouting that surplus armaments are useless. All the world knows that we overstock conventional and nuclear weapons. Many other nations do likewise. Right-wing and paid lobbyist groups utter platitudinous nonsense about curbing the arms race. It is with such a backdrop that many leaders of our commercial community are still willing to join with others to urge that we take advantage of the presently favorable conditions for terminating the senseless arms race.

The SALT talks between the superpowers got bogged down by the reactionary politicians, but each day we all realized the absolute necessity for action. We can adopt practical programs designed to equalize the economic and social welfare of the planet's peoples. There are obstacles, but it is within our power to build an ordered international community in which future issues will be addressed and settled by conference and multinational action.

There are those who boast of our national "superiority" and rationalize our national actions. It becomes pertinent to ask why people shouldn't worry more about their everyday world while the condition of the habitat is so rapidly deteriorating. Auto fumes bury us; sewage drowns us. Growth and expansion are beginning to reach limits. We have abused our resources, and now all we have left is a dirty, noisy, tense, exhausted world. It's about time we caught hold of our globe—if only to prolong the life of our species.

Let us go back a few short hundred years in the Western world to study our present system of law and order. At Runnymede on Monday, June 15, 1215, King John agreed to the terms of the Magna Carta, setting up the charter of English liberties, an event of vast political and legal significance. Seven hundred and thirty years later, on October 24, 1945, the United Nations Charter was signed in San Francisco. The United Nations system came to be considered the offspring of man's scientific, technological, and intellectual accomplishments. It is the organization primarily geared to the external world and to solving man's physical and mental needs and development.

Only five years later the superpowers were again hellbent on bankrupting and destroying themselves by "defense spending." They claimed to be protecting themselves from their former allies—and a new threat of communism. The United States spent billions defending itself against China and Russia. Nuclear weaponry, which could despoil the land, skies, and seas, became the threat, the balance wheel among the giants.

Americans, who talk so much about democracy, placed in the finger of one man the power to destroy the world! The rest of the world wasn't sympathetic to superpower domination. They sensed our proclivity for meddling in the affairs of other nations. The cartels in various raw materials, including oil, nickel, coffee, copper, and foodstuffs were also beginning to show that the United States was dependent on other nations. We gave political, financial, and military aid only to our "friends." We boycotted Cuba, the Soviet Union, and the socialist nations in the Far and Middle East. Through it all, the underdeveloped but rich-in-resources third and fourth worlds began to emerge as political factors. A few conservative Americans, like Barry Goldwater and Richard Nixon, still believed that their free-enterprise system could operate under a nuclear umbrella—and survive forever. It was a case where our technology and market dominance blinded us to our shortcomings.

Three-quarters of the world's population, hungry, unorganized, and deprived, now saw the opportunity to come together in one institution. Like the poor of all ages, they were not inclined to oblige, submit, or even watch the affluent nations flaunt their wealth. The one-nation, one-vote concept gave them power and muscle. In Asia, Latin America, and Africa economic and social dislocation were prolonged by our military and commercial maneuvering. Pious words about nonviolence became meaningless. Preachments about "democracy," "human rights," or America's "security" seemed ridiculous. Presidential interpretations of our right to intervene in the affairs of other nations to protect such ideological rights were unappreciated—a hypocritical exercise in futility.

The inspiring opening words of the Preamble to the Charter of the United Nations begins, "We the peoples."

Not presidents, senators, generals, or ambassadors, but peoples. America, host to the birth of the United Nations, has been especially slow in accepting the world organization. But experience develops an interest in its possibilities—there have been many exciting accomplishments. New working agencies were set up to attack the problems of food, environment, and education. With more knowledge of its work and achievements, a vast majority of humanity is pressing aggressively for a truly effective world institution.

It is an international body, not the agency of any single nation. It exists for the benefit of tens of millions of our fellows around the globe. Each person who helps build such an institution is making a significant contribution to his times. At first we thought of the United Nations as a peacekeeping instrument. It expanded its horizons, and we watched the dream unfold. More and more people of the world became builders and supporters. There were carping critics and detractors, but through it all there was being forged a truly important human institution.

The world asked itself, "If not the United Nations, what is the alternative?" Future peace cannot be achieved if the U.N. is an instrument for domination by a clique of the big industrialized states. If all humanity and all states are interdependent, then isn't this the place to look for the answers to common problems? The work of the U.N.'s great agencies, like the World Food Organization, the World Health Organization, the International Labor Organization, the United Nations Development Program, UNESCO, UNICEF, the World Bank, the International Monetary Fund, and a dozen other agencies, began to bring about organized rational global systems. At last we had found a forum, a common table for all peoples to sit down together and carry on rational negotiation.

Producing nations sit down with consumer nations. Rich and poor nations confer to discuss tariffs and trade. The United Nations has ushered in a new, revolutionary and sane era. Its remarkable accomplishments need to be brought to the attention of more peoples.

I am a member of various United Nations–support organizations. I have appeared several times before congressional committees urging increased congressional appropriations for the U.N. I write letters, and I make speeches. I help campus, business, and labor groups tour the United Nations. There they learn and study the U.N. activities in New York City, in Geneva, and throughout the world. Exposure to the work of the international body presents exciting challenges. United States senators and high school seniors are all affected by seeing and understanding the extent of international cooperation. It's a pleasure to see the pilgrims from around the world who proudly visit the great edifice in New York City.

American ambassadors to the United Nations are the highest-ranking officers in our diplomatic service. Prestigious, competent men and women find themselves carrying out strict instructions of the president and the State Department. The delegates have precious little to do with policy. I remember having breakfast one morning with Paul Hoffman, then director of the United Nations Development Program (UNDP), and our Ambassador to the U.N., Adlai Stevenson. It was shortly after the Bay of Pigs fiasco in April of 1961. Stevenson admitted that he had told the U.N. Security Council a blatant falsehood. He had said that the planes attacking the shores of Cuba and carrying Cuban emblems were "rebel" forces. Hoffman said that he suspected, as did many of us, that the planes were merely U.S. planes repainted and piloted by American forces. It was a degrading chore for Stevenson, and he let us know that he was terribly upset at having to follow diplomatic instruction by lying. He was on the point of resigning. He contemplated the pleasant prospect of being on the outside of government, where he would have a touch of independence and the hope of influencing policy makers. What a better world organization we would have had if Stevenson had been the American secretary of state.

There were few other outstanding American ambassadors to the United Nations until a remarkable Andrew Young came along. His discerning and daring comments presented a better picture of America to the rest of the world.

In tomorrow's world we won't stop with a five-year plan. We'll reach out into the newer, wider term spans. We will contemplate what will happen regarding democracy, resources, the climate, and the human condition. As we take a bird's-eye view of the United Nations system, with its present dozen and a half specialized agencies and major programs like a United Nations University, we realize that an impressive start has been made toward a true world system of diagnosis, monitoring, and warning. It becomes the manager of our global human affairs. In our world these UN agencies rationalize the whole human condition. As we reach into outer space and understand our relations with the sun, we begin to encompass the atmosphere and the biosphere and the wherefores of the world climate. Man begins to understand the seas and the oceans, the continents and their subdivisions, and their resources right down (or up) to our individual cosmos. At no time in history has man had such an opportunity to make decisions affecting his own destiny. It is a time for searching!

Isn't it reasonable that we search for ways to improve the total condition and achieve the reality of a happy, secure existence for all those blessed with the miracle of human life? Finally, we ask ourselves if there is any real need in today's world for morality in government and business. We will expect a higher standard of conduct to be required in a society not motivated by profit.

Thus, we must place the whole evolution of the human species in new perspective. This is the principal challenge of our times. A United Nations system becomes not just a collection of good intentions nor a list of moral or religious precepts. It becomes our roadway to the future!

# CHAPTER
# XXIV

~~~~~~~~~~~~~~~~~~~~~~~~~~~~~~

# Toward Human Survival

In the last analysis, each of us is motivated by the economic consequences of his acts. Like all men everywhere, I want food, housing, work, and recreation. But it seems that when armament superiority is reached, individuals and nations want to own everything in sight: "It's mine, all mine." A social struggle ensues over whether ownership is to be public or private. In this time of nuclear overkill, no nation has superiority.

All men, whether in America or in Africa or in Asia, have a bigger right: the right to survive. Humans, all humans, have the same right.

Along the way we learn that the administration of natural and human resources determines the success of every human institution. We discover the critical role of management.

Americans consume 40 percent of the world's resources. The planet's other people struggle for what's left. This condition of inequality cannot and will not continue. Revolution, violent or nonviolent, will determine our collective destiny. A new system will emerge. The real problem isn't the *form* of the new societal structure. Call it by any name

—socialism, communism, or planned economy—we're going to have a more equitable, a more sharing and representative system. Such a democratic order will exist not to suppress the many or enrich the few. It will distribute the earth's abundance to all humanity.

Nation-states are outmoded. We're realizing our interdependence one with one another. Petroleum, minerals, and even technology are to be found in the Middle or the Far East. Our Midwest is still in the middle of America as we become a have-not nation. Our only hope is that a universal, international organization will devote its efforts against the frightening realities of hunger, ignorance, mediocrity, and sham. We come to the belief that only under such a charter of mankind's liberties can individualism be nurtured. Not abundance for just those north of the equator, not for only those born in the United States, but for all mankind. When man is placed in a proper role in this complex external environment, each concerned human being becomes significant.

In proposing a U.N. University, Secretary General U Thant often suggested that such a world institution could create a bridge where educators might assemble. They would make available the most advanced knowledge to all members of the human society. In such a world university, the U.N.'s political world would be constantly exposed to the thinking of academic circles on all major aspects of the human condition. It would offer a cross-fertilization of knowledge—the great adventure in human evolution.

Even businessmen, including those in the oft-maligned multinational corporations, might one day assemble and deliberate in its halls. It could become the clearing house for gathering systematic information about the thinking, data, diagnoses, and proposed actions of the U.N. system.

The institution will house headquarters for services covering international trade and economic contacts. Already through the World Bank and other international financing institutions, we're discovering, in both the developing and the industrialized worlds, that the great medium exists for furthering human trade relationships. I even urge the most conservative groups, interested in the *status quo,* to recognize this role of the U.N. in bringing stability to the world. It will be possible to establish guidelines for foreign investment and economic development. Religious groups, non-governmental organizations, and all other human institutions established within our society can speak out on the issue. They will want to make a commitment to this evolving world instrumentality.

Students seeking to make a contribution to society may achieve a certain optimism about the fate of our planet when they realize the full extent of the intergovernmental cooperation already existing in the United Nations. Teachers in international affairs, lecturing to the faculties of medicine, ecology, social studies, or trade, must be pleased as they become aware of the work undertaken by the U.N. institutional system. A vast amount of knowledge and experience is already available to the students who seek global information. Worldwide computerization is functioning in various fields, including outer space and ocean matters, nutrition, population, children, and old age, where vast research studies are available. This material needs translating into current and popular books and guides. Millions of these publications are already moving worldwide. The collection, analysis, and dissemination of information adds up to tremendous progress in human affairs.

I grow increasingly proud of my allegiance to the United Nations. Since it is the only institution that represents all mankind, I am more inclined to back its decisions "right or wrong." A master of ceremonies at a United Nations Association conference once flatteringly introduced me as "the man in the private sector who has done the most to build a constituency of support in America for the United Nations." How I wish it were true!

Actually, there are dozens of American organizations dedicated to the support of the United Nations. There are almost two hundred local units aligned within the Council of Organizations of the United Nations Association—U.S.A. Probably the most influential support body in the entire United Nations area is the group known as the Non-

Governmental Organizations (NGO). I have been active in nearly every group trying to advance the work of the United Nations. I may have the only private person's pass (number 957) to the United Nations building.

More and more I try to focus my financial aid to those activities supportive of the world community. I believe that institutions dealing in education and health care should be actively supported by their government. My favorite contributions are those which help the model U.N. conferences on the campuses, various internship and research programs, tours and seminars at the U.N., the advancement of aid to the emerging countries throughout the world, and the programs designed to improve the status of women and children.

My longtime friend William Benton, publisher of the *Encyclopaedia Britannica,* a former U.S. Senator and a former Ambassador to UNESCO, urged that I become a member of the Board of Directors and of the Board of Governors of the United Nations Assocation—U.S.A. (For reasons that are unclear, they have two Boards.) The organization began functioning under the leadership of a dedicated Eleanor Roosevelt. After merging with other support organizations it was able to obtain substantial funding. It moved forward with a competent professional staff.

It then embarked upon a program of building grass-roots chapters throughout the country. It enlisted rather sizable American support for the United Nations. The UNA membership was accused of being confined to a group of little old ladies and such. But at its peak in the early 1970s, the organization had nearly fifty thousand members. It reached out to recruit fresh, alert young people. Then, as in many organizations, a bureaucracy blossomed. Money raisers moved in; missionary enthusiasm for the United Nations waned. Several officers recruited from the U.S. State Department were more interested in justifying American foreign policies than in rallying program support for the United Nations.

The UNA—U.S.A. does have some worthwhile programs. Its "parallel-policy study panels" consist of foreign-policy experts, such as Richard Goodman, Cyrus Vance, Charles

Yost, and William Scranton, who meet with their counterparts in the Soviet Union, Japan, and other countries. Their dialogues were addressed to pertinent international issues. The deliberations of the participants have in some cases helped to ease tensions between nations.

The wars in Korea and Vietnam polarized world opinion against the United States. It was obvious that America blundered in not submitting these issues to the United Nations, mankind's principal peacekeeping organization. We tried to settle the complicated issues of the Arab-Israel dispute in our usual unilateral fashion. We supply weaponry to both sides and keep the other concerned parties out of the negotiations. We found we can't run the world all by ourselves. Thus the United States is unable to find allies or sympathizers for its actions. We have avoided like the plague a meaningful Geneva conference. Such international issues are better understood, certainly, if objective studies are undertaken by international organizations—not to justify a national position, but to understand a world's problems.

After the Helsinki Conference in 1975, the Carter administration latched on to a new-old slogan of human rights. The president may have sought an excuse for our intervention in the affairs of others. We couldn't define human rights, but we seemed hellbent on enforcing them in other countries. We wanted to protect human rights selectively around the world. We ignored such rights for our own Indian or minority groups and emphasized our concern for the status of those in socialist countries, where human rights to food, shelter, and jobs are also important. Eventually "human rights" will be understood and protected when we can all sit around a conference table set in the global headquarters.

As a director and trustee of many corporations and foundations, I know something about the ramifications of interlocking directorates. The test of eligibility is devotion to the Establishment—and the ability to raise money. Often the ripoff is open and flagrant. The motive for big money giving is tax deductibility—and the retention of the American free-enterprise system. A corporation like Atlantic Richfield can even buy a profound report on international energy resources—and have at its fingertips the imprimatur of the UNA—U.S.A. With such a report the company can go before Congress and obtain tariff subsidies or depletion allowances and incentives—all to "stimulate domestic oil exploration and production." It can give a large donation to a peace organization if it will *not* make a report on energy!

The United Nations Association—U.S.A., whose function it is to support the institution of the United Nations, often draws its management officials from the U.S. State Department, the Pentagon, and the U.S. Central Intelligence Agency. Edward Korry retired as ambassador to Chile while the CIA involvement was at its peak. He immediately became president of the United Nations Association—U.S.A. Howls of protest from liberals and U.N. supporters followed.

The election of such people to head up an international peace organization did have obvious shortcomings. Our attempts to destroy Chile's Marxist government backfired. America's efforts to support Latin American dictators were exposed and proved most embarrassing. Edward Korry resigned from the presidency of the UNA—U.S.A. A staff member, James Leonard, recently out of the U.S. State Department Division of Counter-Intelligence, took over as president. After a short interval with the UNA he became America's deputy ambassador to the United Nations under Andrew Young. The presidency was then given to Robert Ratner, whose previous administrative life had been confined to fundraising.

Robert Benjamin, a rich attorney and movie magnate, following the death of Chief Justice Earl Warren, was elected co-chairman along with James McDonnell, president of McDonnell-Douglas, one of the Pentagon's largest suppliers of military hardware. The movement of prestigious names out of the corporate positions and into American nonprofit organizations is common enough. Conservative leaders from special-interest causes take over. The treasury of the UNA now owns thirty-seven thousand shares of McDonnell-Douglas, with a market value in excess of $1.5 million. Chairman of the UNA–U.S.A. was James McDonnell, Chairman of the Pentagon's darling weapons supplier.

With such affluent trustees, substantial sums of money flowed into the organization's coffers. Armand Hammer, a West Coast oil man just excused from jail following a fraud conviction for making illegal political contributions to Richard Nixon, offered $500,000 to the UNA–U.S.A. as consideration for his election to the UNA board of governors. We were told that his election would "help his image in the community." Election to the big foundations and non-profit organizations are like that—largely confined to rich donors. At testimonal dinners the trustees honor each other and sell a thousand tickets at prices of $100 to $1,000 to the company's suppliers. It's an accepted practice. Such dinners raise as much as a million dollars in a single evening.

When I submitted an advertisement in the proposed UNA–U.S.A. anniversary issue saying, "Now is the time to disarm," my ad was turned down by Chairman James McDonnell. My message simply suggested that "this is not a time for killing but a time for Americans to get together and establish a world at peace." At the time, of course, the Pentagon and various aircraft companies such as Lockheed and McDonnell-Douglas were getting publicity because of their pay-offs to foreign officials. Actually the UNA and other such support organizations are often more apologists for American foreign policy than pioneers building the world peace institution. When they accept federal funds for their "research," they become mere subsidized spokesmen for our State Department.

Of course, there are dozens of worthy and dedicated organizations throughout the United States doing a good job in bettering our understanding of the United Nations. I like the work of U.N. We Believe, started by two United Airlines pilots. The very able president, Roger Enloe, directs its activities, which are largely oriented to the American business and labor community. The organization arranges dozens of seminars and meetings devoted to explaining the United Nations. It helps American corporations become

familiar with the many services of the U.N. It takes ambassadors and officials of other countries around to American
communities explaining their relationship to the international organization. Like most successful institutions, it has
a lean, action-programmed staff. It has exposed many thousands of influential Americans to the work of the United
Nations.

As these U.N. support organizations look to the Establishment for their funding, it's natural that the largest contributors call the tune. National advertising firms, without
offending a single corporate client, often donate their talents
and resources to inform Americans on the significance and
accomplishments of the world organization. Decision makers
within American industry are realists. They begin to recognize that only an international institution can set the
guidelines and regulations to govern their multinational
operations. We still must look for help from the economic
leaders, the big bankers and corporate leaders of the United
States, to take us to an international sanctuary guaranteeing
basic rights to all mankind. Yet these are the voices of
effective power in our land. American businessmen are well
informed on many subjects. They know that their own
future security and welfare will be better assured with the
creation of such an international socioeconomic body. The
world organization brings law and order to the globe. It
protects people from the abuses of power, from fear, cruelty,
hunger, and suffering. To the extent that it preserves the
*status quo,* many businessmen see the need for helping the
United Nations.

Trustees of the prestigious American think tanks, universities, and especially the large foundations, all are chosen
because of their financial clout. Having served on many such
boards, I see that they do more than determine policy: a
large percentage of their time is spent in fundraising. In
the UNA—U.S.A., the Center for the Study of Democratic
Institutions, and other such organizations, the technique is
always the same. Policies are controlled by a handful of the
largest donors. James McDonnell of McDonnell-Douglas can
give hundreds of thousands of tax-exempt dollars on a

matching grant to the UNA—U.S.A., even assuring himself that such a peace organization does *not* have a conference on disarmament. It is informative to watch the board members react to their own financial interests. The average American citizen wants only impartial factual news about the world institution. It would be helpful if mass newspapers outlined spot news and U.N. information.

When the Helms Amendment to the appropriation bill squeezed through the closing days of Congress in November 1978, it cut off the U.S. assessed contributions to the United Nations and its agencies—a really frightening threat to the world organization. Our contribution to the World Health Organization alone amounted to $27.9 million. We defaulted. Unfortunately, there seemed little media and public reaction. I pleaded with the board of governors of the UNA— U.S.A that we take action to get the legislation changed: set up appointments with Jimmy Carter, call and organize protest meetings in Washington, and generally raise hell to get the funds restored. Robert Benjamin and Robert Ratner replied that we would be taking part in political action and that the UNA—U.S.A. might lose its tax exemption! Such thwarting of the purposes of U.N. support organizations seemed nothing less than scandalous. It may mean that we need new and more aggressive grass-root support organizations.

I enjoy watching how trustees react. John Leslie, chairman of Bache, Halsey, Stuart, Shields and an officer of the UNA—U.S.A., was neutral on the elimination of the panel-study reports. When I saw him at a meeting on November 19, 1978, I told him that on the following day our Nevada National Bank was issuing ten million dollars of securities through his brokerage firm. Probably there was no connection but his attitude softened as he sensed the merits of my suggestions.

It's difficult to get support for positive programs of the United Nations. Daniel Patrick Moynihan's book *A Dangerous Place* (Atlantic-Little, Brown, $12.50), attacking the peace organization, became a bestseller and a Book-of-the-Month Club selection, and he became a United States senator. Robert Muller, a longtime United Nations official who spent his life in the pursuit of peace and building an effective world organization, published his inspiring work *Most of All They Taught Me Happiness* (Doubleday, $7.95). This outstanding work exists in almost total obscurity. But isn't it true that in worthwhile causes the attacker, destroyer, and nonbeliever get the headlines? However, posterity, if not our contemporaries, will reward the builders of the world community.

It would be quite unfair if I did not mention the totally dedicated workers for peace in and out of the support organizations.

Many important organizations are aggressive in pushing the blossoming world organization. Unfortunately, profound pronouncements from the ivory towers and executive suites often point out the deficiences, rather than the merits, of the United Nations. Such an organization can carry out many positive programs, including such matters as the preparation of a curriculum for schools. Many high schools and colleges initiate major projects dealing with the functions and opportunities of the world body. I hope that more courses on the United Nations will be added to the curriculum. National essay contests with prestigious judges can make the United Nations a matter of great student interest. We produce dozens of television programs and motion pictures based on the activities of the United Nations in which name stars gladly participate. I see that every one of these films appears on many TV stations.

Thousands of corporations and individuals are toured through the United Nations. Career opportunities are available for prospective international servants. The United Nations University set up in Japan will become activated when the United States drops its opposition. We do have to lobby for American-government support for such programs. We can establish a United Nations Peace Fellows Internship— and know that we are training the future leaders of the world! I have campaigned to get the United Nations to honor Citizens of Peace. Such awards could be the most prestigious honors ever offered.

The charter of the United Nations may need change and amendment, but I doubt that we can alter it in the present shaky condition of the world. Now building step by step, it represents the preferred world order in embryonic form. It isn't perfect, but what are the alternatives? Chaos and anarchy? Those who criticize the present organization must realize that the U.N. is merely the gilding on an obsolete system of nation-states. In this transition period in which we seek corrections of the world organization, we search for methods that will achieve justice under an orderly world institution. Any impartial observer must admit the United Nations, in this respect, has established a splendid and positive record of accomplishment. We've come a long way in a few decades. The UN's offspring agencies are forming a world rule of law in the various fields of human endeavor.

Movements toward multinational organization started a long time ago—after the Thirty Year War ended in 1648 with the Peace of Westphalia. The League of Nations and the United Nations were born after World Wars I and II. By the 1970s 150 independent states were joined in the global society. The stability of these independent states has become a priority of the United Nations. Thus the stabilization of national borders has been partially accomplished. My feeling is that such an effective social system has within itself the capacity for drastic system change and ability to meet new challenges. After all, man eliminated cannibalism and slavery, created the nation-state, carried out social revolutions in France, the United States, and the Soviet Union, and saw the collapse of Western colonialism. Quite an accomplishment! Global reform, transition, amendment, and growth are not going to stop at this point in the history of the world's most important social evolution.

The United Nations and its agencies are becoming a vital part, maybe the very essence, of our lives. If there is a global problem—food, status of children, environment, or whatnot —the U.N. has set up facilities to cope. Its vastness is hardly appreciated. The United Nations Development Program has a billion-dollar budget, triple that of the UN itself. It has some eighty-five hundred projects going on at all times.

But the true significance of the U.N. lies in its ability to move us closer to our dream of a more equitable habitat. It may bring us nearer to an international socialist society, nearer to a sharing society.

The United Nations is getting stronger and more effective every day. It has become the one human institution in which I place my faith.

My plea, my sales pitch for the United Nations is three-fold: (1) the ethical philosophy of U Thant, secretary general of the U.N., who emphasized that the aims of the U.N. charter and all religions are compatible; (2) the self-interest of all peoples is furthered by preserving a world at peace. The international laws of space, the seas, and the environment are only a few examples of our cooperative efforts; (3) a reaffirmation of the basic rights of all mankind.

It's probably true that the more countries industrialize, the more they must trade with each other. In furthering world trade and exchange among nations, the United Nations is doing more than setting patterns for the future—it is assuring humanity's survival. We are seeing the shifts taking place in international institutions and shaping the form of the world economy. New industrializing countries, such as Yugoslavia, Taiwan, Singapore, Mexico, Rumania, and the Koreas, have differing political systems. Such countries have tremendous potentials for export. During the 1970s they almost doubled their share of the rich-country market. Imagine the possibilities if international planning can be established to contribute resources, climate, labor force, capital, and technological know-how to all economies of the future. The United Nations and its agencies might just temper man's ardor for shooting wars and tariff wars. Certainly it provides an orderly forum for the economic guidance and governance of the world. The rest is up to the intelligence of all of us.

We face the future not knowing the ultimate form or details of our social order. We may call it communistic, socialistic, or capitalistic; it matters not. What we will have is a world with a more equitable all-nation, planned economy, sharing the world's human and natural resources. Every movement we undertake, be it peaceful or disorderly, that builds the instrument for accomplishing these changes must be a truly giant benefit to the security and happiness of every present and future inhabitant of this planet.

Now, at last, I walk the corridors of the all-nation, flag-bedecked building at United Nations, New York. I visit with friends from the global perimeters. We move through hallways and meeting rooms. We're traveling a common path together in this symbolic home of all mankind. To me this is the most important building in the world. We are witnessing conferences involving the great social, economic, and political questions of our times. As equals we can join others around these very tables and become a part of the positive dialogue of peace and human welfare.

Finally, the United Nations is right for our times. It is the rational, sensible solution for the common problems of mankind. It is achievable. The United Nations brings us a world of order, free of anarchy. It gives us the opportunity to achieve the fullness of the human lifespan. I join my fellow humans in pleading for the success of the world community.

# INDEX

Agnew, Spiro, 29, 48, 201
Aker, George E., 131, 132
Allende, President Salvador, 26, 196
Alliance for Progress, 201
Alumatic Corp., 101
American Dream, 39
American Management Association, 211
Amsterdam, Morey, 86
Anderson, Jack, 212

Bancorporation Leasing, 138
Barth, Carl, 52, 53
Batesville Rubber Company, 108
Batista, Colonel, 203
Bay of Pigs, 199, 200, 201, 210, 225, 252
Benjamin, Robert, 260, 263
Benton, Marge, 90
Benton, William, 241, 258
Benny, Jack, 86
Berle, Milton, 86
Birley, Lady Annabel, 126
Bobrakov, Yuri I., 155, 238
Bogota, 25
Bolsheviks, 41, 65
Bolshevik Revolution, 73
Bonaparte, Napoleon, 25, 182
*Boston Herald*, 56
Brezhnev, Leonid, 237
Brophy, John, 42
Brown & Geddes, 39
Brown, Dr. Courtney, 156
Budenz, Louis, 187
Burton, Pierre, 235

Caesar, Julius, 25
Camp David, 164
Carlson, Chester, 241
Carter, Jimmy, 120, 263
Castro, Fidel, 17, 65-67, 172-75, 182, 190, 193-94, 199-200, 203-08, 210-25
Center for Natural Resources, Energy and Transport (CNRET), 92
Center for the Study of Democratic Institutions, 48, 180, 183, 194, 213, 220, 241, 262
*The Center* Magazine, 183
Chambers, Whittaker, 186
Chaplin, Charlie, 55

Chase, Stuart, 153
Chiang Kai-shek, 203
Chilegate, 29
China, People's Republic of, 33, 62, 66, 149, 160
Church, Frank, 172, 212
Churchill, Winston, 154
*The Churchman*, 172
CIA, 17-19, 22, 48, 65, 149, 170-74, 176, 178, 180-84, 186, 188-89, 192-97, 202, 205-06, 215, 260
Clark, Dr. Kenneth, 67
Colby, William, 176
Committee for Industrial Organization (CIO), 42, 44
Commoner, Barry, 228
*Congressional Quarterly*, 46
Constitution (U.S.), 14, 242, 248
Copolymer, Inc., 107
Cordon de Habana, 205
Cornell University, 13
Cuba, 17, 22, 33, 48
Cubana Airlines, 202

Dartmouth College, 32, 53, 216
Darwin, Charles, 13
Debs, Eugene V., 53
Declaration of Independence, 12
Delgato, Arturo, 219
Dornan, Robert F., 46
Dreiser, Theodore, 234
Dortegas, President, 221
Douglas, William O., 48, 194, 212, 242
Dow-Jones Stock Averages, 248
Dubois, René, 228, 229
Dudley's Massacre, 234
Dumont, Allen B., 85
Duranty, Walter, 75

Eaton, Cyrus, 48, 184, 241
Eccles, Marriner, 48, 130, 133, 144
Eisenhower, Dwight D., 188, 203
Engels, Friedrich, 30
Enloe, Roger, 261
*Erie Dispatch Herald*, 87
Establishment, 23, 87, 146, 259
Export-Import Bank, 149

Farber, J. Eugene, 125-26
FBI, 17-19, 170, 176, 178-79, 183-87